Divine Lives

The Descending Current of Bhakti

sarasī-taṭa-sukhadoṭaja-nikaṭa-priya-bhajanam
lalitāmukha-lalanākula-paramādara-yajanam
vraja-kānana-bahu-mānana-kamala-priya-nayanam
guṇa-mañjari-garimā-guṇa-hari-vāsana-vayanam
śubhadodaya-divase vṛṣa-ravijā-nija-dayitam
praṇamāmi ca caraṇāntika-paricāraka-sahitam

Near the banks of Śrī Rādha Kuṇḍa at Svānanda Sukhada Kuñja, she is devoted to the service of her Beloved, and is very dear to the gopi girls of Vraja headed by Śrī Lalitā. She (Nayanamaṇi Mañjari) is the favourite of Kamala Mañjari (Śrīla Bhaktivinoda Ṭhākura) who is preeminent in Vṛndāvana.

She joyfully sings the divine qualities of Guṇa Mañjari (Śrīla Gaura Kiśora Dāsa Bābaji) and the spiritual threads of those qualities entwine, weaving a tent where Śrī Kṛṣṇa likes to dwell.

I bow down to the appearance of the beloved companion of Śrī Vṛṣabhānu-nandini (Śrī Rādhīkā) and the servitors at his holy lotus feet.

—*Śrī Dayita Dāsa Praṇati Pañcakam,* Verse 4

Divine Lives

The Descending Current of Bhakti

MANDALA
San Rafael • Los Angeles • London

P. Bhadra 98.

Contents

Foreword

It is an immense privilege for me to have the opportunity to write the foreword for this publication, which is being presented on the momentous occasion of two significant anniversaries. Firstly, we celebrate the 150th appearance ceremony of my revered grand spiritual master, His Divine Grace Śrīla Prabhupāda Bhakti Siddhānta Sarasvatī Gosvāmī Ṭhākura, who is the founder *ācārya* of the entire Gauḍīya community. Secondly, we honour the 125th appearance ceremony of my spiritual master, His Divine Grace Śrīla Bhakti Pramode Purī Gosvāmī Ṭhākura, the founding *ācārya* of Śrī Gopinātha Gauḍīya Maṭha.

In our spiritual community, we observe the presence of numerous spiritual masters, also known as gurus, and various spiritual organizations. According to the scriptures, the Supreme Lord Śrī Kṛṣṇa is the ultimate maintainer and protector of the entire universe, making Him the ultimate guru. All initiating gurus (*dīkṣā-gurus*) and instructing gurus (*śikṣā-gurus*) are representatives of Śrī Kṛṣṇa. As part of this festival, an important ceremony known as guru puja will be performed. It is essential to understand that guru puja goes beyond honouring an individual guru. Rather, it signifies the recognition that all representatives of Lord Kṛṣṇa should be regarded as equal to the Lord Himself. It is through my grand spiritual master, my spiritual master, and all the pure devotees of the Lord gathered in this divine assembly (*divya-samāgam*) that Kṛṣṇa's mercy descends upon us.

We are aware that Lord Kṛṣṇa eternally resides in the hearts of His pure devotees, and they are His heart and soul. This fact has been explained by one of our previous teachers, Śrīla Narottama Dāsa Ṭhākura. Although many pure devotees are physically present at this ceremony, we can be certain that all our previous teachers are also spiritually present here.

I humbly offer my prayers at their feet, seeking their blessings to bestow mercy upon all of us. With their grace, may we faithfully carry out the loving mission of Lord Caitanya, chant the Hare Kṛṣṇa Mahā-mantra without committing any offenses, and embody true unity in diversity by maintaining amicable relations with one another.

Vaiṣṇavas are known for their magnanimity and lack of fault-finding. In the arrangements for this three-day gathering, there may be inconveniences and shortcomings that guests and devotees might encounter. I earnestly request everyone to overlook any shortcomings and kindly forgive our mistakes.

Furthermore, I pray that this three-day spiritual gathering will be a spiritually uplifting and invigorating experience for all the attendees. I express my heartfelt gratitude to everyone for their participation, which will contribute to the success of this festival.

I forever desire a mere particle of the dust from the feet of the pure devotees.

An unworthy servant,
B.B. Bodhayan Swami
Śrī Gopinātha Gauḍīya Maṭha

Introduction

In the early years of this century, Śrīla Prabhupāda Bhaktisiddhānta Sarasvatī Gosvāmī Ṭhākura inspired a devotional revival that spread rapidly throughout Bengal, India, and eventually around the world. He brought into question the very foundations of current theistic thought in a way that has little comparison anywhere in the dialogue of spirituality, East or West. Through him, the world awakened to the teachings of Śrī Caitanya Mahāprabhu and the movement of pure devotion (*śuddhā-bhakti*).

To orchestrate this modern bhakti revolution, Śrīla Prabhupāda gathered into his circle some of the greatest spiritual luminaries of the age. Such a convergence of exalted spiritual personalities can only be compared to the assembly of Śrī Caitanya's direct followers in the sixteenth century. His Divine Grace Bhakti Pramode Purī Gosvāmī Mahārāja was one such titan of pure devotion who entered Śrīla Prabhupāda's sacred orbit.

The keystone of success in practicing devotion is to perfectly hear the holy words spoken by one's spiritual preceptor. Śrīla Prabhupāda would often say, "All that is required of you is that you lend me your ears." Śrīla Purī Mahārāja was fully committed to this maxim. He had the great good fortune to associate closely with Śrīla Prabhupāda for thirteen years, and during that time he served him personally by making a record of his lectures and conversations. These notes were later published. The greater part of the words spoken by Śrīla Prabhupāda today come from transcriptions of Śrīla Purī Mahārāja's notes. At the same time, Śrīla Purī Mahārāja cultivated a deep knowledge of the Vaiṣṇava scriptures, and so he became a veritable storehouse of the wealth of the preceptorial line coming from Śrī Caitanya and His followers. This led to his becoming one of the most prolific writers and influential teachers in all of Gauḍīya Vaiṣṇava history. His writings reflect the disciplined eye of a scholar who expresses with grace and directness the purest scriptural conclusions supported by his own uncommonly profound realizations.

In all, our venerable teacher's wisdom is embodied in over sixty years of writings on Vaiṣṇava philosophy and theology. He penned a rich variety of texts, bringing *bhāgavata-dharma* to life through hundreds of poems, essays, narratives, diaries, editorials, and personal letters; thus creating a treasure house of pure devotion for his disciples and the world.

Śrīla Purī Mahārāja taught through his every action. He excelled in all aspects of devotional practice, and there was no area in which he did not exhibit utmost expertise, diligence, and foresight, from his encyclopedic knowledge of scripture to maintaining the printing press to his beautiful singing of *kīrtana*. He was especially recognized for his sensitivity and attention to detail in the performance of deity worship and devotional rites, and was thus widely called on to be the head priest at most Gauḍīya Maṭha deity installations and ceremonial functions. He was rarely known to rest; he served in an uninterrupted flow. Even in his later years, he remained awake through the night, writing and chanting, while his youthful disciples slept. When his personal servants arrived in the morning, they would invariably find him already risen, before everyone else in the ashram, chanting the holy name.

Śrīla Bhakti Pramode Purī Mahārāja had outstanding love for his godbrothers and was inspired in his glorification of others. He found richness in everyone he met. He had the quality of making others feel so wanted and their life so valued. At the same time, he paid almost no attention to himself. He was the emblem of humility and simplicity, and his generosity of spirit and his kindness touched the hearts of the whole Vaiṣṇava community. Among his lifelong intimate companions were Śrīla Bhakti Rakṣaka Śrīdhara Deva Gosvāmī Mahārāja, Śrīla Bhakti Prajñāna Keśava Gosvāmī Mahārāja, and Śrīla Akiñcana Kṛṣṇa Dāsa Bābājī Mahārāja. Toward the end of his sojourn in this world, in 1995, he was honored by the Gauḍīya Vaiṣṇava community for his learning and long life of service and devotion and made president of the World Vaiṣṇava Association.

"He has love for his guru; and let it be known that his life is one with his words." This tribute by Śrīla Prabhupāda himself is the most revealing statement about Śrīla Purī Gosvāmī Mahārāja's personality and qualities. He ascribed all credit for his accomplishments to the mercy of his *gurudeva* alone. Through the blessings of Śrīla Bhaktisiddhānta Sarasvatī Gosvāmī Ṭhākura, Śrīla Bhakti Pramode Purī Mahārāja attracted the hearts of so many to the path of *bhāgavata-dharma*. People from so many different backgrounds and countries found in him a true spiritual guide and shelter. He upheld the principles of pure Vaishnavism and delineated the path of *śaraṇāgati* (wholehearted surrender). He so embodied pure devotion and service to his spiritual master that one of his disciples once remarked that he was able to "silently lay down Śrīla Prabhupāda's entire *siddhānta*."

We are greatly indebted to His Divine Grace for his gift—a lifetime of pure devotion, spanning more than a century—which we can learn from, discuss for our own spiritual nourishment, and aspire to. In years to come, as more of his words and vision are translated, the world outside Bengal and India will gradually come to know the spirit of the true Vaiṣṇava religion he so tirelessly shared. May the gentle rain of his perfect, nectarean teachings continue to bring auspiciousness into this world.

—*Śrīla Bhakti Bibudha Bodhāyan Mahārāja*

(Excerpted from the forthcoming biography of Śrīla Bhakti Pramode Purī Gosvāmī Mahārāja, *A Century of Devotion: The Life of Śrīla B.P. Purī Gosvāmī Mahārāja*)

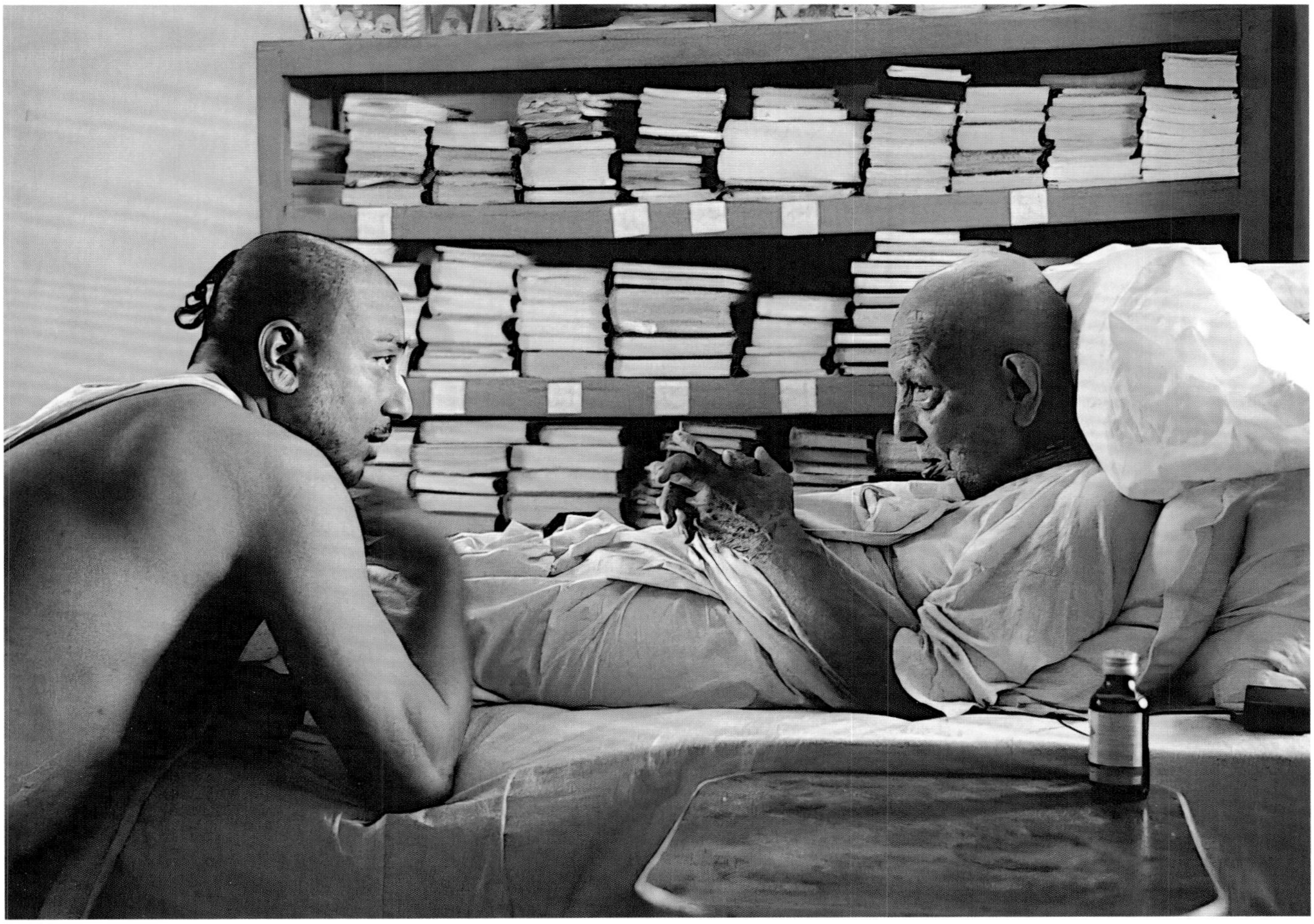

The True Meaning of Vyāsa Pūjā

"The words 'Vyāsa Pūjā' mean nothing more than this acceptance of shelter or surrender at the lotus feet of the spiritual master."

"Vyāsa Pūjā also means offering everything to the service of the spiritual master in the form of works conducive to the fulfillment of his wishes."

"The ultimate object of our desires is to become specks of dust at the lotus feet of the followers of Rūpa Gosvāmī. Remain united in following the āśraya-vigraha in order to satisfy the transcendental senses of the one, non-dual supreme truth."

– *Śrīla Prabhupāda*

INVOCATION

PRABHUPĀDA PRAṆĀMA

nikhila-bhuvana-māyā-chhinna-vichchhinna-kartrī
vibudha-bahula-mṛgyā-mukti-mohānta-dātrī
śithilita-vidhi-rāgārādhya-rādheśa-dhānī
vilasatu hṛdi nityaṁ bhakti-siddhānta-vāṇī

WITH HIS FIRST STEP, HE CUT TO PIECES THE WHOLE PLANE OF EXPLOITATION, AND WITH HIS SECOND, HE CRUSHED THE SPECULATION OF SCHOLARS OF SALVATION AND LIBERATION. WITH HIS THIRD, HE SOFTENED VAIDHĪ-BHAKTI WITH A TOUCH OF DIVINE LOVE (RĀGA MĀRGA). TAKING US BEYOND VAIKUṆṬHA, HE HAS INTRODUCED US TO THE HIGHEST WORSHIP OF ŚRĪ RĀDHĀ AND ŚRĪ GOVINDA.

"With the softness of Vṛndāvana within, and the hardness of a devastator without, he created havoc in the world—fighting with one and all. Singlehandedly fighting against the whole world—cutting everything to pieces—that was his external attitude. And his second attitude was to stop the boasting research of the scholars and doctors of different schools of thought; and third, to minimize and slacken the grandeur of the worship of Nārāyaṇa, and establish the service of Rādhā-Govinda as the highest attainment. He caused the domain of love to descend into this plane, with the service of Rādhā-Govinda, establishing the flow of divine love from the heart as all in all.

"That was his history—the real existence of Śrīla Bhaktisiddhānta Sarasvatī Ṭhākura Prabhupāda. May his divine teachings, *bhaktisiddhānta-vāṇī,* dance eternally within the core of our hearts."

-Śrīla Bhakti Rakṣaka Śrīdhara Deva Gosvāmī

Sree Vyas Puja Offering

Adore adore ye all
The happy day,
Blessed than heaven,
Sweeter than May.
When He appeared at Puri
The holy place,
My Lord and Master
His Divine Grace.

Oh ! my Master
The evangelic angel.
Give us Thy light,
Lit up Thy candle.
Struggle for existence
A human race.
The only hope
His Divine Grace.

Misled we are
All going astray,
Save us Lord
Our fervent pray.
Wonder Thy ways
To turn our face
Adore Thy feet
Your Divine Grace.

Forgotten **Krishna**
We fallen souls,
Paying most heavy
The illusion's toll.
Darkness around
All untrace.
The only hope
His Divine Grace.

Message of service
Thou hast brought.
A healthful life
As **Chaitanya** wrought.
Unknown to all
It's full of brace.
That's your gift
Your Divine Grace.

Absolute is sentient
Thou hast proved,
Impersonal calamity
Thou hast moved.
This gives us a life
Anew and fresh
Worship thy feet
Your Divine Grace.

Had you not come
Who had told,
The message of **Krishna**
Forceful and bold.

That's your right
You have the mace.
Save me a fallen
Your Divine Grace.

The line of service
As drawn by you,
Is pleasing and healthy
Like morning dew.
The oldest of all
But in new-dress
Miracle done
Your Divine Grace.

Abhay Charan Das.

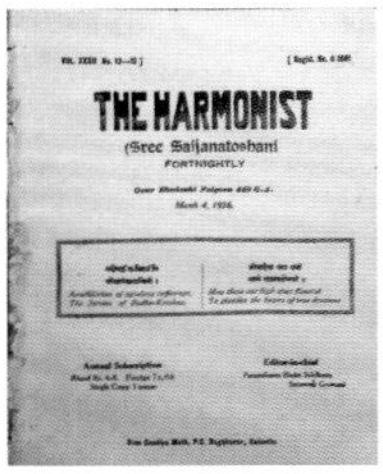

This poem was originally published in 1936 in the Harmonist (Volume 32, Issue 12-13) as a Vyāsa Pūjā offering by Śrīla A.C. Bhaktivedanta Swami Prabhupāda, then known as Abhaya-caraṇa Dāsa, to his spiritual master, His Divine Grace Śrīla Bhaktisiddhānta Sarasvatī Ṭhākura Prabhupāda. (Courtesy of Bhaktivedanta Research Center)

Part 1
Śrīla Prabhupāda

A Brief Biography Of Śrīla Prabhupāda

A Divine Life

śrī siddhānta-saraswatīti viditau gauḍīya-gurv-anvaye
bhāto bhānur īva prabhāta-gagane yo gaura-saṅkīrtanaiḥ
māyāvāda-timiṅgilodara-gatān uddhṛtya jīvanimān
kṛṣṇa-prema-sudhābdhi gāhana sukhaṁ
prādāt prabhuṁ taṁ bhaje

"In the great Gauḍīya Vaiṣṇava teachers' line, as Śrīla Bhaktisiddhānta Saraswatī he's renowned. Like the radiant sun in the morning sky, he appeared to rescue all souls swallowed by the all-devouring impersonal philosophy. By spreading the teaching of Lord Gaurāṅga to sing the holy name of Lord Kṛṣṇa, he gave all the chance to dive in the ocean of love for Śrī Kṛṣṇa, the Supreme Person. Śrīla Bhaktisiddhānta, my lord, divine master—at his feet do I pray to serve him forever."

—*Śrīla Bhakti Rakṣaka Śrīdhara Deva Goswāmī*

Divinity can be seen by its own light. The transcendental life of Śrīla Prabhupāda Sarasvatī Ṭhākura can be known to us only by his own causeless mercy—for such is the nature of the Supreme Lord and His representatives who come to this world. Śrīla Prabhupāda was an infinite ocean of divine treasure; if we are fortunate enough, perhaps we can touch the waves of that ocean as they lap the shore of our mortal plane. Within that ocean are his innumerable transcendental qualities such as scholarship, genius, spiritual realization, humility, magnanimity, compassion, mercy, and divine love, to name only a few. The essence of Śrīla Prabhupāda's life cannot be revealed in many volumes—let alone a single chapter—if they are merely a catalog of facts and figures. It takes the dedication of a lifetime to attain a true glimpse of his message, and his life is his message.

We are about to stand in front of a divine personality; we are about to catch sight of that reality which is eternal and infinite. Yet in our meeting with the eternal we have to retrace the footsteps of time, because we must begin somewhere.

Childhood, 1874–1892

Śrīla Prabhupāda Bhaktisiddhānta Sarasvatī Ṭhākura made his appearance in Puruṣottama Kṣetra (Jagannātha Purī) in the state of Orissa, at 3:30 in the afternoon on Friday, the 6th of February, 1874. He was born in his family home, which was next to the holy site called the Nārāyaṇa-chhātā of Śrī Jagannātha Temple, and which always reverberated with the chanting of the holy name. He was the fourth son of Śrīla Bhaktivinoda Ṭhākura and Śrīmatī Bhāgavati Devī. Śrīla Bhaktivinoda Ṭhākura firmly established the concept of pure Vaiṣṇavism in the hearts of many educated and spiritually inquisitive people of Bengal in the latter part of the nineteenth century. Śrīla Prabhupāda Bhaktisiddhānta Sarasvatī Ṭhākura was a beautiful child with all the bodily symptoms of a great personality that are described in the scriptures. Everyone was amazed to see that the child was born with his umbilical cord wrapped around his neck like a *brāhmaṇa's* sacred thread. Śrīla Bhaktivinoda Ṭhākura named his son Śrī Bimalā Prasāda, meaning "the mercy of the transcendental potency of Lord Jagannātha, Śrīmatī Bimalā Devī."

Śrī Bimalā Prasāda

When Śrī Bimalā Prasāda was six months old, Lord Jagannātha's annual chariot festival took place. That year the chariot stopped in front of Śrīla Bhaktivinoda Ṭhākura's house and could not be budged an inch for three days. So, while Lord Jagannātha stayed in front of the house, *kīrtana* was continuously performed there under the leadership of Śrīla Ṭhākura Mahāśaya ("Mahāśaya" is an honorific title). On one of these days, Śrī Bimalā Prasāda, in his mother's arms, went to see Lord Jagannātha, and extended his hand towards the Deity as if to offer his obeisance. At that moment a garland fell from the neck of Lord Jagannātha and encircled the child. The crowd was jubilant witnessing Lord Jagannātha's blessing on the child. Amid the tumultuous sound of "Haribola!", Bhaktivinoda Ṭhākura fed Bimalā Prasāda some of Lord Jagannātha's *mahāprasād*, and thus observed the child's *anna-prāśana* ("grain ceremony"—first feeding of grains) under the most auspicious circumstances.

Śrīla Prabhupāda's birthplace

Śrī Bimalā Prasāda lived in Jagannātha Dhāma for ten months with his mother. Then they traveled to Bengal and resided first at Rāṇāghāṭa and then at Śrīrāmpura. Once, when Śrīla Bimalā Prasāda was a small boy, he took a mango without first offering it to the Lord. When his father chastised him for this, he became very remorseful and immediately vowed never to eat a mango again—a vow which he observed his whole life. In 1881 Śrīla Bhaktivinoda Ṭhākura had a house built in Calcutta at Rām-bāgān and named it Bhakti Bhavan. As the foundation was being dug, a Deity of Śrī Kūrma Deva manifested Himself from the ground. Śrīla Bhaktivinoda Ṭhākura gave this Deity to his son Śrī Bimalā Prasāda when he was eight or nine years old, and taught him the mantra and the method of deity worship. The child duly started his deity worship with great care and devotion.

Śrīmatī Bhāgavati Devī

When Śrī Bimalā Prasāda was in fifth grade, he invented a new method of shorthand which he called Bicanto (or Vikṛnti). His teachers were always amazed by his mastery of Bengali and Sanskrit, his extraordinary intelligence and memory, and his pure moral and devotional nature. At this time Śrīla Bhaktivinoda Ṭhākura gave him *Śrī Caitanya Śikṣāmṛta* to read. Śrī Bimalā Prasāda also displayed extraordinary ability in mathematics and astrology. He studied astrology under the tutelage of the famous astrologer Mahesh Candra Churamani, and impressed his teacher with his mastery of the subject and his exceptional talent. He also studied astrology with Paṇḍit Sundar Lāl. Seeing his scholarship in many different subjects, including the scriptures, his teachers named him Śrī Siddhānta Sarasvatī—"master of scriptural conclusions." When Śrīla Sarasvatī Ṭhākura was a student in the seventh grade in Śrīrāmpur, Śrīla Bhaktivinoda Ṭhākura gave him *harināma* (the holy name) on *Tulasī-mālā* (rosary made of *Tulasī* beads), as well as Śrī Nṛsiṁha mantra.

In 1885 Śrīla Bhaktivinoda Ṭhākura founded the Vaiṣnava Depository, a press which was housed in his own home. Śrīla Sarasvatī Ṭhākura learned about the printing press and began assisting his father in proofreading. At this time, Śrīla Ṭhākura Mahāśaya's magazine, *Sajjan Toṣaṇī,* resumed publication. In that same year Śrīla Sarasvatī Ṭhākura accompanied Śrīla Ṭhākura Mahāśaya on his pilgrimage to such places as Kulīngrām and Sargrām. At these places he heard extensive discussions on the holy name. Also in 1885, Śrīla Ṭhākura Mahāśāya established his "Viśva-Vaiṣṇava-Rāj-Sabhā" ("great assembly of the Vaiṣṇavas of the world") in the house of Śrī Rāma-gopāla Basu on Bethune Row in Calcutta. Many well-known personalities such as Madan-gopāla Gosvāmī, Nīla-kānta Gosvāmī, Bipina-bihārī Gosvāmī, Rādhikā-nātha Gosvāmī, and Śiśira Kumāra Ghoṣa attended the meetings of the society and participated in discussions. Śrīla Sarasvatī Ṭhākura used to carry *Bhakti-rasāmṛta Sindhu (The Ocean of the Nectar of Devotion)*, by Śrīla Rūpa Gosvāmī, to these meetings, and listen to the discussions there with rapt attention.

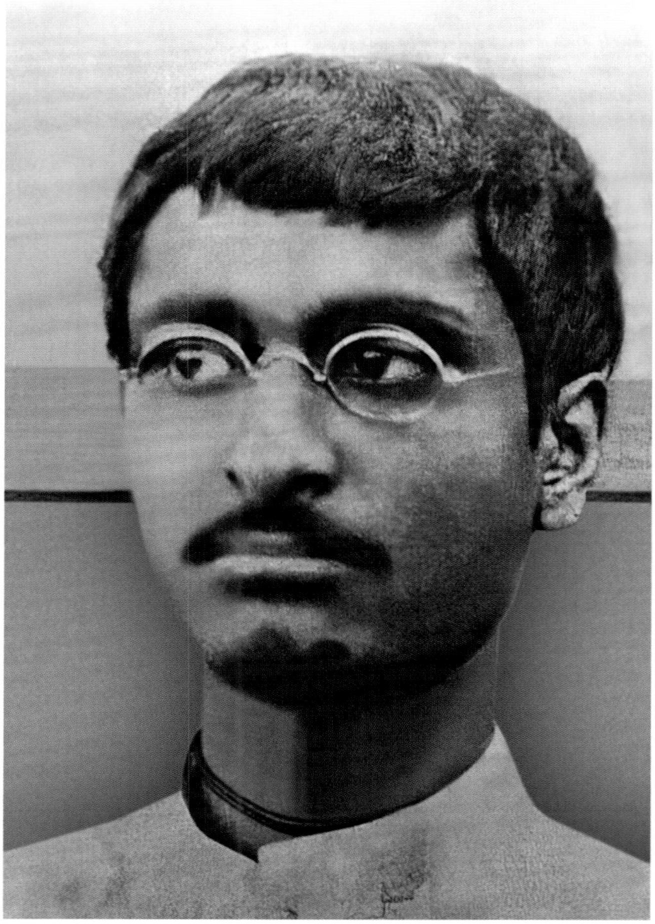

Śrīla Bhaktivinoda Ṭhākura (left) and Śrī Bimalā Prasāda (right)

Śrīla Sarasvatī Ṭhākura was not interested in associating with other boys of his age unless they were interested in spiritual matters. His two favorite books were *Prārthanā* and *Prema-Bhakti Candrikā* by Śrīla Narottama Dāsa Ṭhākura. As a young boy he published books on astrology, such as *Sūrya Siddhānta* and *Bhakti Bhavana Pañjikā.* In the afternoons he spent hours debating about religion and philosophy with other students in Calcutta's Beadon Square. Later, while still a teenager, he founded the August Assembly. All members of the Assembly had to take a vow of lifelong celibacy. Many educated people, both young and old, took part in the Assembly.

Sanskrit College & Work in Tripura, 1892–1905

In 1892 Śrīla Sarasvatī Ṭhākura finished high school and enrolled in the Sanskrit College. He was more interested in reading many different books in the college library than in reading his own textbooks. He studied the Vedas under Paṇḍita Pṛthvī-dhara Śarmā after college. He also studied the *Siddhānta Kaumudī* within a very short time. As a student in Sanskrit College, he refuted some of the concepts of Professor Pañcānana Sāhityācārya. Subsequently, no one wanted to debate with Śrīla Sarasvatī Ṭhākura, for fear of defeat. But his spiritual interests did not allow him to stay in college for very long. He wrote in his autobiography: "If I keep studying at college with great attention, then I will be under a lot of pressure to enter family life. But if I am seen as a stupid, incompetent person, then no one will try to influence me towards material progress. Thinking this, I left the Sanskrit College, and in order to live a life of devotional service, I wanted a pious occupation so I could have a modest income."

In 1897 Śrīla Sarasvatī Ṭhākura established the Sārasvata Catuṣpāṭhī (The Saraswat Academy) at Bhakti Bhavan. Many prominent and educated men such as Lālā Hara-Gaurī-Śaṅkara, Dr. Ekendra-nātha Ghoṣa, Sātkari Caṭṭopadhyāya, Śyāma-lāla Gosvāmī, and Śaratcandra Vidyāvinoda came to study astrology and mathematics there. From Sārasvata Chatuṣpāṭhī, Śrīla Sarasvatī Ṭhākura published astrological magazines such as *Jyotirvid* and *Bṛhaspati,* as well as quite a few ancient astrological texts. Śrīla Sarasvatī Ṭhākura's reputation as a very knowledgeable

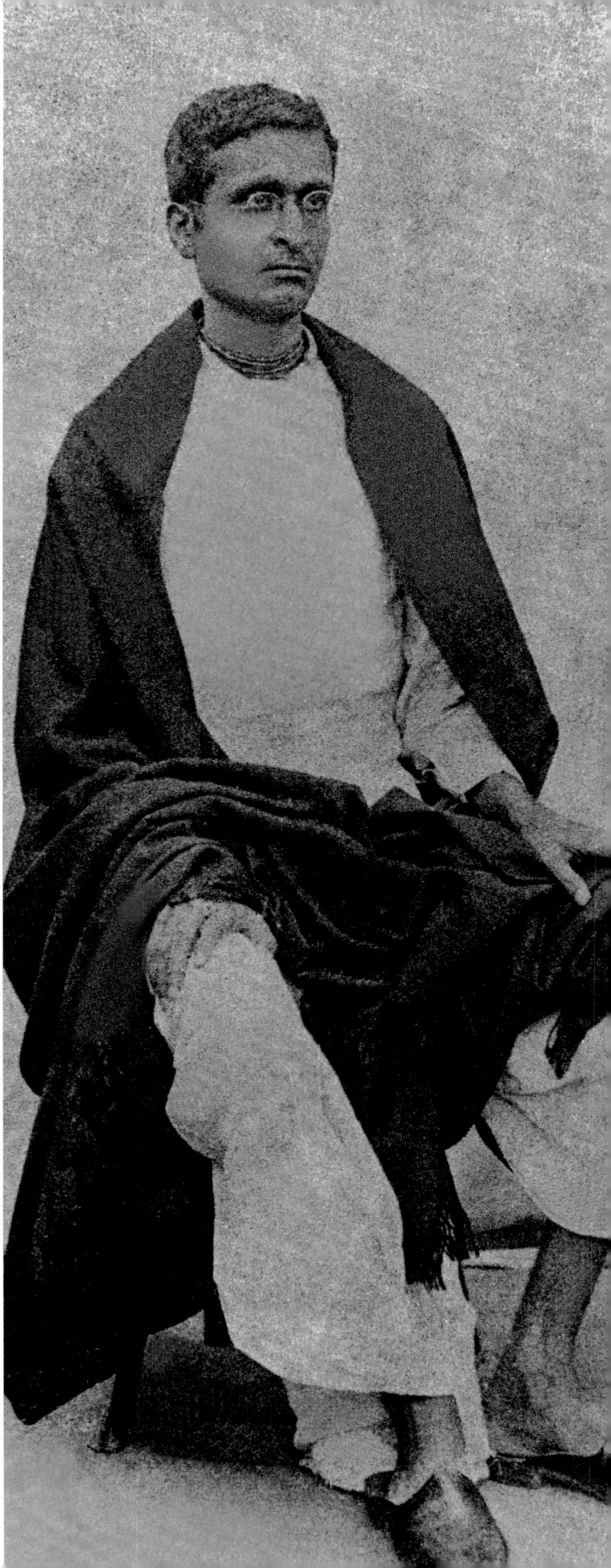

astrologer spread in the educated society of Calcutta. Later Sir Āśutoṣa Mukhopādhyāya, the Vice Chancellor of the University of Calcutta, said that the chair of astronomy at the University of Calcutta would be reserved for Śrīla Sarasvatī Ṭhākura.

In 1895 Śrīla Sarasvatī Ṭhākura accepted a job with the independent state of Tripura, as a scholar and tutor for the royal family thereof. After King Vīracandra passed away in 1896, his son, King Rādhā-kiśora Māṇikya Bāhādur, requested Śrīla Sarasvatī Ṭhākura to tutor the princes, and later to supervise the estate in Calcutta. But Śrīla Sarasvatī Ṭhākura soon wished to retire from this job, and the King allowed him to do so in 1905 with full pension. Śrīla Sarasvatī Ṭhākura accepted that pension until 1908.

Bhajana Life & Initiation, 1898–1905

Previously, in 1898, Śrīla Sarasvatī Ṭhākura had visited different places of pilgrimage such as Kāśī, Prayāga, and Gayā. At Kāśī (Benares), he had an extensive discussion with Rāma Miśra Śāstrī about the Rāmānuja *sampradāya*. During this period the renunciate nature of his devotional life became very apparent. As early as 1897 he was observing the four months of *cāturmasya* with great austerity and devotion. He would eat only boiled food (*haviṣyānna*) which he cooked himself, and sleep on the floor without pillows. In 1899 he wrote various articles to preach Vaiṣṇavism in a magazine called *Nivedan*, published in Calcutta. In 1890 his scholarly book *Baṅge Samājikata*, consisting of research on society and religion, was published in Calcutta.

In 1897 Śrīla Bhaktivinoda Ṭhākura established his own *bhajana-kuṭīra* (cottage for reclusive devotional practice), called Ānanda-sukhada-kuñja, on the Godruma island of Navadvīpa on the bank of the river Sarasvatī. There, in the winter of 1898, Śrīla Sarasvatī Ṭhākura met with an extraordinary, exalted Vaiṣṇava saint, Śrīla Gaura-kiśora Dāsa Bābājī, who captured his heart. Sarasvatī Ṭhākura wanted to take shelter at the lotus feet of Śrīla Gaura-kiśora Dāsa Bābājī, and by the order of Śrīla Bhaktivinoda Ṭhākura he surrendered at the lotus feet of Śrīla Gaura-kiśora Dāsa Bābājī and received *bhāgavatī-dīkṣā* (initiation) from him in 1900.

Shortly before this, in March of the same year, Śrīla Sarasvatī Ṭhākura had gone to Remuṇā via Baleswar to see the Deity of Kṣīracorā Gopīnātha (Gopīnātha who stole the *kṣīra*, or milk pudding, for his devotee Śrī Mādhavendra Purī). Then he went to Purī via Bhubaneswar. Śrīla Sarasvatī Ṭhākura became very attached to the holy city of Purī. His great desire was to establish a *Maṭha* in front of the *samādhi* of Śrīla Haridāsa Ṭhākura. The subregistrar of Purī, Jagabandhu Paṭṭanāyaka, and others requested him to take charge of the service of the Deity of Śrī Giridharī at Sātāsana Maṭha. In 1902 Śrīla Bhaktivinoda Ṭhākura started to build his *bhajana-kuṭīra* called Bhakti Kuṭī near the *samādhi* of Śrīla Haridāsa Ṭhākura. The King of Kasim Bazar, Mahārāja Maṇīndra Candra Nandī, who was grief stricken due to some personal tragedy, used to live there in a tent and listen to the *hari-kathā* of Śrīla Bhaktivinoda Ṭhākura and Śrīla Sarasvatī Ṭhākura. At this time Śrīla Sarasvatī Ṭhākura regularly used to read and explain the *Caitanya-caritāmṛta* to the audience in Bhakti Kuṭī, in front of Śrīla Bhaktivinoda Ṭhākura. During this time he labored to collect material for *Vaiṣṇava Mañjuṣā*, a Vaiṣṇava encyclopedia.

One Bābājī, Rādhā-ramaṇa-caraṇa Dāsa, who lived in Purī, had concocted a song: "*Bhaja nitāi gaur*

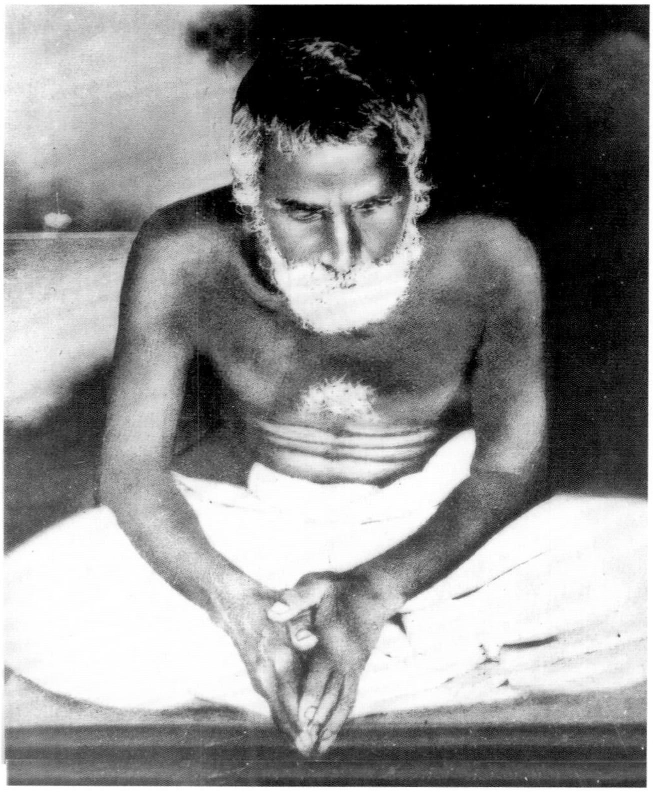

Śrīla Gaura-kiśora Dāsa Bābājī Mahārāja

rādhe śyāma, japa hare kṛṣṇa hare rāma." Śrīla Sarasvatī Ṭhākura not only protested against this but presented a very strong argument and proved it to be inauthentic and against Vaiṣṇava scriptures. This Bābājī also introduced the *sakhī-bekhi* concept by dressing one of his followers as Lalitā Sakhī. This was against Mahāprabhu's teachings since an ordinary *jīva* was being worshiped as though he were an expansion of Śrīmatī Rādhārāṇī. Śrīla Sarasvatī Ṭhākura was always a fearless and forthright speaker, and thus opposed the Bābājī. Therefore, those who opposed him, unable to defeat him in argument, tried other ways to suppress his preaching. Although Śrīla Sarasvatī Ṭhākura silently tolerated this oppression, Śrīla Bhaktivinoda Ṭhākura asked him to go to Māyāpura and practice his *bhajana* there, without obstacles.

In Śrī Māyāpura Dhāma, 1905–1910

In February 1905, Śrīla Sarasvatī Ṭhākura went on pilgrimage to various holy places in South India. After visiting Siṁhācala, Rājamahendrī, Madras, Peremvedur, Tirupati, Kāñcipuram, Kumbhakoṇam, Śrīraṅgam, Madurai, etc., he returned to Calcutta and then went on to Śrī Māyāpura. In Peremvedur he gathered information about the practice of *tridaṇḍa-vaiṣṇava-sannyāsa* from a *tridaṇḍi-swāmī* who belonged to the Rāmānuja *sampradaya*.

In 1905, Śrīla Sarasvatī Ṭhākura began preaching Śrīman Mahāprabhu's message while residing in Śrī Māyāpura. Following in the footsteps of Śrīla Haridāsa Ṭhākura, he would take the holy name 300,000 times a day. He would sleep on the floor for only a few hours, eat very simply, and take the holy name day and night. In the afternoon he would speak *hari-kathā* to the assembled devotees. On some days he would go to Kuliyā to have *darśana* of Śrīla Gaura-kiśora Dāsa Bābājī and receive his instruction. Śrīla Gaura-kiśora Dāsa Bābājī was very pleased to see the great renunciation of Śrīla Sarasvatī Ṭhākura. He used to say, "In my Prabhu I see the same kind of renunciation that was seen in Śrī Rūpa and Śrī Raghunātha." Śrīla Bābājī Mahāśaya used to address his disciple Śrīla Sarasvatī Ṭhākura as "my Prabhu" ("my master"). Śrīla Sarasvatī Ṭhākura also received the blessings of Śrīla Vaṁśī-dāsa Bābājī Mahārāja in Navadvīpa. Seeing Śrīla Sarasvatī Ṭhākura, Śrīla Vaṁśī-dāsa Bābājī Mahārāj would say, "Someone very close to my Gaura has come to me."

Śrīla Sarasvatī Ṭhākura began his intense preaching of pure devotional principles in a society in which the authority of the *brāhmaṇas* was unquestioned, and the concept of pure devotion was misinterpreted and misrepresented by the imitators of Vaiṣṇavism (the Sahajiyās). In India in the 19th and early 20th centuries, most *brāhmaṇas* were more concerned about rules and regulations that were separated from the concept of devotion and not based on the injunctions of authentic scriptures than they were about what was spiritually and morally beneficial for the rest of society. A *brāhmaṇa* was no longer a person with brahminical qualities, but simply a person born in a family of *brāhmaṇas*. Since the caste system was rotting at its core, it had become meaningless and was in fact detrimental to the spiritual and moral welfare of society. The *brāhmaṇas* opposed any ideas that might threaten their preeminence, which was bereft of any moral or spiritual basis. Although many educated people had lost their faith in the beneficial role of the

Śrīla Vaṁśī-dāsa Bābājī Mahārāja

brāhmaṇa class, they did not know who could take their place. The pure Vaiṣṇavas led reclusive lives hidden from the public eye, and the Sahajiyā Vaiṣṇavas aroused more hatred and suspicion than respect. In this context, Śrīla Prabhupāda wanted to establish the principles of *daivī-varṇāśrama-dharma*—the system in which the service of the Lord is placed in the center of society, a Vaiṣṇava is respected by everyone else, and one's caste is ascertained according to one's natural tendency, not according to one's birth.

A photograph of Bhaktivinoda Ṭhākura. Signed, "To Babu Bimala Prasad Dutt with affection Kedarnath Dutt Bhaktivinod, 21st March 96."

A Letter from Bhaktivinoda

In the meantime Śrīla Bhaktivinoda Ṭhākura was very concerned that pure Vaiṣṇavism was being overshadowed by many other wrong concepts and also by imitators. He felt that among all his sons and disciples, Śrīla Sarasvatī Ṭhākura was the most qualified person to preach pure Vaiṣṇavism; he had more enthusiasm, courage, and qualification than anyone else. Therefore, Ṭhākura Mahāśaya wrote him a letter:

Sarasvatī!

People of this world who are proud of their own aristocratic birth cannot attain real aristocracy. Therefore they attack the pure Vaiṣṇavas, saying, "They have taken birth in low-class families because of their sins." Thus they commit offenses. The solution to this problem is to establish the order of daivī-varṇāśrama dharma—something you have started doing; you should know that to be the real service to the Vaiṣṇavas. Because pure devotional conclusions are not being preached, all kinds of superstitions and bad concepts are being called devotion by such pseudo-sampradāyas as sahajiyā and atibāḍi. Please always crush these anti-devotional concepts by preaching pure devotional conclusions and by setting an example through your personal conduct.

Please make great effort so you can start the parikramā [circumambulation] of Śrīdhāma Navadvīpa as soon as possible. It is by those actions that everyone in this world will receive kṛṣṇa-bhakti [devotional love for the Lord]. Please try very hard to make sure that the service to Śrī Māyāpura will become a permanent thing and will become brighter and brighter every day. The real service to Śrī Māyāpura can be done by acquiring printing presses, distributing devotional books, and preaching congregational chanting (not reclusive bhajan). Please do not neglect to serve Śrī Māyāpura or to preach for the sake of your own reclusive bhajan.

When I am not present anymore, please take great care to serve Śrī Māyāpura Dhāma which is so dear to you. This is my special instruction to you. People who are like animals can never attain devotion; therefore, never take their suggestions. But don't let them know this, directly or indirectly.

I had a special desire to preach the significance of such books as Śrīmad Bhāgavatam, Ṣaṭ Sandarbha, and Vedānta Darśan. You have to accept that responsibility. Śrī Māyāpura will prosper if you establish an educational institution there. Never make any effort to collect knowledge or money for your own enjoyment. Only to serve the Lord will you collect these things. Never engage in bad association, either for money or for some self-interest.

All the Vaiṣṇava devotees who were in contact with Śrīla Bhaktivinoda Ṭhākura and Śrīla Sarasvatī Ṭhākura knew that the relationship between them was not mundane, like that between an ordinary father and son. Their relationship with each other was completely transcendental, like that between *guru* and disciple, as is evident in this letter.

Śrīla Sarasvatī Ṭhākura became more enthused now to preach pure Vaiṣṇavism. Apart from delivering *hari-kathā* and leading congregational chanting, he also started collecting facts about the four Vaiṣṇava *sampradāyas* (branches of disciplic lineage). He started writing and publishing articles about Vaiṣṇava *ācāryas* in *Sajjana Toṣaṇī*.

In 1906, one gentleman called Śrī Rohiṇī Kumāra Ghoṣa came to visit Śrīla Sarasvatī Ṭhākura. He was the nephew of a High Court judge, Śrī Candra Mādhava Ghoṣa of Barishal. Rohiṇī Bābu gave up his home life to have a devotional life in Navadvīpa. He found a *guru* from the Bāul *apasampradaya* (one of the pseudo-Vaiṣṇava groups) and started residing in his *āśrama*. One afternoon he came to Śrīla Sarasvatī Ṭhākura and heard some invaluable devotional instructions from him. Rohiṇī Bābu was deeply touched by this discussion, and when he came back to the *āśrama* that night, it was all he could think about. Without taking his meal, he went to bed. That night, he had a dream in which that Bāul Guru and his female companion came as tigers to attack him, but Śrīla Sarasvatī Ṭhākura came to rescue him from this danger. The next morning when Rohiṇī Bābu was awakened by the sunlight streaming through his window, he immediately left that *āśrama* and set off for Māyāpura to beg Śrīla Sarasvatī Ṭhākura for shelter at his lotus feet. He was the first disciple of Śrīla Prabhupāda (Śrīla Sarasvatī Ṭhākura was thus addressed by his disciples).

Bhajana Kuṭīra at Śrī Vrajapattana, 1909

In February 1909, Śrīla Prabhupāda built a small *bhajana-kuṭīra* near the *bhavana*, or residence, of Śrī Candraśekhara Ācārya, who was the maternal uncle of Śrīman Mahāprabhu. Remembering Mahāprabhu's *vraja-līlā* that was performed here, he called this Śrī Vrajapattana. Śrīla Prabhupāda continued his service at Śrī Yogapīṭha (the birthplace of Śrīman Mahāprabhu), but stayed at Śrī Vrajapattana. At this time his mother, Śrīmatī Bhagavatī Devī, was staying at Yogapīṭha and assisting him in his service to Śrī Māyāpura Dhāma.

While he was staying there by himself, two very young boys came to him and took shelter at his lotus feet. One of them, Aśvini Haldār, came from nearby Ballaldighi. Even though he was illiterate when he first came, by the grace and guidance of Śrīla Prabhupāda he became a great scholar of scripture. Later when Śrīla Prabhupāda gave him initiation, he named him "Vaiṣṇava-dāsa" ("servant of the Vaiṣṇavas"). Śrīpāda Vaiṣṇava-dāsa Prabhu served Śrīla Prabhupāda for the rest of his life. He was known as a very expert *kīrtana* singer.

The second boy, Śrī Pañcānana Samāddār, came from the village of Vinodnagar, in Jessore district. His father, Śrī Tāriṇīcaraṇa Samāddār, had had the good fortune of associating with Śrīla Bhaktivinoda Ṭhākura. Śrīla Ṭhākura Mahāśaya had visited their village once as well. The little boy Pañcānana was very attracted to *hari-kathā*, and at the age of twelve he left home one night during the predawn hours and set forth in search of his devotional destiny. Somehow he came to Navadvīpa and, as if by some unknown attraction, came to Māyāpura and met Śrīla Prabhupāda. Hearing from Śrīla Prabhupāda, he knew his destiny was at the lotus feet of this great personality. So he stayed there with Śrīla Prabhupāda. Later Prabhupāda sent him to different schools, including the Sānagar School in Calcutta and the Hindu School in Navadvīpa. But his main teacher was Śrīla Prabhupāda himself. Later he was known as a great scholar and writer, and talented in many arts. In 1913, Śrīla Prabhupāda gave him initiation and named him "Paramānanda Vidyāratna." Throughout his life, he was always by the side of Śrīla Prabhupāda and he served his spiritual master in every capacity. Śrīla Prabhupāda made him one of the trustees of the Gauḍīya Maṭha.

Brāhmaṇas and Vaiṣṇavas, 1911

In 1911 the Vaiṣṇava devotees were confronted by a great deal of hostile criticism from the orthodox *brāhmaṇas* of Bengal, known as the Smārta Samāja. These *brāhmaṇas,* although bereft of real scriptural knowledge, were very proud of their own birth and social position, and their doctrines of rules and regulations. Because of their elevated social status, it was easy for them to influence the masses, who were ignorant of pure devotional conclusions. Even some Vaiṣṇava devotees supported the *brāhmaṇas* in order to get some favor from them. At this time Śrīla Bhaktivinoda Ṭhākura was ill and bedridden. But he was still very concerned about the situation and wanted someone to confront the *brāhmaṇa-paṇḍitas* face to face. In accordance with Śrīla Bhaktivinoda Ṭhākura's desire and having been so requested by the famous scholar Śrī Madhusūdana Gosvāmī of Vṛndāvana, Śrīla Prabhupāda arranged a meeting with the *brāhmaṇa-paṇḍitas* at the town of Balighai, in Medinipur district. Paṇḍita Śrī Viśvambharānanda Deva Gosvāmī presided over this meeting.

Śrīla Prabhupāda read there his famous article, "Brāhmaṇa and Vaiṣṇava." When he arrived, the assembled scholars were sitting in two different groups: those who believed in the superiority of *brāhmaṇas* over all other classes of people, and those who believed in the superiority of Vaiṣṇavas, irrespective of birth or social position, over all other classes of people. At first Śrīla Prabhupāda quoted from many scriptures glorifying *brāhmaṇas*. The joy of the assembled *brāhmaṇas* knew no bounds, because even they did not know that there was so much glorification of *brāhmaṇas* in so many different scriptures. But then Śrīla Prabhupāda started his glorification of Vaiṣṇavas, again based on scripture, which far exceeded the glorification of *brāhmaṇas* in quality and quantity. This time the *brāhmaṇa paṇḍitas* were not so pleased. Unable to respond to the evidence presented by Śrīla Prabhupāda, they started shouting. One or two of them desperately tried to present new arguments, but Śrīla Prabhupāda crushed those also by dint of his scriptural knowledge and irrefutable logic. He personally answered all questions and refuted all arguments by the *brāhmaṇas,* and thus established the superiority of pure devotees over all classes of people.

The Gaura Mantra, 1911

In that same year, at a meeting attended by many devotees and scholars of religion, Śrīla Prabhupāda established the truth that the Gaura mantra is eternal and should be chanted by all devotees. He based his conclusions on the evidence of many scriptures, such as the *Caitanyopaniṣad* from the *Atharva Veda* as well as other *Upaniṣads* and *Purāṇas*. Thus he crushed the theory that the name Gaura is not an eternal name of the Supreme Lord and that Śrī Caitanya Mahāprabhu was not an incarnation of the Supreme Lord. Unbeknownst to Śrīla Prabhupāda, his Gurudeva Śrīla Gaura-kiśora Dāsa Bābājī was also present in the audience and ecstatic to hear his conclusions.

Kasim Bazar Religious Conference, 1912

In March 1912, Śrīla Prabhupāda was invited by the Mahārāja of Kasim Bazar, Calcutta, Śrī Maṇīndra Candra Nandī, to deliver *hari-kathā* at the "Kasim Bazar Sammilani," an annual religious conference. But when Śrīla Prabhupāda arrived there, he saw that the organizers were more interested in their mundane concept of religiosity and in pleasing other people than in promoting the concept of pure devotion. To protest these concepts, which were contradictory to pure devotion, Śrīla Prabhupāda fasted during his entire stay there and accepted *prasādam* (food that has been offered to the Supreme Lord) only after his return to Śrī Māyāpura Dhāma.

Pilgrimage & Preaching, 1912

On November 4, 1912, Śrīla Prabhupāda, in the company of a few devotees, set out to visit the holy places where Śrīman Mahāprabhu and his associates had their pastimes, such as Śrīkhaṇḍa, Yājigrām,

Kāṭwā, Jhāmatpur, Chākhandi, Daihāt, and so forth, and preached about pure devotion there. In Śrīdhāma Māyāpura and the surrounding areas, and sometimes in other villages of Bengal and in Calcutta, Śrīla Prabhupāda constantly preached and answered spiritual questions.

The Printing Press & the Anubhāṣya, 1913–1915

In 1913, Śrīla Prabhupāda established a press called Bhāgavat Yantrālaya at 4 Sānagar Lane, Kalighat, Calcutta, and began publishing and printing such books as *Śrī Caitanya-caritāmṛta* with his *Anubhāṣya* commentary, *Śrīmad-Bhagavad-gītā* with the commentaries of Śrī Viśvanātha Cakravartī Ṭhākura, the *Gaura-kṛṣṇodaya* by the Oḍiyan poet Govinda Dāsa, and so forth. In the evenings he would lead *saṅkīrtana* and afterwards deliver *hari-kathā*. Many distinguished gentlemen of Calcutta would come to listen to him. In 1914 Śrīla Bhaktivinoda Ṭhākura disappeared from this world to enter into the transcendental abode of his eternal pastimes. In January 1915, Śrīla Prabhupāda moved the printing press to Śrī Vrajapattana at Māyāpura, and continued publishing and printing books from there. He finished his commentaries on *Śrī Caitanya-caritāmṛta* on June 14, 1915.

Editing Sajjana-Toṣaṇī, 1915

After the disappearance of Śrīla Bhaktivinoda Ṭhākura, his famous and widely distributed Vaiṣṇava magazine, *Sajjana Toṣaṇī*, continued publication under the editorship of Śrīla Prabhupāda. In July 1915 he moved the Bhāgavat Yantra press to the town of Krishnanagar, and began publishing Śrīla Bhaktivinoda Ṭhākura's books.

Disappearance of His Spiritual Master, 1915

On November 17, 1915, on the holy day of Utthāna Ekādaśi, Śrīla Prabhupāda's *dīkṣā-guru*, Śrīla Gaura-kiśora Dāsa Bābājī Mahārāja, disappeared from this world. Śrīla Prabhupāda immediately set forth for Navadvīpa from Māyāpura. Śrīpāda Kuñja-bihāri Vidyābhūṣaṇa (later Śrīmad Bhakti Vilāsa Tīrtha Mahārāja) has described this incident in the biography of Śrīla Prabhupāda, *Sarasvatī Jayaśrī*. A few so-called Bābājīs of Navadvīpa began arguing with each other about who would give *samādhi* to the transcendental body of Śrīla Gaura-kiśora Dāsa Bābājī. They all had some ulterior motive, namely to own this *samādhi* temple themselves so they could make money in the future from devotees and pilgrims. Apprehending a breach of the peace, the Inspector of Police, Śrī Barīndra Nātha Siṁha, arrived there.

After much argument these Bābājīs said that Śrīla Prabhupāda was not a *sannyāsī* and therefore did not have the right to give *samādhi* to Śrīla Gaura-kiśora Dāsa Bābājī Mahārāja. Śrīla Prabhupāda responded in a thunderous voice, "I am the only disciple of Śrīla Bābājī Mahārāja. Although I am not a *sannyāsī*, I have observed *brahmācārya* (celibacy) all my life. By the grace of Śrīla Bābājī Mahārāja, I have not lived a secret life of illicit conduct and debauchery, like some 'monkey' renunciates. If there is someone among those present here who has a genuinely pure character and who is a renunciate, then he can give *samādhi* to Śrīla Bābājī Mahārāja and we have no objection to that. If there is anyone here who, in the last one year, or six months, or three months, or one month, or even in the last three days, did not have any illicit contact with a woman, then he can touch this blissful transcendental body. If anyone else touches this body, he will be ruined."

Hearing this the inspector asked, "What will be the proof of this?" Śrīla Prabhupāda replied, "I will believe their words." Everyone present was amazed to see that all the so-called Bābājīs left the scene, one by one. The Inspector of Police was dumfounded.

Then by the order of Śrīla Prabhupāda, the Vaiṣṇava devotees with him were fortunate enough to carry the transcendental body of Bābājī Mahārāja. Some people said, "When Śrīla Bābājī Mahārāj was alive, he said, 'My body should be dragged on the ground of Navadvīpa so it can be covered by the dust of Navadvīpa.' His instruction should be obeyed."

Then Śrīla Prabhupāda said, "Even though we are stupid, ignorant, and offensive, we should still be able to understand the significance of these humble words of my Gurudeva, which were spoken to destroy the pride and arrogance of materialistic people. Even Lord Kṛṣṇa considers Himself fortunate to carry the body of my *gurudeva* on His shoulders or head. After the disappearance of Śrīla Haridāsa Ṭhākura, Śrī Gaurasundara took his blissful body in his own arms and danced; such was the reverence he showed him. Therefore, following in the footsteps of Śrīman Mahāprabhu, we shall also carry Śrīla Bābājī Mahārāja's blissful body on our heads."

On November 17, 1915, Śrīla Prabhupāda gave *samādhi* to his Gurudeva, on the Nutan Charā of Navadvīpa, on the banks of the Gaṅgā. Sixteen years later, the moving currents of the Gaṅgā arrived at that holy place. By his instruction, on August 21, 1932, some of his disciples from Śrī Caitanya Maṭha, including Śrīpāda Narahari Prabhu and Śrīpāda Vinoda Bihārī Prabhu (later Śrīla Bhakti Prajñāna Keśava Mahārāja) and others, removed this *samādhi* by boat across the Gaṅgā from Navadvīpa to Śrī Caitanya Maṭha, Māyāpura.

The Divine Vision of Śrīla Prabhupāda, 1915

After the disappearance of Śrīla Bhaktivinoda Ṭhākura and Śrīla Gaura-kiśora Dāsa Bābājī Mahārāja, Śrīla Prabhupāda was grief-stricken and was feeling the pangs of separation. At that time a wonderful incident took place. Śrīpāda Paramānanda Vidyāratna has described this in *Sarasvatī Jayaśrī*:

Śrīla Prabhupāda was feeling very discouraged in the absence of Śrīla Ṭhākura Mahāśaya and Śrīla Bābājī Mahārāja, seeing the helpless condition of the spiritual section in the country and the propaganda of the sahajiyās (imitators). He was thinking, "How will I fulfill the desire of my spiritual masters? How will I be able to preach the message of Śrī Caitanya Mahāprabhu? I do not have enough money or manpower. Nor do I have any knowledge or talent that would enchant the public. I have no material skill or wealth. How can this grave task be performed by me? I won't be able to preach the message of my spiritual masters."

Thinking all this, Śrīla Prabhupāda displayed his pastime of gloom and depression. Then one night he saw in a visionary trance that Lord Gaursundar had arrived from the east side of the Yogapiṭh temple with His associates. Amid the sound of saṅkīrtana, *He was ascending to His birth site. With Him were the six Gosvāmīs. Śrīla Jagannātha Dāsa Bābājī, Śrīla Bhaktivinoda Ṭhākura, and Śrīla Gaura-kiśora Dāsa Bābājī were also present in their effulgent transcendental forms. Addressing Śrīla Prabhupāda directly, they said, "Why are you in such a state of anxiety? Begin your task of establishing pure religion. Everywhere preach the message of Śrī Gaura and spread the service of the holy name, abode, and desire of Śrī Gaura. We are always ready to help you, being eternally present with you. In your mission of establishing pure devotional service, you will always receive our help. Behind you innumerable people, unlimited wealth, and extraordinary scholarship are waiting to help you. Whatever you need at any time will immediately appear to serve your mission of pure devotion. With full enthusiasm, proceed with your preaching of the message of pure devotion as it was preached by Śrīman Mahāprabhu. No material problems can impede you. We are always with you." The next morning Śrīla Prabhupāda told us about this visionary trance with great ecstasy.*

Sannyāsa and Founding Śrī Caitanya Maṭha, 1918

Even though Śrīla Prabhupāda was already a great renunciate and an eternally liberated (*nitya-siddha*) spiritual personality, in order to preach extensively as a travelling mendicant (*parivrājaka*) and to set an example of *daivī-varṇāśrama dharma*, he decided to take *sannyāsa* in the year 1918. By accepting the saffron cloth, he actually took a humble position below his two gurus, Śrīla Bhaktivinoda Ṭhākura and Śrīla Gaura-kiśora Dāsa Bābājī, who had both accepted the *paramahaṁsa-veśa* (the white cloth of a renunciate Vaiṣṇava who has given up *varṇāśrama dharma*; *sannyāsa*, which requires wearing a saffron cloth, is part of *varṇāśrama dharma*). On the full moon day of March 7, 1918, on the auspicious occasion of the appearance festival of Śrīman Mahāprabhu, Śrīla Prabhupāda took *sannyāsa* in Śrī Māyāpura according to Vedic rites. Early in the morning he shaved his head and then went to bathe in the old Gaṅgā, near Vāmana Pukura. Śrī Rāma-gopāla Vidyābhūṣaṇa, Śrī Ananta Vāsudeva Prabhu, Śrīkānta Dāsādhikārī (later Śrīmad Bhakti Prakāśa Āraṇya Mahārāja), and a few other devotees accompanied him. On the way Śrīla Prabhupāda spoke on such topics as the story of Ajāmila, the *sannyāsa* pastime of Śrīman Mahāprabhu,

Old temple of Śrī Caitanya Maṭha in Māyāpura

and some verses from the *Śrīmad-Bhāgavatam*. After bathing he offered his *daṇḍavats* and returned to Vrajapattana. The devotees had collected and arranged all the necessary paraphernalia there. Śrīla Prabhupāda went inside the temple and, remembering his Gurudeva, he took *tridaṇḍi-sannyāsa* (the word "*tridaṇḍi*" signifies the threefold vows of serving the Supreme Lord with body, mind, and soul).

In the meantime all the devotees were waiting outside. Among them were Śrīpāda Paramānanda Vidyāratna and Śrīpāda Kuñja-bihārī Vidyābhūṣaṇa. A big crowd had also assembled to celebrate the appearance festival of Śrīman Mahāprabhu. When Śrīla Prabhupāda emerged as a *sannyāsī*, everyone became very sad and remembered the *sannyāsa* pastime of Śrīman Mahāprabhu. Overwhelmed with devotional emotion, all started crying.

That same day, Śrīla Prabhupāda established Śrī Caitanya Maṭha and installed the Deities of Śrī Śrī Guru Gaurāṅga and Śrī Śrī Rādhā Govinda there. This Śrī Caitanya Maṭha in Māyāpura is the Ākara Maṭha (the original or parent *Maṭha*) of all the Gauḍīya Maṭhas all over the world. In the afternoon he delivered a lecture about the appearance of Śrīman Mahāprabhu to the assembled crowd. The next day he initiated some of the surrendered devotees, such as Śrīpāda Haripada Vidyāratna, Śrīpāda Ananta Vāsudeva Prabhu, and Śrīpāda Bhakti Prakāśa Prabhu.

After taking *sannyāsa*, Prabhupāda displayed his extraordinary pastimes of renunciation and austerity. This was described in the memoir of Śrīpāda Ananta Vāsudeva Prabhu quoted in *Sarasvatī Jayaśrī*:

Before taking sannyāsa he used to wear a top garment twenty-four hours a day. No one ever saw his upper body. But after sannyās he would wear a chādar most of the time. He gave up wearing sandals. Walking everywhere without sandals made his feet bleed, but he still would walk without sandals. Seeing his example of great renunciation, we were amazed. During cāturmāsya (the four months of the rainy season) he would sleep on the floor and would only eat during the day, never after sunset. In the heat of summer in Māyāpura he would close his door and chant night and day.

Later that month Śrīla Prabhupāda gave a very scholarly lecture called "Vaiṣṇava Darśana" ("The Vaiṣṇava Philosophy") at a literary meeting in the Krishnanagar town hall. In May he took some of his disciples with him to preach in different places. In Daulatpur he stayed in the house of Vanamāli Poddar and preached continuously for several days. There he initiated quite a few devotees including Śrīpāda Yaśodānandana Prabhu and Śrīpāda Narahari Prabhu.

At this time, his disciple Śrīpāda Nayanābhirāma Prabhu (later Śrīmad Bhakti Viveka Bhārati Mahārāja) earnestly assisted Śrīla Prabhupāda with his preaching activities. Śrīmad Bhārati Mahārāja would preach in very simple language and present the Vaiṣṇava concept in a simple, but attractive, way. Śrīla Prabhupāda engaged Śrīmad Bhārati Mahārāja to speak to the general public. Śrīmad Bhārati Mahārāja would sometimes make them laugh and sometimes make them cry. His preaching captured their hearts and they would come by the thousands to listen to him. He was an expert *kīrtana* singer. Śrīla Prabhupāda always knew the greatest strength of each of his disciples, and he would engage them accordingly. Before he left this world, he told Śrīmad Bhārati Mahārāja that he was a hard-working, practical person, and should serve the mission.

Śrī Kṣetra-maṇḍala Parikramā, 1918

To celebrate the fourth disappearance anniversary of Śrīla Bhaktivinoda Ṭhākura, Śrīla Prabhupāda set forth for Purī Dhāma on June 2, 1918, along with twenty-three other devotees. Before going to Purī Dhāma, Śrīla Prabhupāda accepted the invitation of Śrīpāda Kuñja-bihārī Vidyābhūṣaṇa and went to his residence in Gauribāḍi Lane, Calcutta, with all the devotees to take *prasādam* for two days. Śrīpāda Kuñja-bihārī Prabhu was an ordinary impoverished postal employee. Despite this fact, he arranged for a sumptuous feast of many courses for Śrīla Prabhupāda and his entourage. On his way to Purī Dhāma Śrīla Prabhupāda also preached at different places such as Sāuri, Kuāmārā, and so forth. Then he went to Remuṇā to see the Deity of Kṣīracorā Gopīnātha. At a meeting in Baleswar, he gave a lecture on the *Śikṣāṣṭaka* verses of Mahāprabhu. On his way to Purī he became overwhelmed with the mood of separation of Śrīman Mahāprabhu. Many distinguished government officers and citizens came to listen to his lectures, and some of them invited him to lecture in their homes.

After celebrating the disappearance festival of Śrīla Bhaktivinoda Ṭhākura with extensive preaching and *saṅkīrtana* in Purī, Śrīla Prabhupāda came back to Calcutta. For a little while he stayed at No. 3 British Indian Street. He delivered lectures there, and his disciples used to visit him daily. Sometimes Śrīpāda Kuñja-bihārī Vidyābhūṣaṇa would cook for Śrīla Prabhupāda there. During August and September 1918, a representative of a group of opponents of Vaiṣṇavism presented Śrīla Prabhupāda with twenty-nine questions. He answered all of them on the basis of scripture and logic and thus silenced his opponents. These questions and answers were subsequently published in an article called "The Answers to the Questions of the Critics." Later Śrīla Prabhupāda came back to Bhakti Bhavan.

Bhaktivinoda Āsana 1918–1919

In the next few months and years, something unprecedented took place. The big city of Calcutta, previously thought by Vaiṣṇavas to be a very unfavorable place, became the center of preaching for Śrīla Prabhupāda's mission of pure devotion. It started when his disciple Śrīpāda Kuñja-bihārī Prabhu, who was always burning with fervent enthusiasm to serve Śrīla Prabhupāda, submitted a new proposal at his lotus feet. One day in Māyāpura, he said, "Prabhupāda, how many people can come here and listen to your glorious, powerful, and unparalleled message about Śrīman Mahāprabhu? On the other hand, people from all over the world come to Calcutta or pass through that city. If we can arrange for a residence for you in Calcutta, faithful people from many places will have the good fortune of listening to you." Śrīla Prabhupāda granted this request. Śrīpāda Kuñja-bihārī Prabhu rented a two-story house in November 1918 on No. 1 Ultadanga Junction Road, next to the famous temple of Pareśanātha.

That same month Śrīla Prabhupāda established the spiritual institution called Bhaktivinoda Āsana there. The temple room and Śrīla Prabhupāda's room were upstairs, and three or four devotees, including Śrīpāda Kuñja-bihārī Prabhu, lived downstairs. The rent was Rs. 50 per month. This was beyond the means of an impoverished postal employee. Other devotees staying there tried to help Śrīpāda Kuñja-bihārī Prabhu, but most of the time they also found it difficult to come up with that money. But Śrīpāda Kuñja-bihārī Prabhu always went out of his way to supply whatever was necessary to serve his *gurudeva*, even if he had to incur a substantial debt in order to do so.

Śrīla Prabhupāda now started his regular preaching program in the newly established Bhaktivinoda Āsana. More and more people came to listen to him. On February 5, 1919, on the auspicious appearance day of Śrīmatī Viṣṇupriyā Devī, Śrīla Prabhupāda re-established the Viśva-Vaiṣṇava-Rāja-Sabhā. He gave a scholarly lecture on the ancient history of this assembly. On June 27, in Svānanda-sukhada-kuñja (the *bhajana-kuṭīra* of Śrīla Bhaktivinoda Ṭhākura), the worshipable deity form of Śrīla Bhaktivinoda Ṭhākura was installed.

Preaching in East Bengal, 1919

On October 4, 1919, Śrīla Prabhupāda set forth to preach in East Bengal (now Bangladesh) and north Bengal. Right before this, natural disasters, a strong hurricane and flood, had hit East Bengal. Thousands of people became homeless and many people died. Usually autumn is a season of festivity in Bengal, since during this time of year Bengalis celebrate their Durgā Pūjā festival. But this year grief and loss took the place of festivity in many places. Śrīla Prabhupāda chose this time to preach his message of pure devotion. He decided that this was the proper time to sing the verse:

tat te 'nukampāṁ susamīkṣamāṇo
bhuñjāna evātmakṛtaṁ vipākam
hṛdvāg vapubhir vidadhan namaste
jīveta yo muktipade sa dāyabhāk

—*Śrīmad-Bhāgavatam* 10.14.8

"My dear Lord, one who earnestly waits for You to bestow Your causeless mercy upon him, all the while patiently suffering the reaction of his past misdeeds and offering you respectful obeisances with his heart, words, and body, is surely eligible for liberation, for it has become his rightful claim."

Śrīla Prabhupāda preached in many different towns and villages in East Bengal. Wherever he went, many people came to listen to his lectures. In many places special meetings were arranged where Śrīla Prabhupāda was requested to speak. Many distinguished gentlemen invited Śrīla Prabhupāda to their homes to deliver *hari-kathā*. He led *saṅkīrtana* processions in different towns and villages. Śrīla Prabhupāda visited such places as Damurhuda, Kushtia, Pabna, Satberia, Sagar Kandi, Belgachi, Rajbari, Louhajang, Domsar, Narayanaganj, Dhaka, Sirajdigha, Kotchandpur, Sripat Maheshpur, and so forth.

Questionnaire for the Kasim Bazar Conference

In April 1920 the religious conference "Kasim Bazar Sammilani" took place in Kummilā, East Bengal. The members of the Viśva-Vaiṣṇava-Rāja-Sabhā were invited to participate in that conference. But when they saw the agenda, which included the discussion and singing of Lord Kṛṣṇa's very intimate pastimes with the *gopīs*, by the order of Śrīla Prabhupāda they sent a questionnaire to that conference, care of the gentle and humble Mahārāja of Kasim Bazar, Śrī Maṇīndra Candra Nandī. Seven questions were posed regarding the propriety of such discussions of the intimate pastimes of Śrī Śrī Rādhā-Kṛṣṇa among conditioned souls. The Mahārāja duly presented the questionnaire to the assembled *paṇḍitas*. But no one dared to answer those questions.

Disappearance of Śrīmatī Bhagavati Devī, 1920

In June 1920 Śrīla Prabhupāda's worshipable mother, Śrīmatī Bhagavati Devī, left this world to enter the abode of her eternal pastimes. Six years earlier on that very day Śrīla Bhaktivinoda Ṭhākura had left this world. For many years, Śrīmatī Bhagavati Devī had dedicated herself to assist the divine mission of Śrīla Prabhupāda. Before she left this world, she called Śrīla Prabhupāda to her bedside and expressed her last desire, that the message and the holy name of Śrīman Mahāprabhu be preached all over the world.

Śrī Gauḍīya Maṭha, 1920

On September 6, 1920, Prabhupāda founded Śrī Gauḍīya Maṭha at Bhaktivinoda Āsan and installed the Deities of Śrī Śrī Guru Gaurāṅga and Śrī Śrī Rādhā Govinda. Śrīla Prabhupāda's movement gained great momentum immediately after he chartered the Gauḍīya Maṭha. Śrīla Prabhupāda wanted to start a great mission which would propagate Śrīman Mahāprabhu's teachings in their purest form. He wanted to preach that the goal of life is to love and serve Kṛṣṇa, and that the only way for the fallen souls of Kali-yuga to be delivered is to chant the holy name and render unconditional devotional service. He wanted to preach his concept of pure devotion to all classes of people—the educated and the uneducated, the rich and the poor, the orthodox *brāhmaṇas* and the young people influenced by Western ideas. He wanted hundreds of people to come to his lectures and thousands of people to read the books and magazines published by the Gauḍīya Maṭha. In short, he wanted to start a spiritual revolution, a seemingly ambitious goal for someone who had only a handful of men to help him and hardly any money to spend. But the Gauḍīya Maṭha grew at an amazing speed. People came from all fields of life, and most of them were highly educated. Many people came to join his mission with many different talents and skills to contribute—scholars, writers, editors, administrators, doctors, engineers, lawyers. Śrīla Prabhupāda's unique personality and his powerful speeches touched many people's hearts and changed their lives forever. A spiritual revolution was indeed taking place in Bengal.

The devotees of the Gauḍīya Maṭha worked very hard to propagate Śrīla Prabhupāda's preaching mission. They begged from door to door, worshiped the Deities, performed *kīrtana* inside the temple, and went on *nagara-saṅkīrtana* on the streets of Calcutta. They also preached at various places, being so instructed by Śrīla Prabhupāda. In 1920, Śrīpāda Kuñja-bihārī Vidyābhūṣan Prabhu suddenly left for Basra (in present-day Iraq) to take a temporary position, so that he could pay off the huge debt he had incurred in trying to serve the Gauḍīya Maṭha.

On November 1, 1920, Śrīla Prabhupāda gave *sannyāsa* to Śrīpāda Jagadīśa Bhakti-pradīpa, who was a disciple of Śrīla Bhaktivinoda Ṭhākura. He was the first devotee to receive *sannyāsa* from Śrīla Prabhupāda. Now he was called Śrīla Bhakti Pradīpa Tīrtha Mahārāja.

On March 14, 1921, Śrīla Prabhupāda revived Navadvīpa Dhāma Parikramā. At the end of March he once more went to preach in Purī Dhāma. At this time Śrīmad Bhakti Pradīpa Tīrtha Mahārāja published a book called *Āchār O Ācārya (The Spiritual Master and His Conduct)*, by Śrīla Prabhupāda. This book introduced revolutionary ideas by criticizing the contemporary practices of those gurus who had turned religion into a money-making profession.

From the 1920s onward, Śrīla Prabhupāda's movement started spreading steadily. Preaching went on continuously, not only in Bengal, but in other parts of India. Scholars of every field came to listen to Śrīla Prabhupāda's lectures and ask him spiritual questions.

Śrī Caitanya Maṭha, Māyāpura, 1920

As Śrīla Prabhupāda was spending more and more time away from Māyāpura while preaching at the Bagbazar Gauḍīya Maṭha or going on preaching tours of different places in Bengal, Bihār, and Orissa, in 1920 he decided to establish some of his disciples at Śrī Caitanya Maṭha in Māyāpura. He directed two devotees, Śrīpāda Narahari Dās Brahmacārī and Śrīpāda Vinoda-bihārī Brahmacārī, to take charge of that *maṭha*.

Gauḍīya Maṭha in East Bengal, 1921

In 1921, Śrīla Prabhupāda preached at different places in Bihar, including Dhanbad, and then returned to East Bengal to preach extensively there. Some of his disciples who were influential speakers, such as Śrīmad Bhakti Pradīpa Tīrtha Mahārāja, also delivered many lectures and answered questions. In the beginning considerable opposition to Śrīla Prabhupāda's outspoken preaching arose. The professional speakers of *Śrīmad-Bhāgavatam* did their best to launch a powerful campaign to mislead the common people against Śrīla Prabhupāda's mission. Initially it worked, when some people refused to open their doors to Śrīla Prabhupāda's disciples. But being empowered by his blessings, Śrīla Prabhupāda's disciples were very determined to preach. They decided that if there was no food and shelter for them, then they would just go hungry and drink the water of the Buriganga river. But they would go on preaching tirelessly. Such determination was rewarded by a renewed interest in Gauḍīya Vaiṣṇavism among the spiritually inquisitive. The ground for Śrīla Prabhupāda's preaching in East Bengal was made fertile by the advance work of Śrīla Prabhupāda's disciples.

When Śrīla Prabhupāda went to East Bengal, he gave realizations to the inquiring public that were beyond their dreams. For example, Śrīla Prabhupāda resided in the city of Dhaka for one month and gave thirty different interpretations of the following verse from *Śrīmad Bhāgavatam*:

oṁ namo bhagavate vāsudevāya
janmādy asya yato 'nvayād itarataś
chārtheṣv abhijñaḥ svarāṭ
tene brahma hṛdā ya ādi-kavaye
muhyanti yat sūrayaḥ
tejo-vāri-mṛdāṁ yathā vinimayo
yatra tri-sargo 'mṛṣā
dhāmanā svena sadā nirasta-kuhakaṁ
satyaṁ paraṁ dhīmahi

—*Śrīmad Bhāgavatam 1.1.1*

"O my Lord, Śrī Kṛṣṇa, son of Vasudeva, O all-pervading Personality of Godhead, I offer my respectful obeisances unto You. I meditate upon Lord Śrī Kṛṣṇa because He is the Absolute Truth and the primeval cause of all causes of the creation, sustenance, and destruction of the manifested universes. He is directly and indirectly conscious of all manifestations, and He is independent because there is no other cause beyond Him. It is only He who first imparted the Vedic knowledge unto the heart of Brahmāji, the original living being. By Him even the great sages and demigods are placed into illusion, as one is bewildered by the illusory representations of water seen in fire, or land seen on water. Only because of Him do the material universes, temporarily manifested by the reactions of the three modes of nature, appear factual, although they are unreal. I therefore meditate upon Him, Lord Śrī Kṛṣṇa, who is eternally existent in the transcendental abode, which is forever free from the illusory representations of the material world. I meditate upon Him, for He is the Absolute Truth."

Even great scholars were amazed to hear these interpretations. Many sincere souls took initiation then from Śrīla Prabhupāda. One of the disciples who came from Dhaka was Śrīpāda Sundarānanda Vidyāvinoda, who later became one of the main writers in the preaching mission of the Gauḍīya Maṭha.

That same year, Śrīpāda Kuñja-bihārī Vidyābhūṣaṇa Prabhu returned from Basra and joined Śrīla Prabhupāda's preaching mission in Dhaka. Śrīla Prabhupāda had been missing him greatly, and had already made plans to take Śrīpāda Kuñja-bihārī Vidyābhūṣaṇa Prabhu with him to different places.

On October 13, 1921, Śrīla Prabhupāda established the Śrī Madhva Gauḍīya Maṭha in Dhaka, and on October 31 he installed the Deities there. In Faridabad Śrīla Prabhupāda delivered *hari-kathā* in the house of Śrī Saratcandra Bandopādhyāya, who was grief-stricken by his son's death. Hearing Śrīla Prabhupāda's *hari-kathā*, he felt relieved and took initiation from him. Later his two daughters, Śrīmatī Āparaṇā Devī and Suṣamā Devī, also took initiation from Śrīla Prabhupāda. Śrīmatī Āparaṇā Devī was a poet and a writer. She subsequently wrote quite a few articles in the *Gauḍīya* magazine. Much later she translated Śrī Rūpa Gosvāmī's *Stavamālā* and Śrī Raghunātha Dāsa Gosvāmī's *Stavavali* into Bengali poetry, which was much appreciated by the Vaiṣṇava devotees.

On his return from Dhaka, Śrīla Prabhupāda renovated some ruined temples and places of pilgrimage from the time of Śrīman Mahāprabhu's pastimes, and reestablished regular worship there. Among them were the famous Gaura-Gadādhara temple in Campāhāṭi, the birth site of Śrī Vṛndāvana Dāsa Ṭhākura, the guesthouse in Modadruma-dvīpa, etc. In 1933, Śrīla Prabhupāda put Satīśa Prabhu (Śrīpāda Satprasaṅgānanda Brahmacārī, later Śrīmad Nayanānanda Bābājī Mahārāja) in charge of the Gaura-Gadādhara temple in Champāhaṭi.

Puruṣottama Maṭha in Purī, 1922

"Hy utkale puruṣottamāt – From Utkal (Orissa) the concept of pure devotion will spread to the whole world." To honor this prediction of the scriptures, Śrīla Prabhupāda founded the Puruṣottama Maṭha in Purī in June 1922. Following in the footsteps of Śrīman Mahāprabhu, he participated in the pastime of cleansing the Guṇḍicā temple and in *parikramā* of Purī Dhāma along with his disciples. He sent his disciples to preach in various parts of Orissa.

Publication of the Gauḍīya Magazine, 1922

On August 19, 1922, Śrīla Prabhupāda began publishing a magazine called *Gauḍīya* from the Krishnanagar Bhagavat Press, which would become the most famous and widely distributed spiritual Bengali magazine and one of the chief instruments of Śrīla Prabhupāda's preaching mission. In its first year the magazine was jointly edited by Śrīpāda Atulcandra Bandopādhyāya Bhakti-sāraṅga (Śrīpāda Aprākṛta Prabhu—later Śrīmad Bhakti Sāraṅga Gosvāmī Mahārāja) and Śrīpāda Haripada Vidyāratna (later Śrīmad Bhakti Sādhaka Niṣkiñcana Mahārāja). In its second year, Śrīpāda Sundarānanda Vidyāvinoda became the assistant editor. Subsequently Śrīpāda Bhakti-sāraṅga was editor-in-chief, Śrīpāda Sundarānanda Vidyāvinoda was editor, and Śrīpāda Haripada Vidyāratna was assistant editor. From 1930 onward, Śrīpāda Praṇavānanda Brahmacārī (later Śrīmad Bhakti Pramoda Purī Mahārāja) became joint editor of *Gauḍīya*.

In each issue of *Gauḍīya* there was an editorial; sometimes there would be an article by Śrīla Prabhupāda or an article based on his lectures. All together each issue would comprise three or four articles, short paragraphs on current topics and recent events or information on upcoming events, and a column of questions and answers. Browsing through old issues of *Gauḍīya,* one can find the names of Bhakti Rakṣaka Śrīdhara Mahārāja and Śrīmad Praṇavānanda Brahmacārī as those who answered questions from the readers.

For a few years, Śrīpāda Sundarānanda Vidyāvinoda was posted in Dhaka as a teacher in a high school there. But he used to send one or two articles every week. Śrīpāda Praṇavānanda Prabhu also used to write articles, and would proofread the whole magazine. Śrīla Prabhupāda trusted him with the proofreading because he would work very hard and frequently stay up all night to make the text free from errors. The result was a perfect production every week. Devotees used to distribute *Gauḍīya* with great enthusiasm. One devotee from Śrī Caitanya Maṭha in Māyāpura, Śrīpāda Satyen Brahmacārī (later Śrīmad Bhakti Nilaya Giri Mahārāja) used to take the first train to Calcutta every morning to sell and distribute *Gauḍīya*. The philosophical and literary standard of *Gauḍīya* was unsurpassed.

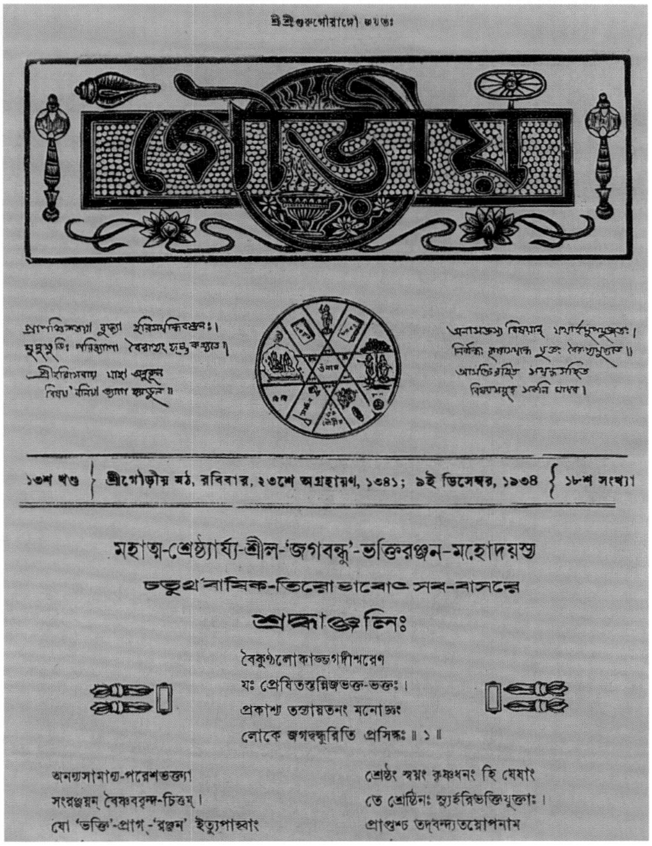
গৌড়ীয়

১৩শ খণ্ড | শ্রীগৌড়ীয় মঠ, রবিবার, ২৩শে অগ্রহায়ণ, ১৩৪১; ৯ই ডিসেম্বর, ১৯৩৪ | ১৮শ সংখ্যা

মহাত্ম-শ্রেষ্ঠ্যার্য্য-শ্রীল-'জগবন্ধু'-ভক্তিরঞ্জন-মহোদয়স্য

চতুর্থ-বার্ষিক-তিরোভাবোৎসব-বাসরে

শ্রদ্ধাঞ্জলিঃ

বৈকুণ্ঠলোকাজ্জগদীশ্বরেণ
যঃ প্রেষিতস্তন্নিজভক্ত-ভক্তঃ।
প্রকাশ্য তত্তায়তনং মনোজ্ঞং
লোকে জগদ্বন্ধুরিতি প্রসিদ্ধঃ ॥ ১ ॥

অনন্যসামান্য-পরেশভক্ত্যা
সংরঞ্জয়ন্ বৈষ্ণববৃন্দ-চিত্তম্।
যো 'ভক্তি'-প্রাগ্-'রঞ্জন' ইত্যুপাখ্যাং

শ্রেষ্ঠং স্বয়ং কৃষ্ণধনং হি যেষাং
তে শ্রেষ্ঠিনঃ স্যুর্হরিভক্তিযুক্তাঃ।
প্রাপ্তশ্চ তদ্বন্দ্যতয়োপনাম

Gauḍīya magazine

Dr. Dinesh Candra Sen, Professor of Bengali literature at the University of Calcutta, was a well-known scholar and writer. Some of his books, such as *Rāmāyaṇī Kathā (Topics of the Rāmāyaṇa)* were prescribed textbooks for the students of Bengali literature. The editor of *Gauḍīya* wrote an article criticizing some of his ideas. When Dr. Dinesh Sen read that article, he was so impressed by its literary standard that he wrote a letter of praise to the writer. That letter was kept in the archives of the Gauḍīya Maṭha. But more importantly, *Gauḍīya* helped to keep the fire of devotional inspiration burning in the hearts of many Bengalis, when another big fire was burning in the heart of Bengal and the rest of India.

Gauḍīya Maṭha and the Freedom Movement of the 1920s

That other fire that was burning in the hearts of the masses of India was the desire for freedom. On one hand was Mahātmā Gāndhi's nonviolent movement for freedom. On the other hand was the more radical guerrilla group. There were little pockets of guerrilla resistance everywhere in India. The British government, which was very reluctant to give up India, "the jewel of the crown of the British empire," was intimidated by both groups.

In Bengal one of the groups of guerilla freedom fighters was called the "Anushilan Samiti" (Organization for the Cultivation of Freedom). Actually, "*anuśilana*" means cultivation, but what was to be cultivated was not specified, for obvious reasons. Hundreds and thousands of young, educated, and talented men, with the support of their mothers, sisters, and wives, gave up their education, family life, and profession, and risked their lives to join one of these two movements: Mahātmā Gāndhi's nonviolent movement or the guerrilla movement. If there was one desire that was shared by the whole nation, it was the desire for freedom from the British.

But Śrīla Prabhupāda wanted to preach about another kind of freedom which transcends any freedom of the mundane world: the freedom of the soul. While nationalistic leaders were preaching that it is the birthright of a nation to have freedom and sovereignty, Śrīla Prabhupāda was preaching that it is the birthright of every soul to seek freedom from material bondage and find its rightful place in the realm of eternity. The nationalistic leaders would argue that that could wait, but Śrīla Prabhupāda insisted one should not waste one minute while reaching for the supreme goal of human life, because it can end at any moment.

Śrīla Prabhupāda said, "First of all we have to know who we are. After that it will become very easy to find out what is our foremost duty. The only path to our eternal welfare is to serve the Lord and have His grace. The human birth is the root of devotional service. It is not possible to render devotional service in animal life.... We all have to become free. But the state of freedom is nothing other than the state of cultivating Kṛṣṇa consciousness with the support of all our senses, being fixed in our real identity." (*Upadeśāmṛta,* p. 462–463)

As one can imagine, it is easier to arouse the oppressed masses to seek political freedom than to arouse the soul to look for its eternal prospect. Yet many young men gave up the nationalistic movement and came to Śrīla Prabhupāda's spiritual movement.

Śrīpāda Vinoda-bihārī Prabhu was formerly a member of the secret organization called the Anushilan Samiti. He gave up his affiliation with it and joined Śrīla Prabhupāda's movement, and so did a few others. But the British police remained very suspicious of their activities. So they sent undercover agents to the Gauḍīya Maṭha to spy on the activities of its members. One such undercover agent listened to Śrīla Prabhupāda's lectures with rapt attention, and gave up his profession to become Śrīla Prabhupāda's disciple. Before begging for Śrīla Prabhupāda's mercy, he disclosed that he had come as a spy. He became Śrīpāda Gaurendu Brahmacārī (later Śrīmad Bhakti Vardhana Sāgara Mahārāja).

After this incident, in 1924 or 1925, another very learned gentleman, Śrī Rāmendra Candra Bhaṭṭācārya, who was not known to any of the devotees, began coming to the *maṭha* regularly. He would silently listen to Śrīla Prabhupāda's lectures with rapt attention. One day Śrīpāda Praṇavānanda Brahmacārī was giving a lecture when he arrived. One devotee, Śrīpāda Kīrtanānanda Brahmacārī, cautioned Śrīpāda Praṇavānanda Prabhu about this gentleman. He said, "I have noticed that he does not ask anything, but listens to every word with rapt attention. He must be a spy."

Śrīpāda Kīrtanānanda Prabhu started keeping an eye on this gentleman. But it so happened that very soon Śrī Rāmendra Candra Bhaṭṭācārya attracted Śrīla Prabhupāda's attention. It was discovered that he was no spy, but in fact was formerly in Mahātmā Gāndhi's freedom movement. Śrīla Prabhupāda gave him initiation, and later named him Śrī Rāmānanda Dāsa Brahmacārī. Within a few years he gave him *sannyāsa*, naming him Śrīmad Bhakti Rakṣaka Śrīdhara Deva Gosvāmī Mahārāja. Śrīla Prabhupāda was very fond of him, and so were his other disciples. Śrīmad Bhakti Rakṣaka Śrīdhara Mahārāja was known for his extraordinary scholarship, his poetic talent, his powerful preaching, his saintly character, and his wholehearted dedication to serving his *gurudeva*.

Many distinguished citizens of Calcutta admired Śrīla Prabhupāda's unprecedented and extraordinary contribution to the Vaiṣṇava movement of Bengal. But not everyone shared their sentiment. The famous Bengali leader of the freedom movement, Netaji Subhash Chandra Bose, complained to Śrīla Prabhupāda that he was diverting the attention of the youth from the freedom movement to his devotional mission. Śrīla Prabhupāda appeased him by saying, "These men are not so physically strong. They will not be of much use to you." Of course, he did not think that Netāji would be interested in the concept of spiritual freedom at that moment.

The Ācārya Who Could Inspire And Engage

Freedom fighters or not, intelligent and spiritually inquisitive young men were coming to Śrīla Prabhupāda, giving up their family ties and material prospects. To cite only one example: Before he took initiation, Śrīpāda Praṇavānanda Brahmacārī used to go to Śrī Gauḍīya Maṭha every day after work. One day, just as he was about to leave for Śrī Gauḍīya Maṭha, he was stung by a scorpion hidden in his shoe. Two days previously a man had died from a scorpion's sting. Although

Śrīla Prabhupāda with the devotees at Ultadingi Junction, Śrī Gauḍīya Maṭha on 4th February 1924. (Gauḍīya, Vol. 4, Issue 2, 22nd August 1925.)

Śrīpāda Praṇavānanda Brahmacārī was bleeding profusely, and the blood was blackish with venom, he told his weeping mother he was all right and set forth for Śrī Gauḍīya Maṭha as if nothing had happened. There he listened to Śrīla Prabhupāda's lecture, and although the intense pain continued throughout that evening and the rest of the night, his mind was on Śrīla Prabhupāda's words, not on his pain. When his godbrothers refer to this incident, he says, "That was my time of *navānurāga* [the first stage of love, when any separation seems risky and unbearable]."

Śrīla Prabhupāda's transcendental personality was extremely attractive, and his powerful preaching could plant the seed of divine love in one's heart—with tangible results. The proof of this was to be found in the atmosphere of the Gauḍīya Maṭha, which was always lively with the sights and sounds of uninterrupted, wholehearted devotional service. Śrīmad Bhakti Rakṣaka Śrīdhara Mahārāja said in his memoir, "When I went there again, I saw many things that touched me. Śrīla Prabhupāda was delivering a lecture to so many gentlemen—educated persons. In another place the elderly Śrīpāda Bhakti Pradīpa Tīrtha Mahārāja was giving a lecture. Elsewhere Śrīpāda Bhakti Svarūpa Parvata Mahārāja was found writing receipts, collecting funds from the people. It was a hive of activity. I felt a transcendental happy atmosphere there."

At the center of this transcendentally happy hive of activity was the *ācārya* who was known to be "softer than a flower and harder than a thunderbolt." Nothing escaped Śrīla Prabhupāda's keen eyes. His affection for his disciples was also all-encompassing. Śrīla Prabhupāda would personally supervise the distribution of *prasādam* to his disciples; he would stand there and make sure everyone ate well. When his disciples' family members came to visit, he would personally welcome them, make them comfortable, and spend considerable time with them.

Śrīla Prabhupāda's deep humility was reflected in his thoughts, words, and actions. He called his disciples "Prabhu" ("master"). He never asked any of them to do anything for him, personally. Yet each of them was eager to render some service to him, for he was their supremely worshipable lord ("Paramārādhya Śrīla Prabhupāda"). Not only was he worshipable to them, but so was anyone who served him with total dedication. Because Śrīpāda Kuñja-bihārī Vidyābhūṣan had a long history of selfless dedicated service to Śrīla Prabhupāda, the *brahmacārīs* staying at the Maṭha would stand in line to eat his remnants (a traditional Vaiṣṇava devotional practice), in the hope that it would give them *guru-sevā-kuñja* (the grove of devotional service to Gurudeva—*kuñja* means "grove").

Vraja-maṇḍala, Śrī Caitanya Maṭha, 1922–1923

On September 28, 1922, Śrīla Prabhupāda went to Vraja-maṇḍala (Mathurā and Vṛndāvana) with the goal of establishing centers for preaching the pure devotional concept of Śrīman Mahāprabhu as preached by Śrīla Gaura-kiśora Dāsa Bābājī and Śrīla Bhaktivinoda Ṭhākura. Later he went back to Dhaka, East Bengal, to preach there again. Then he went to Kuliyā, Navadvīpa, and Santal Pargana (in Bihar).

On March 2, 1923, Gaura-Purṇīmā day, construction of the new temple of Śrī Caitanya Maṭha in Māyāpura began. As per Śrīla Prabhupāda's plan, the Deities on the main altar were Śrī Śrī Guru Gaurāṅga and Śrī Śrī Rādhā Govinda, and outside on the four sides were altars to Śrī, Brahmā, Rudra, and Chatuḥ-Sana, as well as the four *ācāryas* of the four Vaiṣṇava *sampradāyas*, Śrī Rāmānujācārya, Śrī Madhvācārya, Śrī Viṣṇusvāmī, and Śrī Nimbarkācārya.

Later Śrīla Prabhupāda went to Purī Dhāma with many devotees for Śrī Jagannātha's Ratha-yatra (chariot festival), and following in the footsteps of Śrīman Mahāprabhu, he sang and danced in front of the chariot of Śrī Jagannātha in the mood of separation. Later he lectured to a huge crowd consisting of many distinguished gentlemen from Calcutta. He also sent some disciples to preach in Orissa and Madras.

On "Bhaktisiddhanta Road" with disciples in Māyāpura

Publication of Scriptural Texts, 1923

In 1923 Śrīla Prabhupāda started printing *Śrīmad Bhāgavatam* at the Calcutta Gauḍīya Printing Works. Eventually all twelve cantos were published, with summaries of each chapter and various commentaries.

The First Vyāsa-Pūjā, 1924

On February 24, 1924, the fiftieth birth anniversary of Śrīla Prabhupāda, his disciples celebrated his *vyāsa-pūjā* for the first time. In response to their homage, Śrīla Prabhupāda gave a speech, which is regarded as a jewel in Vaiṣṇava literature. He addressed his disciples as *"āmār vipad-tāraṇ bandhu-gaṇ"* ("my friends who rescue me from danger").

Preaching, 1924

The same year, during Gaura-Purṇīmā, the first edition of *Śrī Caitanya Bhāgavat*, by Śrī Vṛndāvana Dāsa Ṭhākura, was edited by Śrīla Prabhupāda and published by Śrī Mādhva-Gauḍīya Maṭha, Dhaka. In July, Śrīla Prabhupāda established Tridaṇḍi Maṭha in Orissa. Later he established the Sāraswat-Āsan in Śrī Gauḍīya Maṭha, a devotional school in which the devotees could study scripture and study and distribute Śrīla Bhaktivinoda Ṭhākura's books. In October, he went to Dhaka for the fifth time. There he gave an erudite lecture about Śrī Mādhva-Gauḍīya *sampradaya* and its concept of Vaiṣṇavism. On December 16, he gave a lecture at the Benares Hindu University on "The Place of Vaiṣṇavism in the World of Religion." This lecture was very much appreciated by such distinguished professors of Oriental Studies as Prof. Pramathnāth Tarkabhuṣaṇ and Prof. Phanībhuṣaṇ Adhikārī. He searched for the places in Benares that were visited by Śrī Caitanya Mahāprabhu. Later he indicated to his disciples the location of the Daśāśvamedha Ghāṭ in Prayāg where Śrīman Mahāprabhu instructed Śrī Rūpa Gosvāmī. He went to preach in the village of Āḍāil, which had previously been visited by Śrīman Mahāprabhu.

Two of Śrīla Prabhupāda's *Brahmacārī* disciples, Śrīpāda Praṇavānanda Brahmacārī (later Śrīmad Bhakti Pramoda Purī Mahārāja) and Śrīpāda Nandasunu Brahmacārī (later Śrīmad Bhakti Hṛdaya Bon Mahārāj), visited one of Śrīla Prabhupāda's *gṛhastha* disciples, Śrīpāda Vaikuṇṭhanāth Dāsādhikārī, for a few days, to attend a preaching program in his house. During this time, Śrīpāda Vaikuṇṭhanātha Prabhu's eleven-year-old son would always stay close to the *brahmacārīs*, listening avidly to their spiritual discussions. He seemed to have a voracious appetite for devotional topics. So the *brahmacārīs* told his father, "Your son is very extraordinary. Unlike other children of his age, he is not so interested in playing as in listening to *hari-kathā*." Śrīpāda Vaikuṇṭhanātha Prabhu said, "This is how he has always been. Would you like to take my son to the *Maṭha*?" The *brahmacārīs* answered, "We would love to have a boy like this in our mission."

So the parents decided to send their son to the *Maṭha* with the *brahmacārīs*. Even though the boy was the beloved child of a wealthy landholder, he was very happy at the prospect of a life in the *Maṭha*. When the time came for the *brahmacārīs* to leave, the parents did not deviate from their decision. Referring to this incident later, the *brahmacārīs* said it reminded them of how little Dhruva Mahārāja was dressed by his own mother as she bade him go to the forest to meditate on Śrī Kṛṣṇa.

Śrīla Prabhupāda became very fond of this boy (who later became Śrīmad Bhakti Kumuda Santa Mahārāja). He sent him to school, but he himself also tutored him. Later Śrīmad Santa Mahārāja became known for his powerful preaching.

Devotees Attacked: Gaura-maṇḍala Parikrama, 1925

On January 29, 1925, Prabhupāda took many devotees and went on a *parikramā* of the whole Gaura-maṇḍala to visit and preach at the various places where the pastimes of Śrīman Mahāprabhu and His associates took place. Everywhere Śrīla Prabhupāda preached about the pure devotional concept of Gauḍīya Vaiṣṇavism. The imitators of Gauḍīya Vaiṣṇavism (the Sahajiyās) and the commercial exploiters of the Vaiṣṇava concept were intimidated by Śrīla Prabhupāda's powerful preaching and his ever-increasing following. That year, in Navadvīpa, they made plans to launch a vicious attack on the *saṅkīrtana* party.

Hundreds and thousands of devotees assembled at Poḍāmātalā, Navadvīpa, for preaching and *saṅkīrtana*. Their Lordships Śrī Śrī Rādhā Govinda were placed on the back of a decorated elephant and were guarded by two devotees. *Sannyāsīs* were giving lectures and many people assembled to listen to the *hari-kathā*. Unbeknownst to them, some carriages which had been filled with broken bricks and draped with cloth were waiting nearby.

Suddenly the thugs started throwing these broken bricks at the assembled devotees. Śrīpāda Sundarānanda Vidyāvinoda, who was on the elephant, immediately guided the elephant away from the scene, to protect Their Lordships. The Xdevotees first tried to appease the thugs by reasoning with them, but this did not work. Many of the devotees were wounded and began bleeding. All of them tried to look for shelter in the nearby homes, especially for Śrīla Prabhupāda. But all the nearby homeowners had been ordered beforehand not to open their doors. They were also afraid that they too would be attacked by the thugs. Amidst the shock and confusion, somehow Śrīpāda Vinoda Vihārī Brahmacārī managed to take Śrīla Prabhupāda inside a house. There he exchanged his white clothes with Śrīla Prabhupāda's saffron clothes so Śrīla Prabhupāda wouldn't be recognized. Then he very quickly took Śrīla Prabhupāda away to a safer place. Thus Śrīpāda Vinoda Vihārī Prabhu managed to protect his spiritual master by his extraordinary dexterity and presence of mind. Even though Śrīla Prabhupāda was always protected by the Supreme Lord Himself, due to Śrīpāda Vinoda Vihārī Prabhu's sincere love for his *gurudeva*, he got this opportunity to protect him. He risked his own life in order to do so.

Some of those present were completely shocked, and one local resident wrote in the *Ānanda Bazar Patrikā* of Calcutta, "I witnessed the reenactment of what Jagāi and Mādhāi did to Śrīla Nityānanda Prabhu more than four hundred years ago." All over Bengal, many distinguished people protested in magazines and newspapers against this incident. As a result the Chief Inspector of Police of Navadvīpa was fired, and the next year the police department sent 36 police officers to escort the devotees on *parikramā* in Navadvīpa.

Śrīla Prabhupāda's Concern for Women Devotees

On September 21, 1925, Prabhupāda gave a long lecture to the devotees assembled at the Gauḍīya Maṭha about how to lead an exemplary devotional life. An excerpt from that lecture follows:

All of you please perceive everything of this world as ingredients for serving Kṛṣṇa; everything of this world is actually meant for Kṛṣṇa's service. Please see the whole race of women as beloved consorts of Kṛṣṇa, and help them to always engage themselves in the service of Kṛṣṇa. Please do not consider them as objects of your sense enjoyment. They are to be enjoyed by Kṛṣṇa; they are never to be enjoyed by the living entities. Please do not see your fathers and mothers as a means to your own sense gratification, but see them as Kṛṣṇa's fathers and mothers. Please do not see your sons as a means to your own sense gratification, but see them as belonging to the group of servitors of Bāla-Gopāla. With your eyes please see the kadamba tree, the river Yamunā and its sandy bank, and the beauty of the full moon. You won't have any more mundane feelings; you will see Goloka, and the beauty of Goloka will be manifest in your home. Then you won't have any material feelings for your home. You will be relieved from the propensities of householder life.

Our Maṭhas are being built at many places, and many sannyāsīs, vānaprasthas, gṛhasthas, and brahmacārīs are living there all the time and receiving the opportunity to learn spiritual conduct. But we have been trying for a long time to also give the mothers [women] the opportunity for devotional service. Of course, those who have the facility and opportunity for devotional service in their own homes do not need a separate residence. But very often we hear that many of them get impeded in their devotional service due to bad association. It will be very beneficial for them if we can build Śrī Viṣṇupriyā-pallī ["pallī" means "neighborhood"] in Śrīdhāma Māyāpura near the residence of Śrīman Mahāprabhu, and if they can live there separately from their families and render devotional service. They actually belong to the group of Śrī Viṣṇupriyā Devī [the wife of Śrīman Mahāprabhu, who was left behind in Navadvīpa when He took sannyāsa]. Therefore it is proper for them to live in the house of Śrīman Mahāprabhu and to serve Him under the shelter of Śrī Viṣṇupriyā Devī. There should not be any bad association or mundane male association for them there. Only a few devotees like Iśān [the old devotee servant who took care of Śrī Śachīdevī and Śrī Viṣṇupriyā Devī after Śrīman Mahāprabhu left] would stay at a distance and take care of them. It is necessary to have such an exemplary neighborhood so that the mothers [women] can read scripture every day, discuss devotional topics with each other, and have iṣṭa-goṣṭhī about devotional topics, so they can give up all luxury and live an exemplary, saintly life and always chant the holy name and take care of the ingredients of Śrīman Mahāprabhu's service and serve him in every way.

—*Sarasvatī Jayaśrī, p. 339*

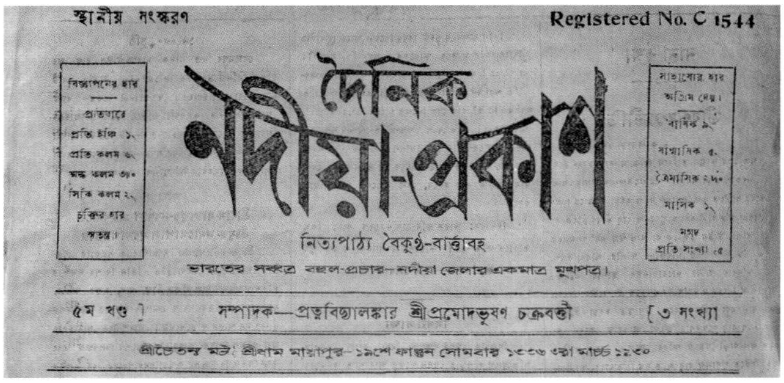
স্থানীয় সংস্করণ
Registered No. C 1544
দৈনিক
নদীয়া-প্রকাশ
নিত্যপাঠ্য বৈকুণ্ঠ-বার্ত্তাবহ
৫ম খণ্ড
সম্পাদক—প্রত্নবিদ্যালঙ্কার শ্রীপ্রমোদভূষণ চক্রবর্ত্তী
৩ সংখ্যা

The Nadiya Prakash showing Pramode Bhushan Cakravartī as the editor (Courtesy of Bhaktivedanta Research Center)

Publication of The Daily Nadiya Prakash, 1926

In 1926, Śrīla Prabhupāda held *nāma-saṅkīrtana* for three days to celebrate the appearance day of Śrī Nityānanda Prabhu. Thereafter this became an annual tradition.

One of Śrīla Prabhupāda's dear disciples, Śrīpāda Bhāgavata Janānanda Dāsa Brahmacārī, had disappeared the year before. In April 1926, Śrīla Prabhupāda established a *Maṭha* in Chiruliyā in his memory and named it "Bhāgavat Janānanda Maṭha". Then he preached at different places in Bengal and sent his *sannyāsī* preachers to different places in Bengal, Bihār, Orissa, and northern and western India. He himself also traveled all over India to preach the message of Śrīman Mahāprabhu, to have discussions with scholars of religion, and to collect facts about the religious traditions of India.

Śrīla Prabhupāda also established the Paramahaṁsa Maṭha in Naimiṣāraṇya, and he established Paravidyāpīṭ in Śrī Māyāpura. He installed the Deities of the *ācārya* and Their Lordships Śrī Śrī Rādhā-Govinda in the newly built temple of Śrī Caitanya Maṭh.

In October 1926, Śrīla Prabhupāda began publishing a new weekly spiritual magazine, *Nadiyā Prakāśa,* in both Bengali and English, at Śrī Bhāgavata Press, Krishnanagar. The joint editors of *Nadiyā Prakāsa* were Paṇḍita Pramoda Bhūṣaṇa Cakravartī (Praṇavānanda Brahmacārī) and Paṇḍita Śrīyukta Caṇḍīcaraṇa Mukhopādhyāya. In its second year, Śrīla Prabhupāda turned it into a daily spiritual newspaper. From this time to its fourth year, Praṇavānanda Brahmacārī was its editor. Then in 1930 Śrīla Prabhupāda made Praṇavānanda Brahmacārī joint editor of *Gauḍīya,* so Atīndranātha Bandyopādhyāya and Kṛṣṇakānti Brahmacārī (later Śrīmad Bhakti Kusuma Śramaṇa Mahārāja) became joint editors of *Nadiyā Prakāśa.*

Publishing The Harmonist Magazine, 1927

On June 15, 1927, Śrīla Prabhupāda started publishing *Sajjana Toṣaṇī* in English, Sanskrit, and Hindi. The English version was called *The Harmonist.* Its editor, Professor Niśikānta Sānnyāl (Śrīpāda Nārāyaṇa dāsa Bhakti-sudhākara) of Ravenshaw College, Cuttack was a learned scholar and a talented writer. Śrīla Prabhupāda was extremely fond of him. Śrīpāda Bhakti-sudhākara Prabhu used to offer his entire salary to Śrīla Prabhupāda each month. Śrīla Prabhupāda would then give it to Śrīpāda Narahari Prabhu and tell him, "Now you manage your household [Śrī Caitanya Maṭha, Māyāpura] with this."

Under the expert editorship of Śrīpāda Bhakti-sudhākara Prabhu, *The Harmonist* enjoyed the same fame and popularity as *Gauḍīya.* Śrīla Prabhupāda considered Śrīpāda Bhakti-sudhākara Prabhu a strong pillar of his preaching mission, and before he left this world he expressed his gratitude to him. Many devotees who were proficient in English, such as Bhakti Pradīpa Tīrtha Mahārāja, Bhakti Rakṣaka Śrīdhara Mahārāja, Bhakti Hṛdaya Bon Mahārāja, and Bhakti Sāraṅga Gosvāmī Mahārāja, regularly

Vol. XXVIII, No. 1.
श्रीश्रीगुरुगौराङ्गौ जयतः
June, 1930.
THE HARMONIST
OR
SREE SAJJANATOSHANI
SRILA THAKUR BHAKTIVINODE (FOUNDER OF THE HARMONIS
EDITED BY PARAMAHANSA PARIBRAJAKACHARYYA
Sri Srimad BHAKTI SIDDHANTA SARASWATI Goswami Maharaj

contributed to *The Harmonist*. From 1933 onwards, Śrīpāda Abhaya Caraṇa Prabhu (later Śrīmad Bhaktivedanta Swāmī Mahārāja) also contributed to *The Harmonist*. The British editor of a British-run newspaper of Calcutta sent a letter of appreciation to the editor of *The Harmonist*.

The following letter appeared in *Gauḍīya*, Vol. 14, No. 24, p. 383:

The Biosophical Institute
250 West 100th Street
New York City
December 10, 1935

Dear Sir,

Since we have been receiving your magazine *The Harmonist*, each issue has given us new joy and inspiration. The spirit pervading the whole magazine is a most unusual one.

Sincerely yours
Sd/ Sylvia Goodwin,
Secretary to Dr. F. Kettner

In September 1927, Śrīla Prabhupāda set forth to preach in North India in different places. Among them were Kāśī, Kanpur, Lucknow, Jaipur, Galatā Parvata, Salimabad, Puṣkara, Ajmer, Dvārkā, Sudāmāpurī, Girṇāra Parvata, Prabhāsa, Avantī, Mathurā-maṇḍala, Indraprastha, Kurukṣetra, and Naimiṣāranya.

Kurukṣetra, Śrī Caitanya Pādapīṭha, 1928–1929

In 1928, Śrīla Prabhupāda edited the fourth edition of *Śrī Caitanya-caritāmṛta*. He went to preach in different places of Assam. On November 4, during the solar eclipse, he went to Kurukṣetra and, following the mood of separation of the *gopīs* and Mahāprabhu, he preached the message of Śrīman Mahāprabhu to millions of devotees who assembled there. At that time he installed a Deity of Śrīman Mahāprabhu at Śrī Vyāsa Gauḍīya Maṭha in Kurukṣetra and opened a spiritual exhibition ("Bhāgavata Pradarśanī") there. He gave Śrīmad Bhakti Rakṣaka Śrīdhara Mahārāja responsibility for the Kurukṣetra *Maṭha*.

In 1929, Śrīla Prabhupāda established the Ekāyana Maṭha in Krishnanagar. In January he discussed Vaiṣṇava religion extensively with Professor Albert E. Suthers of Ohio State University. Śrīla Prabhupāda presented the concept of Vaiṣṇavism as extended and perfect Christianity. At first Professor Suthers was very skeptical and argumentative, but after long discussions he was very impressed by Śrīla Prabhupāda's deep, scholarly, and logical presentation. As a result he decided to visit Śrīman Mahāprabhu's birth site before he left. Later Śrīla Prabhupāda established a Gauḍīya Maṭha in Delhi.

Śrīla Prabhupāda wanted to establish all the sites which Śrīman Mahāprabhu had visited as places of pilgrimage. He called them "Śrī Caitanya Pādapīṭha" and selected 108 such places. He began this task in October 1929 and established the first two sites at Kanai Natshala and Mandar. Later that year he preached extensively in Bihār, in such places as Bhagalpur, Nalanda, and Rajgiri. Subsequently he went to Benares and interpreted *Śrī Sanātana-śikṣā* (Śrī Caitanya Mahāprabhu's instructions to Śrī Sanātana Gosvāmī). Then Śrīla Prabhupāda set forth once more on his North Indian preaching mission, and visited

Faizabad, Ayodhyā, Naimiṣāraṇya, Karauṇā, Miśrika, Sītāpura, and Lucknow. Throughout North India, many took initiation from him. On June 1, 1929, the first post office had opened in Māyāpura. At this time, Śrīla Prabhupāda's disciples had arranged to have electricity at Īśodyāna and electric lights on the domes of Śrī Caitanya Maṭha.

The Māyāpura Exhibition, 1930

On February 3, 1930, Śrīla Prabhupāda arranged a spectacular spiritual exhibition at Māyāpura, which went on until March 17. The famous chemist, Sir Praphulla Candra Roy, opened the exhibition. Thousands flocked to see the exhibition, which contained many stalls depicting stories and lessons from *Śrīmad-Bhāgavatam* through dioramas and paintings.

Śrī Jagabandhu Datta, a rich businessman of Calcutta (originally from Banaripara, Barisol), had the good fortune of associating with some of Śrīla Prabhupāda's disciples. He was an experienced and prudent man in many ways, and he watched the activities and conduct of the devotees at the Gauḍīya Maṭha with a keen eye. Previously he had seen and heard so-called devotees concocting their own philosophy to gratify their senses. Within a short time, he realized this was not the case here. Even though he was wealthy and successful, in the late 1920s he was overwhelmed with physical and emotional problems. He wanted some relief from his material miseries, and he came to visit Śrīla Prabhupāda.

Śrīla Prabhupāda was very merciful to him and spent many hours with him, speaking *hari-kathā* and explaining many things. Śrī Jagabandhu Datta was extremely impressed by Śrīla Prabhupāda's explanations. He began to have a clear concept of Śrīman Mahāprabhu's message of pure devotion. He said of Śrīla Prabhupāda, "What I have heard from him, I have not heard from anyone else." Sometimes he would invite Śrīla Prabhupāda to his home to deliver *hari-kathā* to his friends and relatives. Following is an excerpt from one of Śrīla Prabhupāda's lectures at Śrī Jagabandhu Datta's house:

Śrī Jagabandhu Datta

Śrī Gaurasundara lived in his own house in Navadvīpa only to arouse the devotional consciousness of the people who were attached to their family life. Again when he displayed his pastime of leaving home, that was also to enlighten the ignorant souls. He told his mother and his wife, 'Know Kṛṣṇa as your only son and husband.' Leaving his mother grieving for her son, and his helpless young wife grieving for her husband, he set forth for the eternal welfare of the poor, miserable, and fallen souls of the world. Giving up all his material duty and the vows he had taken at his wedding, he went for kṛṣṇa-kīrtana.

Śrīman Mahāprabhu's sannyāsa-līlā, departing from his household life, was not the same as Śākyasiṁha's [Gautama Buddha's] departure from his house, as Śākyasiṁha was motivated by the selfish desire to attain liberation for himself. Śrīman Mahāprabhu

Srila Prabhupada with his disciples outside Ultadanga Junction, Bhaktivinoda Āsana, Calcutta

displayed his pastime of sannyāsa only to eradicate the eternal poverty of all living beings and to give them an eternal and unequalled gift. He himself was not lacking in anything. He is the only husband of the eternal race of women; He is the only son of the eternal mothers and fathers; He is the eternal friend and master of His servants.

It is not that Śrīman Mahāprabhu's magnanimous gift will remain confined within the perimeters of Bengal; nor is it due only to those who are born in brāhmaṇa families. People of all races—irrespective of whether they are sinful or pious, Hindus or non-Hindus; indeed, all the living entities of the whole world—can accept this magnanimous gift, which was never offered before, if they can give up their pride.

—Sarasvatī Jayaśrī, p. 356

The Bagbazar Gauḍīya Maṭha, 1930

Śrī Jagabandhu Datta begged Śrīla Prabhupāda to give him initiation, and Śrīla Prabhupāda granted his request, giving him the name "Jagabandhu Bhakti-rañjana". Śrīpāda Bhakti-rañjana Prabhu had no children to inherit his wealth, and he wanted to offer his wealth to serve Śrīla Prabhupāda's mission. He wanted a specific service in which his wealth could be utilized, and he begged Śrīla Prabhupāda to give him that service. Śrīla Prabhupāda had been thinking of having a bigger building in Calcutta, where more devotees could stay and more people could come to attend lectures and *saṅkīrtana*. He also wanted to have a printing press on the premises. So he expressed this desire to Śrīpāda Bhakti-rañjana Prabhu.

Bagbazar Gauḍīya Maṭha

Śrīpāda Bhakti-rañjana Prabhu was ecstatic to have the opportunity to finance the new Gauḍīya Maṭha temple. This service became his life and soul. He bought a sizable piece of land in the heart of Calcutta. It was located near the Gaṅgā, on Kali Prasad Cakravarti Street in Bagbazar. Within two years, construction of the new temple was finished. It was a beautiful, palatial marble temple, with many rooms, a conference hall, a library, large kitchens, and a hall for the printing press.

On October 5, 1930, Their Lordships Śrī Śrī Guru Gaurāṅga Gāndhārvikā Giridhāri were taken on a chariot from the Gauḍīya Maṭha at No. 1 Ultadanga Junction Road to the new Bagbazar Gauḍīya Maṭha. A big *saṅkīrtana* procession escorted Their Lordships all the way. A large crowd followed the procession. It was a major event in Calcutta. It was described thus in *Gauḍīya*:

The city of Calcutta has been overwhelmed with joy today. Everyone forgot their daily tasks of earning their livelihood. When the tumultuous sound of kīrtana was heard on the streets of Calcutta, all the people, attracted by that sound, left whatever they were doing and came running into the street. The devotees following the chariot, headed by the sannyāsīs, were singing a special song composed [by Śrīla Prabhupāda] for this occasion, "pūjala rāga patha gaurava bhaṅge, mātala harijana viṣaya raṅge."

—*Gauḍīya, Volume 9, No. 8*

The gist of the song was as follows: "Today, the servants of Hari have become intoxicated by the joy of his divine pastime. They worshiped with great reverence the street on which He rode His chariot."

So many people came to the Gauḍīya Maṭha that day that as people went up the stairs, the iron banister was bent by the pressure of the crowd. Great festivities took place following the Deity installation, *ārati*, *hari-kathā*, and *prasādam*. Thousands of destitute people were also fed sumptuous *prasādam* that day. Śrīla Prabhupāda said in his *hari-kathā*:

Now we have only procured a seat [for hari-kathā]. We have built a castle to preach about the Lord by spending someone's entire savings of a lifetime. But we have to protect ourselves in this castle from the association of materialistic people; we have to defend ourselves from the confusion of this age of Kali (the age of quarrel and hypocrisy). So we have to publish and distribute many more books. Only if we can construct the temple in the form of books and in the form of ideal lives can the idea of devotional service remain permanently in this world.

In the Bagbazar Gauḍīya Maṭha, Śrīla Prabhupāda's preaching mission gained new momentum. More devotees were staying at the *maṭha* now, and more people were coming to listen to *hari-kathā*. The professors and students from prestigious nearby colleges, such as Scottish Churches College and Presidency College, were coming to listen to Śrīla Prabhupāda's lectures. Śrīla Prabhupāda had a core group of eighteen *sannyāsīs* for preaching and organizing. The *sannyāsīs* were always travelling and preaching, and they only stayed at the *maṭha* for a few days at a time while en route to their next destination.

Shortly after the construction of the Gauḍīya Maṭha temple, on November 19, Śrīpāda Jagabandhu Bhakti-rañjana left this material world. Śrīla Prabhupāda was deeply saddened by the departure of his dear disciple. By his instruction, every year the Gauḍīya Maṭha would celebrate the disappearance day of Śrīpāda Jagabandhu Bhakti-rañjana Prabhu, and the *Gauḍīya* would publish a special issue dedicated to his memory. As long as Śrīla Prabhupāda lived in this mortal world, he glorified Śrīpāda Jagabandhu Prabhu with great affection in many of his letters, speeches, and articles.

Before he left this world, Śrīpada Jagabandhu Prabhu wrote a poem to Śrīla Prabhupāda. The translation of that poem is as follows: "What can I give you Gurudeva? The wealth I can give you is yours. You are my treasure and I belong to you. By giving you your property I have nothing to lose. You knew about the sadness in my heart, who else could I talk to? By giving you what belongs to you, I become yours. Jagabandhu dāsa says, 'O you who are the land of nectar personified, you have everything. All I have is you.'"

South India, 1930

In December 1930, Śrīla Prabhupāda went on a preaching mission in South India. Among the places he visited were Kūrmakṣetra, Siṁhācala, Kavoor, and Maṅgala-giri. He established Śrī Caitanya Pāda-pīṭha at Maṅgala-giri. Many distinguished high offiicials, scholars, and professionals were attracted to the message of Śrīman Mahāprabhu as preached by Śrīla Prabhupāda.

Emphasis on Book Publication

Śrīla Prabhupāda called his printing press Bṛhat Mṛdāṅga (the big drum). During *saṅkīrtana* the sound of the ordinary clay drum (*mṛdaṅga*) can be heard only in the immediate vicinity. But the divine message of Śrīman Mahāprabhu can be spread all over the world through the publication of books.

At the opening ceremony of the Bagbazar Gauḍīya Maṭha, Śrīla Prabhupāda said, "...to establish internal *hari-bhajana* in this world, quite a few books have to be written and published. The temple which is within the books and the temple which is within the devotees are more important than the temple built with bricks and stones, because by constructing such temples *hari-kathā* can be preached in this world much longer."

Śrīla Prabhupāda had among his disciples a very talented team of writers and editors, who dedicated their lives to his publication mission. Among them were Śrī Sundarānanda Vidyāvinoda, Śrī Paramānanda Vidyāratna, Śrī Bhakti-sudhākara Prabhu (Professor Niṣikānta Sannyāl), Śrīmad Bhakti Rakṣaka Śrīdhara

Chaitanya Museum
Bag Bazar Gauḍīya Maṭha

The below photos are from the Bhaktisiddhānta Sarasvatī Ṭhākura floor of the Chaitanya Museum located at Bagbazar Gauḍīya Maṭha, Calcutta. The Bagbazar Gauḍīya Maṭha has preserved the temple that Śrīla Prabhupāda established there, including his rooms and numerous artefacts. The museum can be visited as a tirtha for devotees and the public alike. https://www.chaitanyamuseum.org/

Prabhupāda's clock which stopped at the time of his disappearance.

Original Gauḍīya Maṭha printing press.

Wall carving depicting significant life events of Śrīla Prabhupāda.

A wall at the Bhaktivinoda Ṭhākura gallery.

Śrīla Prabhupāda's room at Bagbazar Gauḍīya Maṭha where he made his divine disappearance.

A life-sized statue of Bhaktivinoda Ṭhākura along with his original table and electric fan in the Bhaktivinoda Gallery.

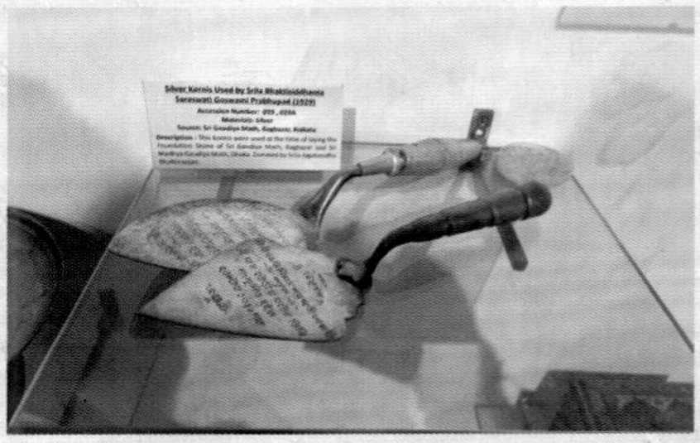

Silver kornis used by Śrīla Bhaktisiddhānta Sarasvatī Prabhupāda.

Śrīla Prabhupāda and several others were present at the Bombay Dock to bid farewell to Śrī Bhakti Pradīpa Tīrtha Mahārāja, Sri Bhakti Hṛdaya Bon Mahārāja, and Samvidānanda Dāsa, who were departing from Bombay Dock on board M.V. Victoria, bound for Genoa en route to London, on April 10, 1933.

Bhaktivinoda Āsana
1 Ultadanga Junction Rd

A Transcendental Place of Pilgrimage

A *tirtha* (place of pilgrimage) is not a static concept in Vedic theology: exalted devotees of the Lord not only visit *tirthas*, but they also create *tirthas* wherever they go.

One such extraordinary *tirtha* is 1 Ultadanga Road in Kolkata, the transcendental ground-zero where Śrīla Prabhupāda Bhaktisiddhānta Sarasvatī Ṭhākura set in motion a global spiritual revolution. There, beginning in 1918, Śrīla Prabhupāda began his worldwide mission, the Gauḍīya Maṭha. Here he enlightened and inspired numerous eminent personalities and scholars, established many temples, and sent out preaching programs to numerous villages, towns and cities of India and Bangladesh. Thus, this site acted as the nodal center for a wide range of dynamic activities for disseminating Gauḍīya Vaiṣṇavism, ranging from worship, preaching and lecture discourses to interactions with devotees and guests, and the editing and publication of Vaiṣṇava periodicals.

In 2019, ISKCON Kolkata succeeded in acquiring this historic building at Ultadanga Junction Road. Extensive research conducted by the Bhaktivedanta Research Center culminated in the establishment of a museum in 2022 at Bhaktivinoda Āsana, 1 Ultadanga Junction. The museum traces the glorious history and evolution of Gauḍīya Vaiṣṇavism and ISKCON through rare photographs, newspaper advertisements, letters personally written by Bhaktisiddhānta Sarasvatī Ṭhākura.

A vintage photograph of Śrīla Prabhupāda with his disciples outside Bhaktivinoda Āsana.

Bhaktivinoda Āsana after restoration in 2022. (Courtesy Sundar Gopal Das)

Showcase of rare artifacts.

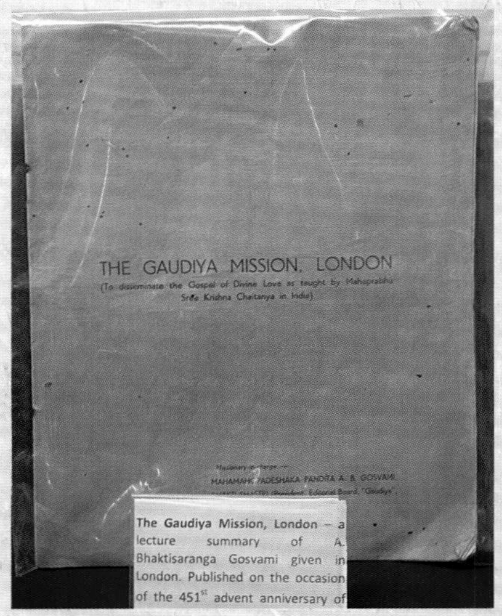

A summary of lectures by Aprākṛta Bhaktisāraṅga Gosvāmī. (Courtesy Bhaktivedanta Research Center Library)

Śrīla Prabhupāda's life-size deity in his room at Bhaktivinoda Āsana.

The renovated ground floor room at Bhaktivinoda Āsana.

The courtyard inside Bhaktivinoda Āsana where devotees would gather and perform saṅkīrtana.

The roof of Bhaktivinoda Āsana where Śrīla Prabhupāda would deliver evening lectures.

Deva Gosvāmī Mahārāja, Śrīmad Bhakti Pradīpa Tīrtha Mahārāja, and Śrī Praṇavānanda Pratnavidyālaṅkāra (later Śrīmad Bhakti Pramoda Purī Mahārāja).

After the disappearance of Śrīla Prabhupāda, another name would be added to this list, that of Śrīla A.C. Bhaktivedānta Swāmī Mahārāja, who published beautifully designed English translations of *Bhagavad-gītā* (as *Bhagavad-gītā As It Is*), *Śrīmad-Bhāgavatam*, *Śrī Bhakti-rasāmṛta sindhu* (as *Nectar of Devotion*), and *Śrī Caitanya-caritāmṛta*. These books would capture the hearts of millions of people all over the world.

The printing presses of the Gauḍīya Maṭha were busy night and day printing books, magazines, and pamphlets. It is not possible within the narrow scope of this chapter to list all the books published by the Gauḍīya Maṭha.

Bhaktivinoda Institute and Sat-Śikṣā Exhibition, 1931

On April 3, 1931, Śrīla Prabhupāda opened a new high school in Śrīdhāma Māyāpura, called the Bhaktivinoda Institute. At a large assembly there he gave a lecture about material education and spiritual knowledge. Later he went to preach at the resort of Darjeeling in north Bengal, in the foothills of the Himālayas. On September 6, during the celebration of the Gauḍīya Maṭha's anniversary, Śrīla Prabhupāda opened a big exhibition in Calcutta, the Sat-Śikṣā exhibition.

Rejection of Sahajiyā Imitationists

Śrīla Prabhupāda preached against the abominable practices and concepts of the pseudo-Vaiṣṇava *sampradāyas* (*sahajiyās*). Inside the Gauḍīya Maṭha as well, he kept a vigilant eye out against any potential for imitation in the path of devotion. Śrīla Prabhupāda preached in very forceful language against any false, external display of devotion. He made it very clear in his lectures that devotion for the Supreme Lord is not some cheap sentiment. Devotion means submission to Gurudeva, self-discipline, self-sacrifice, and wholehearted effort to render devotional service. Unless one is an eternally liberated soul, one cannot attain the platform of spontaneous love (*rāgānugā-bhakti*) without first going through all the stages of regulated practice (*vaidhi-bhakti*).

Even though Śrīla Prabhupāda wanted his disciples to become knowledgeable about scripture, so they could become expert preachers, he did not encourage new devotees to read the intimate pastimes of Śrī Śrī Rādhā-Kṛṣṇa. He made it clear that if a devotee prematurely enters that realm of Kṛṣṇa's pastimes which can be understood only by advanced devotees, then such an act of trespassing will do more harm than good to his *bhajana* life. If one with a propensity for sense-gratification reads about Śrī Śrī Rādhā-Kṛṣṇa's intimate pastimes, then his enjoying propensity will only increase, because he will not realize their transcendental nature. This will be very detrimental to his devotional life. Śrīla Prabhupāda did not even encourage new disciples to read the tenth canto of *Śrīmad-Bhāgavatam*. He also disapproved of indiscriminate displays of paintings of *rādhā-kṛṣṇa-līlā*. An article on this subject, entitled "Ālekhya," appeared in *Gauḍīya*, Volume 13, No. 41. Śrīla Prabhupāda made it very clear that Kṛṣṇa consciousness is not an object of sense enjoyment, but the object of worship and service.

Every spring a festival called "Vasanta-gāna" ("Songs of Spring") or Dhulaṭ used to take place in the town of Navadvīpa. In different public places of Navadvīpa, music concerts would be held in which professional singers would sing songs about the intimate pastimes of Śrī Śrī Rādhā-Kṛṣṇa. These concerts were attended by many local people as well as people from East Bengal. During the concerts, members of the audience would become emotionally aroused and start to dance, roll on the ground, and so forth. Every year some scandals would arise in connection with these concerts. When the festival first started, the audience consisted mostly of uneducated women. Subsequently some educated people, such as writers, also started attending these concerts. They tried to rationalize listening to these songs with the excuse that Mahāprabhu used to like the songs of Jayadeva, Caṇḍidāsa, Vidyāpati, Bilvamaṅgala Ṭhākura, and Rāya Rāmānanda. But Śrīla Prabhupāda quoted from the scriptures written by the Gosvāmīs and cited the examples of the conduct of Śrīman Mahāprabhu and his associates, to establish that if one who is in an illusioned state listens to these songs composed by liberated souls, it is only sense gratification in the name of *śravaṇa-kīrtana*. He particularly mentioned the history over the previous few hundred years of the community of *sahajiyās*, which confirmed this fact. For some people these music concerts were a means to develop reputations as *bhaktas* (devotees) or *rasikas* (connoisseurs of *rasa*), and for others they were a means for commercial exploitation of ignorant people. But by indulging in these practices, one can be deviated from the path of *bhakti*, which is the supreme goal of life. This was discussed in detail in an article called "Vasanta-gāna" which appeared in *Gauḍīya*, Volume 1, No. 22.

Just as Śrīla Prabhupāda was opposed to the enjoying mentality, he also rejected the idea of renunciation for its own sake—without consideration of whether it is favorable for one's devotional service. Instead, he propagated the principle of *yukta-vairāgya* (positive renunciation), according to which one gives up his enjoying propensity but accepts everything that is favorable for devotional service.

North India and Publishing in Hindi, 1931

In October, Śrīla Prabhupāda was invited to preach in Benares at the Mint Palace. Later he went to Lucknow and introduced a new Hindi magazine, *Bhāgavata*. In November he sent one of his *sannyāsī* preachers to the Viceroy of India, Lord Willingdon, in New Delhi. On November 17, he celebrated the anniversary festival of the Delhi Gauḍīya Maṭha for the first time. On December 6, he installed Their Lordships Śrī Śrī Rādhā Govinda there.

Vehement Opposition to Impersonalism

Following in the footsteps of Śrīla Bhaktivinoda Ṭhākura, Śrīla Prabhupāda spoke out against impersonalism through his preaching mission. The impersonalist religious sect of Bengal called the "Brahma Samaj," which was founded by Raja Rammohan Ray in the 19th century, was the greatest opponent of Vaiṣṇavism and the idea of a personal God.

Once the instructor of the Sadharan Brahma Samaj of Calcutta, Śrī Hemcandra Sarkar, came to the Gauḍīya Maṭha to find out about Śrī Caitanya Deva and His successor *ācāryas* from Śrīla Prabhupāda. During the discussion that followed, Śrīla Prabhupāda said, "It is the concept of the Brahmos that is based on idolatry. They have opposed gross idolatry, but they have accepted subtle idolatry. The idol that is made by the material mind on the basis of a material concept of the formless *brahma* is more dangerous than the idolatry of demigod worshippers. Real Vaiṣṇavas are not such idolaters. Gauḍīya Vaiṣṇavism is clearly different from the two kinds of idolatry: iconolatry and iconomachy. The pure Vaiṣṇavas never worship some doll made of wood or clay or a doll fabricated by the material mind. The worshipable Lord of the Vaiṣṇavas is not some imaginary temporary thing."

Hearing this, Śrī Hemcandra Sarkar said, "Then don't you worship idols?" Śrīla Prabhupāda said, "We do not worship any imaginary form or doll whom we are going to break later. We worship the eternal deity form that is manifested by the transcendental knowledge potency of the Supreme Lord, whose potencies are inconceivable."

Then Śrīla Prabhupāda made Śrī Hemcandra Sarkar understand the difference between idolatry and deity worship through a logical presentation. Finally Śrī Hemcandra Sarkar said, "But we see that the Vaiṣṇavas in our village worship many demigods." Śrīla Prabhupāda said, "Considering them to be real Vaiṣṇavas, you criticize us, but they cannot touch the real Vaiṣṇavas or real Vaiṣṇavism. To ascertain the real form of Vaiṣṇavism on the basis of its degenerated form is not an intelligent act. Vaiṣṇavas never become gross or subtle idolaters by worshiping some imagined gross temporary form, as the demigod worshippers do, or some imagined and temporary subtle form or idea, as the impersonalists do. One imagines the absence of God's embodiment of eternity, knowledge, and bliss and of His inconceivable potency by giving him an imagined form based on a material concept or making him formless. This is against the injunctions of the Vedas. Humans have no right to expand their imaginations by thinking that just because God does not have material senses or form, He cannot have transcendental senses or form. Just because the Vedas have denied the material form of *brahma*, some people have thought the Supreme Lord cannot have a transcendental form which is an embodiment of eternity, knowledge, and bliss either. On one hand they are saying '*brahma*', indicating that this worshipable truth is greater than themselves, but on the other hand they are trying to measure that great reality. Raja Rammohan Ray has protested against the ignorant concepts of someone with the title of 'Gosvāmī'. But he did not hear about Vaiṣṇavism from a real Vaiṣṇava *ācārya*—this we can prove with hundreds of logical statements." (*Sarasvatī Jayaśrī*, p. 348–350)

Śrīla Prabhupāda, along with his disciples and South Indian brahmins at the Madras Gauḍīya Maṭha on 27th of January 1932.

Preaching in South India, 1932

Śrīla Prabhupāda went on an extensive preaching mission in South India in 1932. He had already sent some of his disciples to preach in South India. Among them were Śrīmad Bhakti Rakṣaka Śrīdhara Mahārāja and Śrīpāda Hayagrīva Brahmacārī (later Śrīmad Bhakti Dayita Mādhava Mahārāja).

On January 10, 1932, Prabhupāda went to Madras with twenty disciples. A large party of high government officials were waiting to receive him there. Among them was the mayor of Madras, Mr. T. S. Ramaswamī Ayar. A large *saṅkīrtana* procession accompanied Śrīla Prabhupāda to the Madras Gauḍīya Maṭha in Gopālpuram, and there some of the officials gave speeches honoring Śrīla Prabhupāda. On January 23, Śrīla Prabhupāda installed deities at the Madras Gauḍīya Maṭha. He also laid the cornerstone of the new temple at Rayāpeṭṭā. On January 27, the governor of Madras, Sir George Frederick Stanley, came to the Madras Gauḍīya Maṭha to lay the cornerstone of Śrī Kṛṣṇa Kīrtana Hall.

Śrīla Prabhupāda preached with great success in Madras and surrounding areas of South India. Many people took initiation from him. Then he went back to Māyāpura in time for Śrī Navadvīpa *parikramā*. This year, his disciples took such examinations as the Bhakti-śāstri. The purpose of these examinations was to make Śrīla Prabhupāda's disciples familiar with the intimate details of all aspects of Gauḍīya Vaiṣṇavism.

On May 23, Śrīla Prabhupāda returned to Madras. This time he met with the *ācāryas* of different *sampradāyas* and explained Gauḍīya Vaiṣṇavism to them. Later he also preached at Uṭkāmand, Mysore, and Kavoor.

Glorification of Śrīmatī Rādhārāṇī

When asked, "Who are the Gauḍīya Vaiṣṇavas?" Śrīla Prabhupāda replied that they are the devotees of Śrīmatī Rādhārāṇī (*Śrī Upadeśāmṛta*, p. 236). He called himself Śrī Vārṣabhānavī-dayita dāsa (the servant of the beloved of Śrīmatī Rādhārāṇī).

He said that Śrīmatī Rādhārāṇī, who is the transcendental energy of Śrī Kṛṣṇa and the personification of Śrī Kṛṣṇa's pleasure potency (*hlādinī-svarūpa parā śakti*), is the spiritual master of all devotees. Indeed, She is even Kṛṣṇa's guru: Kṛṣṇa learns to be an actor and dancer as Her disciple. All the pure devotees who are not worshiping Śrī Kṛṣṇa in the mellow of conjugal relationship (*madhura-rasa*) know Lord Nityānanda to be their original spiritual master. But the original spiritual master of those who worship Śrī Kṛṣṇa in *madhura rasa* is Śrīmatī Rādhārāṇī. (*Śrī Upadeśāmṛta*, p. 27)

Śrīla Prabhupāda said that Śrīmatī Rādhārāṇī is Śrī Kṛṣṇa's eternal consort; She is the crest jewel of the *gopīs*. No one is more dear to Kṛṣṇa than

Śrīmatī Rādhārāṇī. Śrīmatī Rādhārāṇī is not inferior to Śrī Kṛṣṇa in any way. It is Śrī Kṛṣṇa Himself who enjoys Himself in two separate forms, as the enjoyer and the enjoyed. Śrī Kṛṣṇa's beauty is so stunning that He Himself becomes enchanted by His own beauty. But if the beauty of Śrīmatī Rādhārāṇī were not greater than that of Śrī Kṛṣṇa, She could not enchant Kṛṣṇa, who can enchant the whole universe. That is why She is called Bhuvana-mohana-mohinī. She is the light of the full moon of Śrī Kṛṣṇa, (Kṛṣṇacandra). Śrī Kṛṣṇa is the sum total of all ecstasy, all beauty. He is the original reservoir of all wealth, prowess, and knowledge. So the greatness of Rādhārāṇī, who is the *āśraya* and *viṣaya* of this most perfect Person, Śrī Kṛṣṇa, is beyond the limit of human knowledge—even beyond the limit of understanding of many liberated souls. (*Śrī Upadeśāmṛta,* p. 330–1)

Whenever Śrīla Prabhupāda talked about Śrīmatī Rādhārāṇī, he would become overwhelmed with the symptoms of deep loving ecstasy. Śrīla Raghunātha Dāsa Gosvāmī's famous composition *Vilāpa-Kusumāñjali* consists of verses addressed to Śrīmatī Rādhārāṇī in the mood of intense separation, as Śrīla Dāsa Gosvāmī is an intimate servitor of Śrīmatī Rādhārāṇī in his eternal identity as Śrī Rati-mañjarī. (The *mañjarīs* are young pre-teen girls who serve Śrīmatī Rādhārāṇī.) Śrīla Prabhupāda could quote from memory all 104 verses of *Vilāpa-Kusumāñjali,* and tears would flow from his eyes. He was always in a mood of separation from Śrīmatī Rādhārāṇī.

Every Rādhāṣṭamī day (the appearance day of Śrīmatī Rādhārāṇī), Śrīla Prabhupāda would display the symptoms of deep ecstasy while talking about Śrīmatī Rādhārāṇī. Following is an excerpt from a lecture given by him on the day of Rādhāṣṭamī in 1931 at the Sārasvata Nāṭa-mandira of Śrī Gauḍīya Maṭha.

Let that personification of supreme magnanimity, Śrīmatī Rādhārāṇī, who is always eager to collect the mercy of the Supreme Lord on behalf of all living entities, appear in our hearts and make Her presence known. Let Her appearance be our object of worship. Without submission to the one whom Govinda considers to be everything to Him (sarvasva), we do not realize the meaning of the word "sarva". "Govinda sarvasva"—"sva" means "one's own", "sva" means "wealth". If we have the one who is Govinda's own wealth—the one who makes Him wealthy; that wealth is everything to Govinda—if She becomes the object of our worship, then we will understand what worship is. If after reading the 18,000 verses of Śrīmad Bhāgavatam we do not come to know about Her, then our reading was in vain.

If by some unknown sukṛti we get the association of those who are close to Śrī Vṛṣabhānu-nandinī (Śrīmatī Rādhārāṇī), if we are are fortunate enough to hear about Her, then we can get the inspiration to proceed towards our supremely beneficial goal. She is everything to the son of Nanda who is the reservoir of all ecstasy, and we will never attain devotional service to Govinda without serving Her and Her servitors.

—Prabhupāda Śrī Śrīmad Bhaktisiddhānta Sarasvatī, p. 99–100

Śrī Vraja-maṇḍala Parikramā, 1932

It is in this mood of separation from Śrīmatī Rādhārāṇī that Śrīla Prabhupāda went on Vraja-maṇḍala *parikramā*. In October, Śrīla Prabhupāda started his Vraja-maṇḍala *parikramā* with many devotees. He circumambulated the Vraja-maṇḍala along its 32-mile perimeter. At each place of Kṛṣṇa's pastimes, he gave *hari-kathā*. For the benefit of people who spoke other languages, he himself and many of his followers gave *hari-kathā* in different languages. Śrīla Prabhupāda explained Śrī Rūpa Gosvāmī's *Upadeśāmṛta* to the assembled Vrajavāsīs and scholars.

On November 4, Śrīla Prabhupāda went to Haridwar to lay the cornerstone of the Sārasvata Gauḍīya Maṭha. By his request, the governor of Yukta Pradesh, Sir William Malcolm Haley, laid the cornerstone of Śrī Rūpa Gauḍīya Maṭha.

Preaching Mission to the West, 1933

In 1933, the English book *Śrī Kṛṣṇa Caitanya*, by Professor Niśikānt Sānnyāl, was published in a beautifully bound edition. It was Śrīla Prabhupāda's desire to send a preaching mission to Europe now. Śrīla Prabhupāda wanted to preach Mahāprabhu's message all over the world. He used to tell his disciples, "We'll go on our preaching mission, riding horses, elephants, trains, boats, and airplanes." His dream of preaching all over the West was later greatly fulfilled by his disciple, Śrīmad Abhaya Caraṇāravinda Bhaktivedānta Swāmī, who took initiation from Śrīla Prabupāda in 1933 in Allahabad.

On March 18, 1933, Śrīla Prabhupāda gave instruction to Śrīmad Bhakti Pradīpa Tīrtha Mahārāja, Śrīmad Bhakti Hṛdaya Bon Mahārāja, and Śrīpāda Samvidānanda Dāsa Bhakti-śāstri as they were departing to preach in Europe. At a meeting that was arranged to see them off, Śrīla Prabhupāda gave a farewell address entitled *Āmāra Kathā* ("My Message").

In the beginning of May, Śrīla Prabhupāda's disciples established a preaching center in Kensington, London. At the end of that month, Śrīla Prabhupāda got letters inquiring into spiritual matters from Lord Zetland, who had formerly been the governor of Bengal, and the Marquis of Ludian, to which he replied. In June he got letters of appreciation from Lord Irwin's secretary, the Marquis of Ludian, the editor of the *London Times*, and Sir Stanley Jackson. In July, Śrīla Prabhupāda's disciples met with King George V and Queen Mary at Buckingham Palace, and also with the Archbishop of Canterbury.

In November, Śrīla Prabhupāda's disciples went to preach in Germany and France. At the end of December they returned to London. As one can imagine, this was not a very favorable time to preach Śrīman Mahāprabhu's mission in Europe. Traumatized by the First World War, the West was plagued by the Great Depression, international tension, and the rise of totalitarianism. Furthermore, all of these factors had combined to create a deep cynicism about God and spirituality, which was manifest in the popularity of thinkers such as

Nietzsche and Freud. The atmosphere, particularly in Germany, was one of extreme anxiety, due to the recent collapse of many aspects of the predominant world view, from the way war was waged to the workings of the universe.

Contribution of the Gauḍīya Maṭha

In the meantime, preaching in India was going on in full swing, in the midst of the great national current of the freedom movement. In the same year the Bagbazar Gauḍīya Maṭha was opened (1930), throughout India Mahātmā Gāndhi's followers took an uncompromising stand upholding his nonviolent noncooperation with the British government. That year Gāndhi went on his famous Salt March, which was a decisive turn in the march towards freedom. In Bengal, the guerilla groups also carried on their subversive activities. That same year three young Bengali freedom fighters—Binay, Badal, and Dinesh—launched an open attack on British officials at the Writers' Building in Calcutta. In the chaos that followed, two of them were captured (of whom one later died from his wounds and the other was executed), and one managed to commit suicide. In the heart of Bengal emotions were running high against the British. It might be considered amazing that at a time like this, the Gauḍīya Maṭha managed to win such a favorable position among the educated people of Bengal—

Vraja-maṇḍala parikramā, 1932

that so many people came forward to somehow participate in this mission of pure devotion. Śrīla Prabhupāda hoisted the flag of the Gauḍīya Maṭha to a great height, and he upheld its goal as the most sublime destination of human birth.

Regarding the contribution of the Gauḍīya Maṭha, Śrīla Prabhupāda said:

In the history of spirituality, how many other historical events of great revolution, like the preaching of the Gauḍīya Maṭha, have taken place, the historians of spirituality will determine. What a great revolution this is, that everyone in the Gauḍīya Maṭha is dedicating themselves to preach something that at first sight seems completely unique in the history of the human race. They [the devotees] are not afraid of thousands of people who are proud of their knowledge. Nor are they ready to indulge the deceitfulness and debauchery of the lecherous. The Gauḍīya Maṭha is ready to put to death the mentality of the innumerable living entities of the world who are averse to Kṛṣṇa and who are devising many plans to steal the property of the Supreme Sovereign. They [the devotees] do not want one penny from this world [for themselves]; they want to give the world that which is complete. They want to completely give them Caitanya Deva, who is the full transcendental consciousness.

Preaching in India, 1933

That year, Śrīla Prabhupāda preached extensively in Bombay, and the Bombay Gauḍīya Maṭha preaching center was established on Babulnath Road. In August, Śrīla Prabhupāda gave a lecture about one of his books, *The Vedānta: Its Morphology and Ontology*. Later he preached in Navadvīpa. In November he preached extensively in Bihar and Orissa. At the same time, preaching went on in Karachi, in present-day Pākistān.

Śrīla Prabhupāda with Ananta Vāsudev Prabhu on the way to Naimiṣāraṇya

Building a New Temple At Yogapīṭha, 1934

In January 1934, the King of Tripurā, Mahārāja Bir Vikram Kishor Devavarma Manikya Bahadur, came to the Gauḍīya Maṭha with his retinue and gave a lecture in appreciation of the Gauḍīya Maṭha's preaching mission. On February 4, on the occasion of Śrīla Prabhupāda's *vyāsa-pūjā*, a seminar took place in London, over which Lord Zetland presided. On March 18, Śrīla Prabhupāda laid the cornerstone of the new Yogapīṭha temple in Māyāpura. On April 24, Lord Zetland opened the Gauḍīya Mission Society in London. On May 6, the well-known archeologist, Sir Ramaprasad Chanda, gave a lecture at the Gauḍīya Maṭha called "Navadvīpa At the Time of Śrī Caitanya."

One of Śrīla Prabhupāda's disciples, Śrīyukta Sakhi-caraṇa Rāya Bhakti-vijaya, financed the construction of the Yogapīṭha temple in Māyāpura. Śrīla Prabhupāda greatly appreciated this service. Before he left this world, Śrīla Prabhupāda told Śrīpāda Sakhi-caraṇa Rāya Bhakti-vijaya that his life was successful, as he had done a great service to Śrīdhāma Māyāpura.

On June 13, while the foundation was being excavated, a four-handed Deity of Lord Viṣṇu manifested Himself from the ground. Prabhupāda expressed his opinion that this deity was worshiped by Śrī Jagannātha Miśra. The archeologist Ramaprasad Chanda declared the Deity to be quite ancient.

On August 14, deities were installed at the Pāṭnā Gauḍīya Maṭha. On September 1, on the day of Śrī Kṛṣṇa Janmāṣṭamī, *Sarasvatī Jayaśrī*, a biography of Śrīla Prabhupāda, was published. Different sections of the book were written by different disciples, and the descriptions of many incidents were quoted from the memoirs of other disciples and from *Gauḍīya*. The principal writers of *Sarasvatī Jayaśrī* were Śrīpāda Paramānanda Vidyāratna, Śrīpāda Kuñja-bihārī Vidyābhūṣan, Śrīpāda Ananta Vāsudeva Prabhu, Śrīpāda Sundarānanda Vidyāvinoda, and Śrīmad Bhakti Pradīpa Tīrtha Mahārāja.

In October, Śrīla Prabhupāda went to Mathurā with many devotees to observe Kārtika-vrata, and he established the practice of *śravaṇa-kīrtana* of *aṣṭa-kālīya līlā* (hearing and chanting of Kṛṣṇa's pastimes during the eight periods of the day). On December 6, Śrīla Prabhupāda's disciple from Andhra Pradesh, Śrīyukta Y. Jagannātham, published *Śrī Caitanya Śikṣāmṛta* in Telegu.

Extraordinary Preaching Organization

Śrīla Prabhupāda's unique and unprecedented contribution to the world of Gauḍīya Vaiṣṇavism did not consist solely of his own greatness, but also included the extraordinary preaching organization that he envisioned, built, and nurtured. He alone could bring a spiritual revolution to Bengal and to India—indeed, to the world—but

The governor of Bengal's visit to the mission's headquarters in Māyāpura (top)

Śrīla Prabhupāda with the Mahārāja of Tripura, Mahārāja Bir Bikram Kishore Manikya Debbarma Bahadur at the inauguration of the new temple at the Yogapīṭha (middle)

Yogapīṭha (bottom)

he wanted to leave behind a magnificent spiritual legacy, in the form of a group of dedicated souls who would carry on his mission in his absence in the face of seemingly insurmountable difficulties. He attracted these pure hearts, taught and trained them, and left them behind him to spread his movement throughout the inevitable advancement of Kali-yuga in future decades. Even under the shelter of Śrīla Prabhupāda's lotus feet, they had to face many tests and trials, but with Śrīla Prabhupāda's divine guidance, ultimately fate favored them.

In the Gauḍīya Maṭha, devotees lived very simply. Sumptuous feasts were offered to the Deities on festival days to feed *mahāprasādam* to the guests and to the beggars and destitutes. What the devotees ate every day was nourishing and satisfying, but plain. Their austerity was unsurpassed. They didn't have more than two sets of ordinary clothes each. In eating, sleeping, living, and travelling, they tried to do with the bare minimum. Every penny that came to the Maṭha was recorded, and so was every penny that was spent. Some of these financial statements, which were given in complete detail, can be seen in the old issues of *Gauḍīya*. In Prabhupāda's Gauḍīya Maṭha, his disciples lived in an atmosphere of deep mutual affection and respect. Everyone was always extremely busy with their respective service, and transcendentally happy and peaceful.

Anyone coming to the Gauḍīya Maṭha would be awed by the divine personality of Śrīla Prabhupāda, and then impressed by his team of dedicated disciples. The disciples of a guru are known as his *vaibhāva* (wealth), and Śrīla Prabhupāda was certainly a very wealthy spiritual master. This wealth of his was "in the form of ideal characters." Śrīla Prabhupāda's disciples were known for their unending enthusiasm for preaching, their undefeatable scholarship, their sincere humility, their strong moral character, and their total dedication to serve the mission of Gurudeva. All Śrīla Prabhupāda's disciples who stayed at the different *maṭhas* were intelligent, talented, hardworking, and knowledgeable about scripture.

The core of Śrīla Prabhupāda's preaching mission consisted of eighteen *sannyāsīs*:

Bhakti Pradīpa Tīrtha Mahārāja

Bhakti Hṛdaya Bon Mahārāja

Bhakti Rakṣaka Śrīdhara Mahārāja

Bhakti Sarvasya Giri Mahārāja

Bhakti Sambandha Turyāśramī Mahārāja

Bhakti Viveka Bharatī Mahārāja

Bhakti Śrīrūpa Purī Mahārāja

Bhakti Prakāśa Araṇya Mahārāja

Bhakti Vilāsa Gabhastinemi Mahārāja

Bhakti Bhūdeva Śrautī Mahārāja

Bhakti Svarūpa Parvata Mahārāja

Bhakti Prasuna Bodhāyana Mahārāja

Bhakti Gaurava Vaikhānasa Mahārāja

Bhakti Sambala Bhāgavata Mahārāja

Bhakti Vijñāna Āśrama Mahārāja

Bhakti Sudhīra Yāchaka Mahārāja

Bhakti Vaibhava Sāgara Mahārāja

Bhakti Vardhana Sāgara Mahārāja

They were all expert preachers, and some of them were great scholars, such as Śrīmad Bhakti Gaurava Vaikhānasa Mahārāja, who had been the court *paṇḍita* of Orissa and whom Śrīla Prabhupāda sent to speak with the Viceroy of India.

Śrīla Prabhupāda called Śrīmad Bhakti Rakṣaka Śrīdhara Mahārāja "*Śāstra-nipuṇa* [expert on scripture] Śrīdhara Mahārāja." Śrīmad Śrīdhara Mahārāja was a talented writer of Bengali, English, and Sanskrit. When he wrote his glorification of Śrīla Bhaktivinoda Ṭhākura, Śrīla Prabhupāda described his style as "happy style." Śrīla Prabhupāda also said of this verse to Śrīpāda Aprākṛta Prabhu, "I am satisfied that what I came to say will remain after me; I find in this verse the *siddhānta* (perfect conclusion)." Śrīla Prabhupāda noted the highly philosophical content of Śrīdhara Mahārāja's lectures, and when he himself delivered *hari-kathā* it would always give him great satisfaction to see Śrīdhara Mahārāja in the audience.

Bhakti Prakāśa Araṇya Mahārāja

Bhakti Vilāsa Gabhastinemi Mahārāja

Bhakti Gaurava Vaikhānasa Mahārāja

Bhakti Bhūdeva Śrautī Mahārāja

Bhakti Pradipa Tirtha Maharaja

Bhakti Hṛdaya Bon Mahārāja

Bhakti Rakṣaka Śrīdhara Mahārāja

Bhakti Svarūpa Parvata Mahārāja

Bhakti Sarvasya Giri Mahārāja

Bhakti Sambandha Turyāśramī Mahārāja

Bhakti Viveka Bharatī Mahārāja

Bhakti Vijñāna Āśrama Mahārāja

Śrīla Prabhupāda's auspicious journey to the villages of Cāncuḍī and Puruliyā

On Monday the 21st of Phālguna (1340), which was the 5th of March (1934), at around 9 p.m., Śrī Śrīla Prabhupāda and his associates boarded the Khulnā Mail to travel to Jaśohara (Jessore) Puruliyā, the birthplace of the incharge of Śrī Gauḍīya Maṭha Mahā-mahopadeśaka Ācāryatrika Śrīpāda Kuñjavihārī Vidyābhūṣaṇa Bhāgavata-ratna. From Śrī Gauḍīya Maṭha, the chief editor of the Gauḍīya, Mahā-mahopadeśaka Śrīpāda Bhakti Sāraṅga Gosvāmī Prabhu, Upadeśaka Ācārya Śrīpāda Paramānanda Vidyāratna Bhakti Kuñjara, Parivrājakācārya Tridaṇḍisvāmī Śrīmad Bhakti Viveka Bhāratī Mahārāja, Śrīmad Bhakti Sarvasva Giri Mahārāja, Śrīpāda Bhavabandhacchida Dāsādhikārī Bhakti-saurabha B.L. Mahodaya, Mahopadeśaka Śrīmat Praṇavānanda Brahmacārī Pratnavidyālaṅkāra, Brahmacārī Śrī Sajjanānandajī, Brahmacārī Śrī Hṛdaya-govinda, Brahmacārī Śrī Ghanaśyāma, Śrī Uddhāraṇa, Śrīyukta Gopālacandra Bhaktiratna, the editor of the Gauḍīya, and many other personalities were accompanying Prabhupāda. The devotees from Śrī Māyāpura's Śrī Caitanya Maṭha who had come to join Śrīla Prabhupāda were to board at Vanagrāma station. But something happened. The car traveling from Rāṇāghaṭa to Vanagrāma carrying devotees from Śrīdhāma Māyāpura suddenly got stuck a short distance from the station. In the car coming from Śrī Caitanya Maṭha were eminent personalities like Mahopadeśaka Paṇḍita-pravara Śrī Ananta-vāsudeva Vidyābhūṣaṇa Prabhu, Tridaṇḍisvāmī Śrīmad Bhakti Prakāśa Araṇya Mahārāja, Śrīmad Bhakti Vaibhava Sāgara Mahārāja, Śrīmad Bhakti Svarūpa Parvata Mahārāja, Śrīmad Bhakti Bhūdeva Śrautī Mahārāja, the manager of Śrī Māyāpura estate Śrīpāda Mahānanda Brahmacārī Bhaktyāloka, the overseer of Śrī Caitanya Maṭha Śrīpāda Narahari Brahmacārī Sevāvigraha, Śrīpāda Vinodabihārī Brahmacārī Kṛtiratna and Śrīpāda Siddha-svarūpa Brahmacārī.

Meanwhile, Śrīla Prabhupāda and the other devotees were patiently waiting for the devotees from Śrī Caitanya Maṭha. There was no possibility of the Vanagrāma passengers boarding the Khulnā Mail that day. If the Khulnā Mail train left without the Vanagrāma passengers, the devotees from Caitanya Maṭha would have had to wait till the next day to catch the next Khulnā Mail, and despite enduring this manner of difficulty, it would not have been possible to reach Ācāryatrika Prabhu's house on the designated day and accompany Śrīla Prabhupāda. By Śrīla Prabhupāda's mercy and inspiration, Śrīmat Bhakti Sāraṅga Prabhu spoke with the station authorities and had them help the Vanagrāma passengers reach the station, and shortly all the devotees of Śrī Caitanya Maṭha were able to reach the lotus feet of Śrīla Prabhupāda.

Meanwhile, Śrīpāda Kīrtanānanda Brahmacārī had already reached Puruliyā, and he was waiting at Daulatapura station to welcome Prabhupāda. Adjacent to Daulatapura was a village called Candanīmahala. One of its residents, a disciple of Śrīla Prabhupāda, a retired high official of the P.W.D. engineering department previously based out of Cuttack, Śrīyukta Śaśadhara Bandyopādhyāya, had traveled all the way from Candanī Mahala in order to greet the lotus feet of his spiritual master along with a group of *saṅkīrtana* singers and was waiting for a long time at the Daulatapura station for the train to arrive. Towards the end of the night, the Khulnā Mail arrived at the Daulatapura station. As soon as the train arrived, this devotee and his companions started playing various musical instruments like khola and karatāla and performing *mahā-mantra saṅkīrtana* to greet Prabhupāda. Śaśadhara Bābu, along with his family and friends, welcomed Śrīla Prabhupāda with flowers and garlands, etc. From Daulatpura station, the *saṅkīrtana* party accompanied Prabhupāda to the steamer ghat.

At around quarter to eight the next morning, as the steamer neared the Raghunāthapura ghat, a huge crowd could be seen waiting with flags and posters to conduct an enormous *saṅkīrtana* parade. In this *saṅkīrtana* party were Mahā-mahopadeśaka Bhāgavata-ratna Prabhu, Śrīyukta Advaya-jñānānanda Bhaktiśāstrī, the headmaster of Cāncuḍī and Puruliyā's M.E. School and various other eminent locals. Apart from them, Brahmacārī Śrī Pyārī-mohanajī Kārukovida, Śrī Devakīnandana Brahmacārī, Śrī Pūrṇānanda Brahmacārī and various other Śrī Gauḍīya Maṭha devotees were also present. They had just come to Puruliyā from Kolkata. At the Raghunāthapura ghat, there was a gate and on top of it, the word "Svāgatam" was wrought from colourful cloth, and all manner of auspicious items had been collected to greet the Ācārya. As soon as the steamer docked, cannons were fired in honor of Śrīla Prabhupāda. Mahā-mahopadeśaka Ācāryatrika Prabhu and the previously mentioned headmaster sir boarded the streamer and offered their prostrated obeisance to Śrīla Prabhupāda and greeted him on behalf of the Puruliyā residents with a garland of flowers. As Śrīla Prabhupāda and his associates descended to the ghat, Śrīyukta Pyārīmohana Brahmacārī Kārikovida took a photograph of the party. Seated on a beautiful palanquin decorated with colourful fabric, flowers, etc., Śrīla Prabhupāda made his way toward Puruliyā-grāma amid the *saṅkīrtana* parade and the devotees followed the Ācārya, uttering cries of *jaya-dhvani* for Śrī Śrī Guru-Gaurāṅga. After travelling for nearly one and a half miles, another entrance decorated with colorful flags attracted everyone's attention. Chanting the glories of Śrī Śrī Guru-Gaurāṅga and Mahā-mahopadeśaka Ācāryatrika Prabhu, everyone set down that pathway following Śrīla Prabhupāda in an ecstatic commotion that spread in all directions. Many revered personalities of Puruliyā greeted Śrīla Prabhupāda and accompanied him to a decorated pedestal in a pavilion specially constructed in the courtyard of Ācāryatrika Prabhu's home. As soon as the lotus feet of the Ācārya touched the elevated platform, immediately a roar of exhilarated voices and glorious chanting rose from the crowd. Mahopadeśaka Pratnavidyālaṅkara Śrīpāda Praṇavānanda Brahmacārījī sang prayers to Guru-Gaurāṅga and sang the *kīrtana "Śuddha-bhakata caraṇa-reṇu bhajana anukūla,"* following which, on behalf of the villagers present, the aforementioned headmaster read out a formal greeting card/ welcoming letter, which was then distributed among the audience.

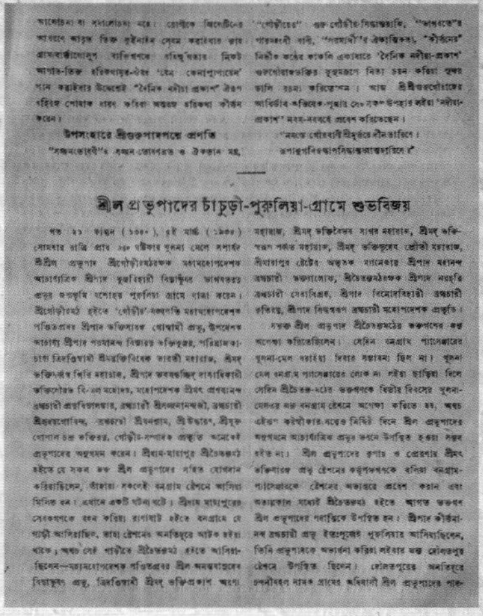

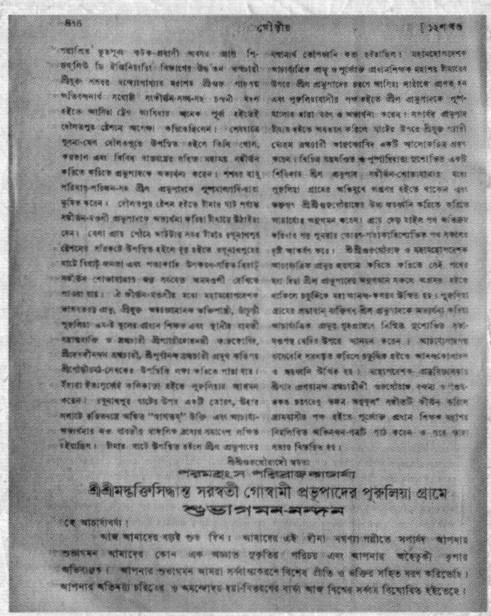

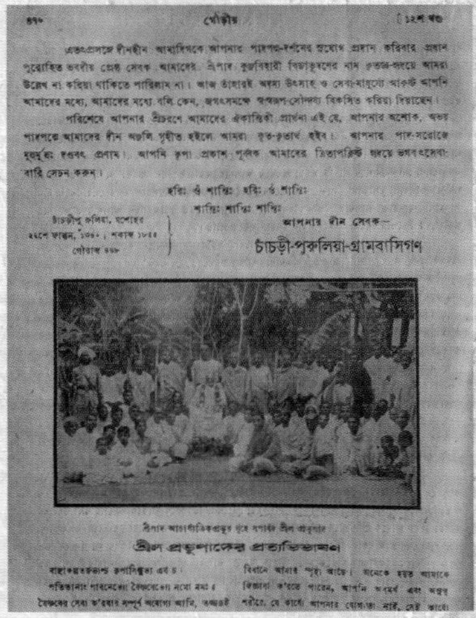

In 1934, Śrīla Prabhupāda visited the birthplace of Kuñjabihārī Vidyābhūṣāna in Jessore, Bangladesh along with several of his disciples and followers. Śrī Praṇavānanda Brahmacārī was one of those attending. Above is the original article published in the Gauḍīya (Volume 12, 17 March 1934), which features a picture taken during the visit. The article on this spread is a translation of the article. (Courtesy Bhaktivedanta Research Center)

Bhakti Pradīpa Tīrtha Mahārāja was also noted for his scholarship. He translated the *Bhagavad-gītā* into English and wrote quite a few other books in English. His powerful lectures in Dhaka became legendary. Śrīla Prabhupāda sent him to preach in the West, along with Śrīmad Bhakti Hṛdaya Bon Mahārāja. Śrīmad Bon Mahārāja's English lectures were so well-reputed that the mere mention of his name would attract high government officials to attend *hari-kathā*.

Śrīmad Bhakti Sāraṅga Gosvāmī Mahārāja was also famous for his scholarship and his lectures. Śrīmad Yāyāvara Mahārāja was known for his ability to quote scripture. Among the Brahmacārī preachers, Śrīpāda Hayagrīva *brahmacārī* (later Śrīmad Bhakti Dayita Mādhava Mahārāja) and Śrīpāda Siddhasvarūpa Brahmacārī were known for their preaching ability. Śrīpāda Hayagrīva Brahmacārī was instrumental, along with Śrīmad Śrīdhara Mahārāja, in opening *maṭhas* in Assam and Madras.

Śrīpāda Svādhikārānanda Brahmacārī (later Śrīmad Kṛṣṇadāsa Bābājī Mahārāja) was also an expert preacher. He was known for his extreme simplicity, incomparable humility, and very austere lifestyle. He was always chanting and singing, and was always in an extremely happy mood. It was impossible to offend him in any way. Pride and anger could not come anywhere near him. Everybody loved him and he loved everybody. He used to make small, inexpensive pamphlets of Śrīla Prabhupāda's lectures and so forth, and distribute them widely during his preaching trips. He was very dear to Śrīla Prabhupāda. He was a very expert singer, and knew many songs and verses by heart. Śrīla Prabhupāda said in one poem, *kanaka kāminī, pratiṣṭhā bāghinī, chāḍiyāche yāre sei ta' vaiṣṇava*—"one who has been released from the clutches of the three tigers representing money, women, and personal ambition is a Vaiṣṇava." By the light of this statement, every devotee who met Śrīpāda Svādhikārānanda Brahmacārī thought of him as a Vaiṣṇava.

Prabhupāda always stressed the importance of preaching. Once Śrīpāda Hayagrīva Brahmacārī asked Śrīla Prabhupāda whether they should learn the local language while preaching in South India. Śrīla Prabhupāda replied, "You

Śrīla Prabhupāda with the governor of Bengal, Sir John Anderson in Mayapur

have to preach in the language you know [in common with the South Indians, e.g., English and Hindi]. I cannot let you waste your precious time learning a new language." Śrīla Prabhupāda sent his preachers all over India and Burma, and to England, France, Germany, and the United States.

Śrīla Prabhupāda told his disciples:

Please preach the kīrtana of the Supreme Lord, even if in doing so you have to incur debt; then in order to pay off that debt, you will have to be even more engaged in sevā. When your creditors put pressure on you, you will be forced to beg more for alms. Again, as the pious householders will not give you alms unless your character and conduct are pure, you will be forced to preserve a pure lifestyle with great determination and care. I will not leave one penny for you, so that in future you won't indulge in laziness and you won't be able to give up your devotional lives full of hari-kīrtana and hari-sevā.

The Maṭha is the center of hari-kīrtana, and hari-kīrtana is life and consciousness. To ensure that there is no place for laziness, bad conduct, trivial thought, gossip, or vulgar desire in the Maṭha, you have to go from door to door, where your hari-kīrtana will be tested by the public. When the public will think that they are the givers of alms and you are the receivers of alms—in other words, that their status is higher than yours—they will criticize you in many ways, thinking you are objects of their mercy. Perhaps some of them will also be ready to kick you out. Then, on one hand, you will be able to become tṛṇād api sunīcha (humbler than a blade of grass) and mānada (respectful to others), and on the other hand, you will take great care to make your lives and characters pure and exemplary. Furthermore, what will be beneficial for you is this: as you will correct the mistakes of the common people by citing the message of sādhu, śāstra, and guru-varga, you will not make those same mistakes.

Please do not be upset if someone criticizes you personally. But your guru-varga, śāstra, and mahājanas are completely faultless, supremely liberated, and eternal associates of the Lord. If, due to ignorance, someone criticizes them, then you should correct that person's mistakes by telling them the real truth. This will be very beneficial for both you and the ignorant people. If you become lazy about begging for alms from door to door to collect ingredients for hari-kīrtana, and if you indulge in laziness and bad habits, preferring reclusive bhajan so you can escape others' criticism, then your character will not be purified. You will not have the life of devotional practice. I will never give you any opportunity to become deceitful in the path of devotion in the privacy of your own home; I will never give you any opportunity to live in a reclusive place so that you can become undisciplined in your heart, thinking no one will come to see or hear you there. You are my dearmost friends. I will never allow you to get into trouble. I will never allow you to give up the path of pleasing the senses of the Lord so you can please the senses of the people of the world, as well as your own, because you received some temporary position or you could not tolerate some temporary criticism.

Radio Broadcasts and Welcoming German Devotees, 1935

On January 15, 1935, the Governor of Bengal, Sir John Anderson, came to Śrīdhāma Māyāpura, visited the holy places of Śrīman Mahāprabhu's pastimes, and gave a speech. On February 23, on the occasion of Śrīla Prabhupāda's 61st appearance anniversary, a big gathering was arranged in Śrī Puruṣottama Maṭha, Purī. The King of Orissa, Gajapati Śrī Rāmacandra Deva himself, presided over the gathering. Before Gaura-purṇīmā that year, Śrīpāda Sakhi-caraṇa Bhakti-vijaya brought electricity to the Yogapīṭha temple. On March 20, on the auspicious occasion of Śrī Gaura-purṇīmā, the King of Tripurā came and opened the newly built temple at Yogapīṭha. In April, Śrīla Prabhupāda established the Gayā Gauḍīya Maṭha. On April 13, he sent a few preachers to Burma to spread the message of Mahāprabhu. On June 9, Śrīla Prabhupāda's disciples preached Mahāprabhu's message on the radio for the first time, at the Indian Broadcasting Service, Calcutta. Among those who delivered *hari-kathā* on the radio were Śrīmad Bhakti Hṛdaya Bon Mahārāja and Śrīpāda Sundarānanda Vidyāvinoda Prabhu. Śrīpada Praṇavānanda Pratnavidyālaṅkāra (later Śrīmad Bhakti Pramoda Purī Mahārāja) sang the collection of verses entitled "Gopīnātha-vijñāpti" by Śrīla Bhaktivinoda Ṭhākura. At this time, Śrīla Prabhupāda was in Darjeeling, North Bengal. But he and his other disciples heard the broadcast from there. When Śrīla Prabhupāda returned, he requested Śrīpāda Praṇavānanda Prabhu to sing "Gopīnātha-vijñāpti" again for him.

On July 8, he installed deities at the Bombay Gauḍīya Maṭha. At this time, Śrīman Samvidānanda Dāsa, M.A., received a Ph.D. from London University in Vaiṣṇava history and literature.

On September 12, the twelve cantos of *Śrīmad Bhāgavatam* with the commentaries of Śrīla Prabhupāda were completed and published. The summaries of each canto up to the ninth were written by Śrīpāda Praṇavānanda Brahmacārī, the summary of the tenth canto was written by Śrīpāda Nanda-lāla Vidyāsāgara, and the summaries of the eleventh and twelfth cantos were written by Śrīmad Bhakti Bhūdeva Śrauti Mahārāja.

On September 18, the devotees in Gauḍīya Maṭha and many distinguished citizens of Calcutta welcomed two German devotees, Ernst George Schulge and H. E. von Queth, who came to Calcutta with Śrīmad Bhakti Hṛday Bon Mahārāja to see Śrīla Prabhupāda. They were each given a decorated cloth scroll welcoming them at a lavish reception in their honor. In October Śrīla Prabhupāda went to Mathurā and observed Kārtik-vrata at Śrī Rādhā-kuṇḍa. On November 7, he went to Delhi, and from there he went to Gayā. At this time, preaching in Burma was going on very successfully.

Preaching in the West, Burma, and India, 1936

On February 12, on his 62nd appearance anniversary, Śrīla Prabhupāda established the Bhaktivinoda Research Institute. In London his appearance anniversary was also celebrated at a special gathering. In the meantime, Śrīmad Bhakti Sarvasva Giri Mahārāja and Śrīmad Bhakti Vilāsa Gabhastinemi Mahārāja were preaching in Burma with great success, and on March 8, a Gauḍīya Maṭha preaching center was established there with the help of the education minister, Dr. Bame, on 29 Brookings Street, Rangoon. On March 15, Śrīla Prabhupāda installed deities in Sarbhog Gauḍīya Maṭha, Assam. On March 29, Śrīla Prabhupāda went to Purī, where a *saṅkīrtana* festival was held for seven days. In June and July, Śrīla Prabhupāda preached at different places in Bengal. Among them were Baliyati, Godruma, Darjeeling, and Bagura. On June 13 and 14, at Dhaka University and the Bar (law) Library of Dhaka, Śrīla Prabhupāda's *sannyāsī* disciples and the two German devotees preached *hari-kathā*. In August, Śrīla Prabhupāda went to Mathurā to observe Puruṣottama-vrata. On September 9, he came back to Calcutta Gauḍīya Maṭha.

Meetings with Scholars and Indologists

Throughout his preaching mission, Śrīla Prabhupāda met with many scholars, national leaders, and Indologists from abroad who were visiting India. At one time or another, Śrīla Prabhupāda met with all the most famous men of Bengal. He also met with high government officials and scholars of religion from all over India. Even though Śrīla Prabhupāda made it very clear through his *pracāra* (preaching) and *āchā*r (conduct) that the supreme goal of life is *kṛṣṇa-prema* (love for Kṛṣṇa), he was still very perceptive of the world situation. In his lectures he would make insightful comments on such diverse subjects as Professor Einstein's findings, medical experiments with monkey glands, the Pope's effort to bring peace to Europe, and so forth. His extraordinary power was that he could make his audience see their surroundings from a Kṛṣṇa-conscious point of view because he could immediately elevate them to that level. They listened to Śrīla Prabhupāda's *hari-kathā* for hours, took part in discussions, and asked him spiritual questions. All of them left him with a sense of reverence for his divine personality and a favorable impression of Vaiṣṇavism. This should not surprise anyone, as Śrīla Prabhupāda's scholarship was unquestionable, his logic was razor-sharp, his concepts were deep and sublime, and his expressions were strikingly beautiful.

What was felt by many of his contemporary scholars in India was thus expressed by Professor Dinesh Candra Sen of the University of Calcutta: "What you have achieved is imperishable. What you have done we could never even have conceived. Everything of ours is going towards degradation. Only you have protected everyone by performing this noble task. What you will do will inspire the whole world, not just Bengal or India."

It is not possible to mention here all those he met, but following are the names of some of them: Raut Ray Saheb, His Excellency General Punya

Samaser Rana Jambahadur of Nepal, Manmathanath Mukhopadhyay (Calcutta High Court Justice), September 1924, Pandit PraMaṭha Nath Tarkabhushan, Professor Phanibhushan Adhikari, December 1924, Pandit Madan-mohan Malavya, April 1925, The Mahanta Mahārāja of Śrī Nāthdvāra, Gokulanāth Gosvāmī Mahārāja of Bombay, the Ācārya of Madhvācārya Maṭha of Uḍupi, the Ācārya of Gādir Maṭha of Salimābād, 1926, Professor Albert E. Suthers (University of Ohio) 1929, A.P. Sen, Professor Rādhākumud Mukhopadhyay, Dr. Rādhākamal Mukhopadhyay, Dr. A.N. Sengupta 1929, Sir P.C. Roy (famous chemist) 1930, Dr. Kalidas Nag (famous historian and professor at the University of Calcutta), Śrī Jatindra Nath Basu, Dr. Dinesh Candra Sen (famous writer and professor at the University of Calcutta), Śrī Birajmohan Mukhopadhyay (Vice Principal of the Law College of the University of Calcutta), Dr. Magnus Hirschfeld (German scholar and world traveller), Dr. Stella Kremrich, A.J. Jacob (American world traveller), Col. Dwaraka Prasad Goel (Principal of Calcutta Medical College), Dr. Ganganath Jha (Vice Chancellor of Āllāhābād University), Vasanta Kumār Chatterjee, 1931, Justice Sundaram Chettiyar of Madras High Court, Sir P.S. Shiva Swami Aiyar, Sir George Frederick Stanley (Governor of Madras), Professor K. Panchapagesan of Purukote College in Madras, Dr. Suniti Chatterjee of the University of Calcutta, Sir William Malcolm Haily (Governor of United Provinces), Dr. Sudhindu Kumar Das (Professor of Krishnanagar College), Śrī Viśvambhara Vyākaraṇa Tīrtha Vedānta Śāstri of Rādhā-kānta Maṭha of Purī, 1932, Śrī Satish Chandra De (Principal of Howrah Nursing College), Professor Ranada Charan Chakravarti, Śrī Sanjiv Kumar Choudhury (professor from Nepal), Śrī Ganesh Candra Chanda (Superintendent, Archaeological Division of Bihar), 1933, Rai Bahadur Ramaprasad Chanda, Śrī Ānanda Mahāpātra (Senior Professor in the Āyurveda Department of the Sanskrit College in Purī), Mr. Junakar (Professor at Dhaka University), Khagendra Nath Mitra (Professor at Presidency College, Calcutta), 1934, Sir Jadunath Sarkar, Dr. Henry Hand and Mr. S.V. Rosetto of California, Mr. S.N. Rudra Bar-at-law, Indirā Devī (Queen of Cochbihar), Mme. M. Potters (French scholar), 1935.

Correspondence With Western Representatives

Śrīla Prabhupāda maintained a steady correspondence with his representatives in Europe. Following are excerpts from some of his letters to Śrīmad Bhakti Pradīpa Tīrtha Mahārāja.

April 4, 1933

"Your conversation with the cultured people of the West following the words of the Divine Lord will surely be appreciated by all sincere souls amidst their busy life. I don't know anybody who was more delighted than myself to hear that at last the Gauḍīya Maṭha Offiice has been opened in the British Isles."

May 5, 1933

"By delivering *hari-kathā* to many people, maybe one or two good people will become interested in devotional topics—this is my expectation."

June 27, 1933

"The esoteric representation need not be placed on the table at the sacrifice of the exoteric code and exposition, as the people are found to be very hasty to judge a person by his external appearance."

July 26, 1933

"We are no mediators, but on the other hand solicitors of congregational meetings. So shifting from the centre of London is now out of the question."

August 21, 1933

"I have much enjoyed learning that the senior Tridaṇḍi Swāmī has been honored and received by Her Majesty, the Queen of England. This unforeseen chance is really a very rare opportunity that hardly falls to the lot of a monk with his triple staff and bowl in his hand.

"We take pride that you are acting as our proxy in a distant land, which our crippled movements have not yet approached."

August 28, 1933

"I learn with great delight that the City of London has found you keeping the fast on Janmāṣṭamī day and am more glad to learn that you could make *pārāyaṇa* (completion) of *Śrī Caitanya-caritāmṛta* on that day."

February 23, 1934

"Though we are distantly placed by the will of Providence, still the symbolic sounds in letters will not keep us at such a distance.

"One does not receive a letter from the Supreme Lord. We hear about Him only from His devotees, and our news also can be sent to Him through His devotees. Such communication took place long before telegrams, air-mail, or radio.

"The benign hand of Śrī Kṛṣṇa is a better judge than our silly selves. We should ever be in the service of the Supreme Lord Kṛṣṇa, whatever troubles we meet in our journey of life."

The Final Days, 1936

On October 24, 1936, Śrīla Prabhupāda bade farewell to Śrīmad Bhakti Śāraṅga Gosvāmī Mahārāja and sent him to preach in England and America. At this time Śrīla Prabhupāda blessed him and gave him *śālagrāma-śīlā*, *gomatī-śīlā*, and *govardhana-śīlā*. That same day Śrīla Prabhupāda set forth from Calcutta for Purī Dhāma. He arrived the following day with many of his disciples accompanying him. Among them were Śrīdhara Mahārāja, Kuñja-bihārī Prabhu, Hayagrīva Dāsa Brahmacārī, Paramānanda Vidyāratna, and Sajjanānanda Brahmacārī.

Many devotees came to the train station to welcome Śrīla Prabhupāda, and they brought a decorated car for him. When Śrīla Prabhupāda arrived at the Puruṣottama Maṭha, a big crowd was assembled there to have his *darśana*.

Śrīla Prabhupāda seemed to be in a meditative mood of deep devotion in Purī. He showed transcendental symptoms of divine ecstasy. From time to time he would tell the devotees, "It is in this life that we have to serve our Lord, so we can gain eternal service at the lotus feet of our eternal Lord. We should not waste any time!"

People started coming from all directions to hear Śrīla Prabhupāda. Śrīla Prabhupāda expressed his desire to celebrate the Annakuṭa festival at Caṭaka Parvata. There was not much time left before the festival, but his dedicated disciples made all the arrangements quickly. The following description was printed in the *Gauḍīya*, 15th Canto, No. 16:

Tridaṇḍi Swāmī Śrīmad Bhakti Rakṣaka Śrīdhara Mahārāja, Śrīpāda Hayagrīva Brahmacārī, Śrīmad Sajjanānanda Brahmacārī, and others took great care to bring sumptuous foodstuffs for the festival and to decorate the place. Sādhunivās was beautifully decorated with fruit, flowers, mango leaves, banana trees, coconuts, and waterpots. On the altar was a very beautiful embroidered canopy. All of the way from the street to Caṭaka Parvata was decorated with flags, banana trees, waterpots, and arches. Different foodstuffs, such as white rice, yellow rice, sweet rice, khichuri, rice pudding, capāṭis, puris, and so forth were arranged in the shape of a mountain. There were other mountains of foodstuffs, such as the Bengali delicacies described in Caitanya-caritāmṛta, the delicacies of Vraja described in Śrī Govinda Līlāmṛta, and all the favorite offerings of Lord Jagannātha. Also an immeasurable amount of mahāprasād, consisting of many vegetable and grain preparations and sweets, came from the Jagannātha temple. Tulasī mañjarīs were placed on all the offerings, and Śrīla Prabhupāda, singing the songs of Śrī Rūpa and Śrī Raghunātha, worshiped Śrī Govardhana. The festival opened with saṅkīrtana. Then, by Śrīla Prabhupāda's instruction, Śrīpāda Sundarānanda Vidyāvinoda read about Śrīpāda Mādhavendra Purī's Annakuta Festival from the fourth chapter of Śrī Caitanya-caritāmṛta: Madhya-līlā.

Hundreds of people were fed mahāprasād that night, and the next morning hundreds of beggars and destitute people were fed.

One day Śrīla Prabhupāda, sitting in his *bhajana kuṭīra*, told the devotees, "All the residents of the *maṭha* should always be engaged in the service of Śrī Hari, Guru, and Vaiṣṇavas. They should always be engaged in hearing *hari-kathā* and discussing *hari-kathā*. If one becomes averse to *hari-kathā* and *hari-sevā* then one will again be entangled by one's material desires. Then one's time will be spent in gossiping, criticizing others, fighting with others and gratifying one's senses. If the residents of the *maṭha* do not understand that *vaiṣṇava-sevā* is the most beneficial thing, then they will not make progress in the realm of devotion. One has to cultivate one's Kṛṣṇa-consciousness by sincerely serving the Vaiṣṇavas and by endeavoring to please the Vaiṣṇavas with body, mind, and soul.

"By the petition of a Vaiṣṇava, merciful Kṛṣṇa will give His mercy to this sinful soul. This we have to remember all the time.

"If a godbrother falls from the platform of service to Hari, Guru, and Vaiṣṇavas, then you should think that your own brother is falling down. Then you have to openly advise him about *hari-bhajana* and nicely make him understand the situation. Sing the beneficial message of Guru and Gaurāṅga to him. If you merely comment on his downfall, then you are not his well-wisher. You have to be merciful to him by talking to him about the Lord. By doing this you will benefit yourself as well as him, and your goal of living in the *maṭha* will be accomplished. We are living together to help each other serve the Lord.

"We will not live in this world very long. If we can die while continuously doing *hari-kīrtana*, then our birth will be successful. We have not come to this world to be carpenters, to deal with wood and stone. We are only carriers of the message of Śrī Caitanyadeva."

On December 7, 1936, Śrīla Prabhupāda left Purī for Calcutta. The next day a huge crowd of devotees was waiting at Howrah Station to welcome Śrīla Prabhupāda. Śrīla Prabhupāda's car was decorated with flowers, and it went to the Gauḍīya Maṭha amid a *saṅkīrtana* procession. While in Purī, Śrīla Prabhupāda had displayed his pastime of illness. So his disciples had engaged the most famous physicians in Calcutta, such as Sir Nilratan Sarkar, Dr. Shivapada Bhattacarya, Dr. Indubhushan Basu, Dr. P. Brahmacari, and Dr. Nagendra Gopal Bishwas, to take care of Śrīla Prabhupāda full-time. As instructed by the doctors, Śrīla Prabhupāda's disciples requested him not to speak for very long at a stretch. When asked how he was, Śrīla Prabhupāda would say that his only problem was that he was not allowed to do *hari-kīrtana*.

Śrīla Prabhupāda told the assembled devotees, "One should not make many disciples. I have not made any disciples. They are all my Gurus. I learn something from all of them. May they give me the opportunity to follow the example of their pure devotion. This is my prayer."

His Final Instructions

On December 23, Śrīla Prabhupāda gave his final instruction to the assembled devotees: "I have caused anxiety for many people. Perhaps many people have considered me their enemy, because I was compelled to tell the unadulterated truth. I asked them to serve the Lord with all sincerity. I have given much anxiety to many people only because I wanted to inspire them to serve Kṛṣṇa sincerely without material desire and duplicity. One day they will understand this."

Preach about Śrī Rūpa and Śrī Raghunātha

"All of you please preach about Śrī Rūpa and Śrī Raghunātha with great enthusiasm. The supreme goal of all our desire is to become specks of dust at the lotus feet of the followers of Śrī Rūpa Gosvāmī. All of you remain united in the shelter of the *āśraya-vigraha* in order to satisfy the transcendental senses of the Supreme Entity of non-dual knowledge. All of you somehow live simply in this temporary world with the single goal of serving the Lord. Please do not give up your devotional service inspite of hundreds of dangers, insults, or persecutions. Please do not be discouraged by seeing that most people of the world are not listening to the transcendental topics of devotional service. Please do not give up *śravaṇa-kīrtana* of *kṛṣṇa-kathā*, which is your own *bhajana* and your sole property. Please always chant the name of the Lord, being humbler than a blade of grass and more tolerant than a tree.

The Fire of Saṅkīrtana

"We only cherish one desire in our hearts: to sacrifice this body, which is only a lump of matter, in the fire of the *saṅkīrtana yajña* of Lord Śrī Kṛṣṇa Caitanya and His associates. We do not wish to be heroes by dint of our action, bravery or religiosity. But let this be our real identity life after life: that we are specks of dust under the lotus feet of Śrī Rūpa. Let that mean everything to us. The Bhaktivinoda current will never be stemmed.

Please take up the mission of preaching the desire of Bhaktivinoda with greater enthusiasm. There are many qualified and accomplished people among you. We have no other desire; our only message is this:

" 'Taking a blade of grass between my teeth, I fall down and pray again and again that I may become the dust at the feet of Śrī Rūpa birth after birth.' "

"Living in this world, one has to face many kinds of difficulties. It is not our job to try to remove those difficulties. Nor should we become depressed by them. After these difficulties are gone, what shall we gain? What will our eternal lives be? While staying here we should have some idea of that. All the things that attract us or repel us, what we want and what we do not want—we have to resolve these things in our minds. The more we distance ourselves from the lotus feet of Kṛṣṇa, the more these things will draw us in. The joy of *kṛṣṇa-sevā* can be realized when one is attracted to His divine name after transcending the happiness and misery of this world. At present, the topic of Kṛṣṇa is startling and perplexing to us. The continuing events of our lives pose obstacles to the realization of our eternal fulfillment. Knowingly or unknowingly, all human beings are struggling to eliminate these. Our only need is to enter that realm of eternal fulfillment, transcending all duality.

"We have no attachment or hostility towards anyone in this world. All arrangements of this world are temporary. Everyone has an indispensable need for the Absolute Truth. May all of you with one goal, and in harmony with each other, attain the right to serve the original *āśraya-vigraha*. Let the currents of thought of the followers of Śrī Rūpa flow in this world. May we never under any circumstances show antipathy towards the seven-tongued fire of *śrī kṛṣṇa saṅkīrtana-yajña*. If we have an increasing attachment for it, then all our goals will be fulfilled. All of you please preach fearlessly about Śrī Rūpa and Śrī Raghunātha with great enthusiasm, under the guidance of their followers."

Then Śrīla Prabhupāda displayed his pastime of illness. At the same time he was incessantly chanting and meditating. Śrīpāda Kuñja-bihārī Prabhu made up a duty roster for some of the devotees who were present, so one of them would be with Śrīla Prabhupāda every hour of the day and night. Among those who had this service were Śrīdhara Mahārāja, Praṇavānanda Brahmacārī, and Kṛṣṇānanda Brahmacārī.

Requests Song Śrī Rūpa Mañjarī Pada

In the morning of December 31, 1936, Śrīla Prabhupāda requested Śrīdhara Mahārāja to sing the song *śrī rūpa-mañjarī-pada sei mora sampada* by Śrīla Narottama Dāsa Ṭhākura. He also asked Śrīpāda Navīna Kṛṣṇa Vidyālaṅkāra to sing the song *tūhu dayā sāgara tārayite prāṇī* by Śrīla Bhaktivinoda Ṭhākura. Then Prabhupāda expressed his appreciation to some of his disciples for their service, and gave some instructions for the future. Finally he said, "Love and rupture both should have the same end in view. Śrīla Narottama Dāsa Ṭhākura lived by the concept of Śrī Rūpa and Śrī Raghunātha. We should also live our lives according to that concept." Then Śrīla Prabhupāda told everyone, "All of you who are present here, as well as those who are not present, please accept my blessings. Please remember that our only duty and religion is to propagate the service of the Lord and His devotees."

Divine Disappearance

At about 5:20 the next morning, Śrīpāda Praṇavānanda Brahmacārī was at Śrīla Prabhupāda's bedside. Suddenly Śrīla Prabhupāda came out of his deep meditation and said, "Who is here?" Praṇavānanda Prabhu said, "It's me, Praṇavānanda, Prabhupāda." Śrīla Prabhupāda said, "Oh, Praṇavānanda Prabhu?" Praṇavānanda Prabhu asked him, "How are you feeling, Prabhupāda?" Śrīla Prabhupāda said, "What can I say? Hare Kṛṣṇa, Hare Kṛṣṇa!" These were his last words. As it was time for the next devotee, Kṛṣṇānanda Prabhu, to take up his post at Śrīla Prabhupāda's bedside, Praṇavānanda Prabhu went back to his room. He sat there thinking, "Is Śrīla Prabhupāda going to leave us now? What will happen if he leaves us now, what shall we do?" His thoughts were interrupted by the sounds of footsteps. It was Kṛṣṇānanda Prabhu. He said, "Come quickly! I think the great disaster has happened to us." Then there was the tumultuous sound of crying all over the

Gauḍīya Maṭha, and amazingly enough, all the clocks in the *maṭha* stopped.

At 5:30 A.M., on Thursday, January 1, 1937, Śrīla Prabhupāda left this world to enter Śrī Śrī Rādhā-Govinda's *niśānta-līlā*. At the predawn hour when Śrī Śrī Rādhā-Govinda are united as one, when the divine pastime of Śrī Gaurasundara is eternally manifest, the most worshipable lord of the Gauḍīya Vaiṣṇavas, Śrīla Prabhupāda, who called himself Śrī Vārṣabhānavī-dayita dāsa (the servant of the beloved of Śrīmatī Rādhārāṇī), entered the abode of his eternal pastime.

The grief and lamentation of the devotees at the Gauḍīya Maṭha were beyond description. Some were sobbing as if their hearts would break, some were chanting loudly with eyes flooded with tears, some were falling at Śrīla Prabhupāda's lotus feet, some were falling on the ground and chanting with their heads bowed down, and some were hitting their foreheads and saying "Oh Prabhupāda! Oh Prabhupāda!" Even though the sun had just risen, it seemed that in the sky of the Gauḍīya Vaiṣṇavas the sun had just set.

The devotees started performing the Vedic rites with great care, in spite of the intolerable burning pain of separation. First of all they bathed Śrīla Prabhupāda with sandalwood water. Then they dressed him in new clothes and decorated him with flowers, garlands, and sandalwood. Crying incessantly, they put *tilaka* on twelve parts of his body. Then Śrīla Prabhupāda was laid on a new bed in front of the Deities. The devotees circumambulated him and performed *pūjā*, *bhoga*, and *ārati* to him amid tumultuous *saṅkīrtana*. Thousands of people started coming to have their last *darśana* of Śrīla Prabhupāda. Flowers and tears were everywhere. Then Śrīla Prabhupāda was taken to Sealdah Station amid a *saṅkīrtana* procession of thousands of people. A devotee of Śrīla Prabhupāda called Śrī Yāmiṇī Mukhopadhyāya arranged for a special train for Śrīla Prabhupāda. The train was fully occupied with thousands of devotees, both men and women. The destination was Krishnanagar, but all the way from Calcutta to Krishnanagar, thousands of people were waiting at every station to see Śrīla Prabhupāda. The devotees were displaying photos of Śrīla Prabhupāda from the windows of the train, and the crowds were offering flowers to those pictures. At Krishnanagar Station, all the high government officials were waiting to offer their obeisances to him. Then he was taken to Navadvīpa Ghāṭa by car, and then they crossed the Gaṅgā on boats to arrive at Māyāpura. A big crowd was already waiting at Māyāpura. When the Calcutta devotees met the Māyāpura devotees, another wave of grief engulfed them.

First Śrīla Prabhupāda was taken to Śrīman Mahāprabhu's birthplace in Yogapīṭha. More devotees were waiting there. Then they laid him down in front of the Deities and offered him *pūjā* and *ārati*. Both the Hindus and the Muslims of Māyāpura were singing his glories with tears in their eyes. Śrīla Prabhupāda was given the garland which had been offered to Śrīman Mahāprabhu. Next he was taken to Śrīvāsa Āṅgana, Śrī Advaita Bhavan, Śrī Bhakti Vijaya Bhavan, the *samādhi mandira* of Śrīla Gaura-kiśora Dāsa Bābājī Mahārāja, and finally Śrī Caitanya Maṭha; at each stop he was offered *pūjā* and *ārati*. When he came to his own Śrī Caitanya Maṭha, the devotees' hearts broke with unbearable pain.

They decided that the place of his *samādhi* would be in between Śrī Caitanya Maṭha and Śrī Bhakti Vijaya Bhavana. Singing *saṅkīrtana, sannyāsī, brahmacārī,* and *gṛhastha* devotees together began digging the foundation of the *samādhi mandira*. Śrīla Prabhupāda was bathed in Gaṅgā water, dressed in new clothes, and decorated with sandalwood. Śrīmad Bhakti Pradīpa Tīrtha Mahārāja wrote the *samādhi* mantra with sandalwood, following the injunction of Śrī Gopāla Bhaṭṭa Gosvāmī. Now Śrīla Prabhupāda was brought to the place of *samādhi*, and amid obeisances, prayer, glorification, and offering of flowers, he was seated on a marble throne covered with delicate cloth. The tumultuous sound of glorification and *saṅkīrtana* resounded as sandalwood, flowers, garlands, and *ārati* were offered at his lotus feet. Devotees were rolling on the ground, crying "Jaya Prabhupāda!" and singing his favorite songs, *śrī rūpa-mañjarī-pada, svānanda-sukhada-kuñja manohara,* and *yaśomati nandana*.

Śrīla Śrīdhara Mahārāja and Śrīpāda Praṇavānanda Brahmacārī offered a fire sacrifice. Śrīla Bhārati Mahārāja read the disappearance pastime of Śrīla Haridāsa Ṭhākura from *Śrī Caitanya-caritāmṛta*, and the devotees circumambulated the *samādhi*, singing *yei ānilo prema-dhana* and *gurudev kṛpā bindu diyā*. Then they sang Śrīla Prabhupāda's *praṇāma-mantra* (*nama oṁ viṣṇu-pādāya kṛṣṇa-preṣṭhāya bhū-tale śrīmate bhaktisiddhānta-sarasvatīti nāmine*, etc.):

"I offer my respectful obeisances unto His Divine Grace Bhaktisiddhānta Sarasvatī, who is very dear to Lord Kṛṣṇa, having taken shelter at His lotus feet.

"I offer my respectful obeisances to Śrī Vārṣabhānavī-devī-dayita Dāsa, who is favored by Śrīmatī Rādhārāṇī and who is an ocean of mercy and the deliverer of the science of Kṛṣṇa.

"I offer my respectful obeisances unto you, the personified energy of Śrī Caitanya's mercy, who deliver devotional service which is enriched with conjugal love of Rādhā and Kṛṣṇa, coming exactly in the line of revelation of Śrīla Rūpa Gosvāmī.

"I offer my respectful obeisances unto you, who are the personified teachings of Lord Caitanya. You are the deliverer of the fallen souls. You do not tolerate any statement which is against the teachings of devotional service enunciated by Śrīla Rūpa Gosvāmī."

Epilogue

Śrīla Prabhupāda is the most magnanimous giver of the message of Mahāprabhu in this age. He took the treasure which had been safeguarded by a few and gave it to many. He revived the *saṅkīrtana* movement of Mahāprabhu by enabling devotees to joyfully assemble together in a modern institution. Now that Vaiṣṇavism was no longer in constant danger from oppressive regimes and reactionary *brāhmaṇas*, and now that the permanence of printing could protect the sanctity of the true and pure Vaiṣṇavism of Mahāprabhu from the corruption of *saahajiyā* interpretation, it could be given out again, freely.

Before Śrīla Prabhupāda began the Gauḍīya Maṭha, the general public had come to regard *sannyāsīs* with contempt or, at best, apathy, for their personal conduct and spiritual backgrounds were considered questionable. But Śrīla Prabhupāda conquered the public's apathy towards *sādhus* and religion. He defeated the *sahajiyās*, who wrongly imitated the pastimes of the Lord, and the impersonalists, who belittled the path of pure devotion. He protected Śrīman Mahāprabhu's mission from those who would dilute and distemper it in the name of adaptation.

Śrīla Prabhupāda knew that while the mundane world had changed greatly since Śrīman Mahāprabhu's time, the path of Vaiṣṇavism was eternal and required no modernization. Instead he modernized its institutions: devotees could assemble freely, to do *saṅkīrtana* in the halls of the Gauḍīya Maṭha and *hari-kathā* in the pages of *Gauḍīya*.

Śrīla Prabhupāda saw and appreciated the inventions of the modern world the way he appreciated anything—as items to be utilized in Mahāprabhu's mission, for devotional service. He preached through the printing press, while simultaneously using it to protect the sanctity and authority of pure Vaiṣṇavism from corruption and misinterpretation. He himself wrote more than 108 essays and books; published the magazines *Sajjana Toṣaṇī*, *Gauḍīya*, *Nadiyā Prakāśa*, *Bhāgavata*, *Paramārthi*, and *Kīrtana*; and established the presses Bhāgavata Yantra, Gauḍīya Printing Works, Nadiyā Prakāśa Printing Press, and Paramārthi Printing Works. He published *Bhagavad-gītā*, *Śrīmad-Bhāgavatam*, *Śrī Caitanya-caritāmṛta Śrī Caitanya-bhāgavata*, and *Śrī Brahma-saṁhitā* with commentaries.

Śrīla Prabhupāda established 64 temples, introduced devotional exhibitions, conducted radio broadcasts, and established organized *parikramās* of the holy *dhāmas*. He was the first *ācārya* to research and compile information on the four Vaiṣṇava *sampradāyas* and emphasize their common ground.

Śrīla Prabhupāda won the respect and admiration of all by inspiring excellence in every spiritual endeavor: the scholarship, integrity, and refinement of the Gauḍīya Maṭha were unquestionable. His standards were unassailable. He was so formidable in debate that he was never defeated. The strength of his conviction and fierce determination earned him the title of *siṁha-guru*, or "lion guru."

Śrīla Prabhupāda was not, however, merely a teacher of strict austerity. He spread compassion and devotion around him like a fountain; he nurtured his disciples with divine affection. As Śrīla Bhakti Kusuma Śramaṇa Mahārāja wrote in his biography of Śrīla Prabhupāda, *Prabhupāda Śrīla Sarasvatī Ṭhākura*, "Wherever he appeared, many people had come there before him in order to see him, and as soon as he arrived the sound of *saṅkīrtana* would reverberate in all directions.

Even when he was walking, he was absorbed in the ecstasy of *hari-kathā kīrtana*. An unearthly, indescribable current of joy would follow Śrīla Prabhupāda everywhere."

The greatest gift of Śrīla Prabhupāda was that he gave the highest concept of devotion to thousands of surrendered souls who took shelter at his lotus feet. Those who came to inquire from him about *kṛṣṇa-prema*, the ultimate goal of their lives, were overjoyed to find out that whatever concept of pure devotion they might have had before, Śrīla Prabhupāda's concept was infinitely higher than that. His disciples saw him as their supreme source of the highest devotion. Śrīla Bhakti Rakṣaka Śrīdhara Mahārāja has expressed this very beautifully in his *Śrī Śrī Dayita Dāsa Daśakam* verses:

"From his lotus feet, the nectarine river of divine love flows throughout the universe; his servitors, like bees, maintain their lives drinking the honey that falls from his lotus feet; and the pure devotees in the shelter of the confidential mellows of Vraja revel in the bliss of singing the glories of his lotus feet.

"Parental affection, so highly esteemed in the world, is a colossal hoax. And without a doubt the reciprocation of conjugal affection shared in matrimony is legal dacoity. And worldly friendship and family relationships are simply cheating in disguise. I have gleaned these thoughts from the rays of light that emanate from the toenails of the holy feet of that great personality, the embodiment of supramundane affection."

Śrīla Bhaktisiddhānta Sarasvatī said, "The Bhaktivinoda current will never be stemmed," and indeed his movement has flowed all over the world, brought and carried on by his disciples and grand disciples. Śrīla Prabhupāda is the personification of Śrīman Mahāprabhu's causeless and perfect mercy. He is the desire tree (*kalpa-vṛkṣa*) of the Gauḍīya Vaiṣṇavas. Not only has he attracted them to Śrīman Mahāprabhu's movement—through his own preaching or the preaching of his followers—but, through his message and the example of his personal conduct, he is also able to provide them with everything they need for devotional service, eternally.

During the inauguration of the exhibition at Śrī Mādhva Gauḍīya Maṭha, Dhaka, Bangladesh.

The Observance of Śrīla Prabhupāda's Vyāsa Pūjā after His Disappearance

Originally Published in Gauḍīya- Vol. 15, Issue 33—34, 27th March 1937
(Courtesy Bhaktivedanta Research Center)

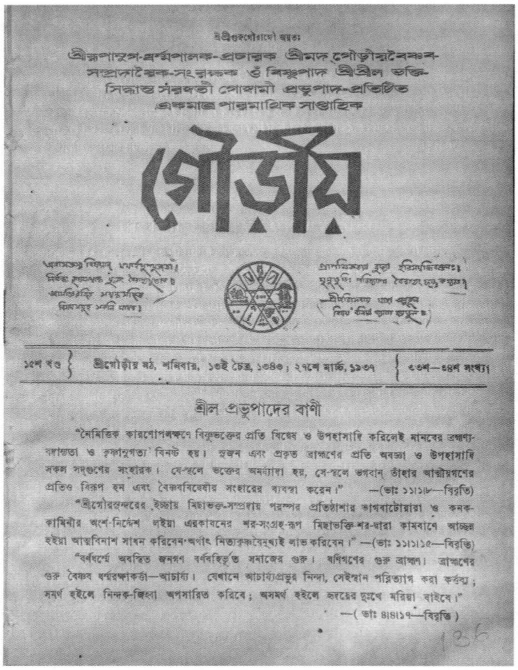

গৌড়ীয়

১৫শ খণ্ড } শ্রীগৌড়ীয় মঠ, শনিবার, ১৩ই চৈত্র, ১৩৪৩; ২৭শে মার্চ, ১৯৩৭ { ৩৩শ—৩৪শ সংখ্যা

শ্রীল প্রভুপাদের বাণী

"নৈমিত্তিক কারণোপলক্ষণে বিষ্ণুভক্তের প্রতি বিদ্বেষ ও উপহাসাদি করিলেই মানবের ব্রহ্মণ্যসদাচারতা ও কৃষ্ণানুগত্য বিনষ্ট হয়। সুজন এবং প্রকৃত ব্রাহ্মণের প্রতি অবজ্ঞা ও উপহাসাদি সকল সদ্গুণের সংহারক। যে-স্থলে ভক্তের অমর্য্যাদা হয়, সে-স্থলে ভগবান্ তাঁহার আত্মীয়গণের প্রতিও বিরূপ হন এবং বৈষ্ণববিদ্বেষীর সংহারের ব্যবস্থা করেন।" —(ভাঃ ১১।১।৮—বিবৃতি)

"শ্রীগৌরসুন্দরের ইচ্ছায় মিছাভক্ত-সম্প্রদায় পরস্পর প্রতিষ্ঠাশার ভাগবাটোয়ারা ও কনক-কামিনীর অংশ-নির্দ্দেশ লইয়া এরকাবনের শর-সংগ্রহ-রূপ মিছাভক্তি-শর-দ্বারা কামবাণে আচ্ছন্ন হইয়া আত্মবিনাশ সাধন করিবেন অর্থাৎ নিত্যকৃষ্ণবৈমুখ্যই লাভ করিবেন।" —(ভাঃ ১১।১।১৫—বিবৃতি)

"বর্ণধর্ম্মে অবস্থিত জনগণ বর্ণবহির্ভূত সমাজের গুরু। বর্ণিগণের গুরু ব্রাহ্মণ। ব্রাহ্মণের গুরু বৈষ্ণব ধর্ম্মরক্ষাকর্ত্তা—আচার্য্য। যেখানে আচার্য্যপ্রভুর নিন্দা, সেইস্থান পরিত্যাগ করা কর্ত্তব্য; সমর্থ হইলে নিন্দক-জিহ্বা অপসারিত করিবে; অসমর্থ হইলে হৃদয়ের দুঃখে মরিয়া যাইবে।" —(ভাঃ ৪।৪।১৭—বিবৃতি)

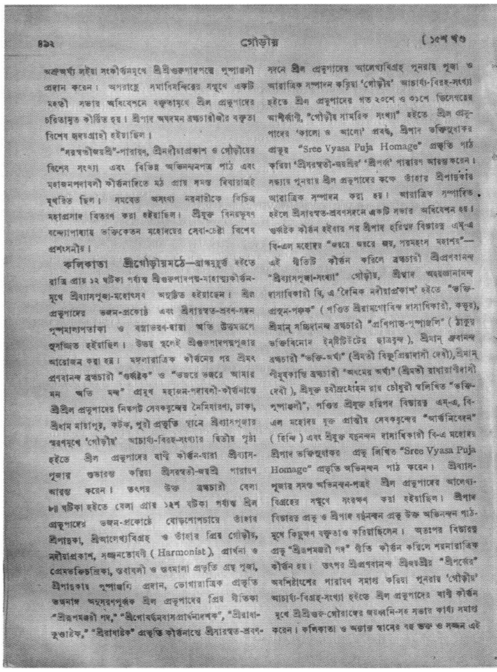

৬১২ গৌড়ীয় [১৫শ খণ্ড

Śrī Gauḍīya Maṭha, Calcutta

From *brāhma-muhūrta* till almost midnight, the festival of Śrī Vyāsa Pūjā was celebrated by way of glorifying Śrī Guru-pādapadma [Śrīla Prabhupāda]. Śrīla Prabhupāda's *bhajana* quarters and the Śrī Sārasvata Śravaṇa-sadana were decorated most excellently with flowers, garlands, flags, fabrics, and ornaments. In both places arrangements for the worship of Śrī Guru-pādapadma were made. After the *maṅgalārātrika-kīrtanas,* Śrīmat Praṇavānanda Brahmacārī sang the *Gurvāṣṭaka* and *"Bhaja re bhaja re āmāra mana ati manda"* and other *padāvalī-kīrtanas* of the *mahājanas*. After the *kīrtana,* he read from the second page of the Ācārya-viraha issue of the *Gauḍīya,* recalling previous Vyāsa Pūjā celebrations in Naimiṣāraṇya, Dhaka, Śrīdhāma Māyāpura, Cuttack, Purī, and other places. Thus he performed *kīrtana* of Śrīla Prabhupāda's words, thereby auspiciously commencing Śrī Vyāsa Pūjā and starting the reading of *Sarasvatī Jayaśrī.*

After that, the aforementioned *brahmacārī* [Śrīla Praṇavānanda Prabhu] performed the Vyāsa Pūjā rituals in Śrīla Prabhupāda's quarters from 8 a.m. to 12 p.m. with all sixteen prescribed items of *arcana*, worshiping Śrīla Prabhupāda's *śrī pāduka* [shoes], his worshipful portrait, as well as his beloved books like the volumes of the *Gauḍīya, Nadiyā Prakāśa, Sajjana Toṣaṇī* (Harmonist), *Prarthanā* and *Prema-bhakti-candrikā, Stavāvalī, Stavamālā,* and other sacred texts. After offering *puṣpāñjali* to Śrīla Prabhupāda's slippers, conducting the *bhogārātrika*, and completing other limbs of such *bhajana,* he sang Śrīla Prabhupāda's favorite *kīrtanas* like *"Śrī Rūpa-mañjarī-pada," "Śrī Govardhana-vāsa-prarthanā-daśaka," "Śrī Rādhā-kuṇḍāṣṭaka," "Śrī Rādhāṣṭaka,"* etc. Then he came down to the Śrī Sārasvata Śravaṇa-sadana temple room and again worshiped the picture of Śrīla Prabhupāda and performed *ārati.* After completing the *ārati,* he read Śrīla Prabhupāda's *āśirvāṇī* ["words of blessing"] from the 23rd and 31st of December from the Ācārya-viraha issue of the *Gauḍīya*. From the *"Gauḍīya Sāmayika*

Saṅkhyā" he read Śrīla Prabhupāda's "Kāla o Ālo" article, Śrīpāda Bhakti-sudhākara Prabhu's "Sree Vyāsa Pūjā Homage," and other articles, before commencing the reading of *Śrī Sarasvatī Jayaśrī's* Śrī Parva.

In the evening, once again *ārātika* was performed of Śrīla Prabhupāda's *śrī-pādukā* in his quarters. After *ārātika* was finished, an assembly was convened in the Śrī Sārasvata Śravaṇa-sadana. After *kīrtana* of the *Gurvāṣṭaka*, Śrīpāda Haripada Vidyāratna Prabhu sang *"Jayare jayare jaya, paramahaṁsa mahāśaya."* After the *kīrtana*, Brahmacārī Śrī Praṇavānanda read the "Vyāsa Pūjā Saṅkhyā" from *Gauḍīya*. Śrīpāda Advaya-jñānānanda Dāsādhikārī read "Bhakti-prasūna-pañcaka" from the *Dainika Nadiyā Prakāśa* (by Paṇḍita Rāma-govinda Dāsādhikārī, T Kovur). Śrīmān Saccidānanda Brahmacārī read the "Praṇipāta-Puṣpāñjali" (by the students of Ṭhākura Bhaktivinoda Institute). Śrīmān Dhruvānanda Brahmacārī read "Bhakti-Arghya" (by Śrīmatī Viṣṇupriyā-dāsī Devī). Śrīmān Pīyūṣa-kānti Brahmacārī read "Adhamera Arghya" (by Śrīmatī Rādhārāṇī-dāsī Devī). Śrīyukta Ravindra-mohana Roy Choudhuri read his own offering "Bhakti Puṣpāñjali." Paṇḍita Śrī Haripada Vidyāratna read "Ārta-nivedana," an offering in Hindi from the devotees of the north. Śrī Yadunandana Dāsādhikārī read Śrīpāda Bhakti-sudhākara Prabhu's "Sree Vyāsa Pūjā Homage" and a few more homages of various devotees. All the written offerings were placed carefully before the worshipful image of Śrīla Prabhupāda. Śrīpāda Vidyāratna Prabhu and Śrīpāda Yadunandana Prabhu also spoke briefly. After this, Vidyāratna Prabhu sang *"Śrī Rūpa-mañjarī-pada"* and the evening *ārati-kīrtanas* were sung. Then Śrī Praṇavānanda Brahmacārī completed the rest of the reading from the Śrī Parva of *Śrī Jayaśrī* and again read Śrīla Prabhupāda's words from the "Ācārya Viraha Saṅkhyā." Then with *jaya-dhvani* for Śrī Śrī Guru-Gaurāṅga, the assembly was concluded. Many devotees and distinguished persons of Calcutta joined the festival to glorify Śrīla Prabhupāda. After the assembly, everyone was served *mahāprasāda*.

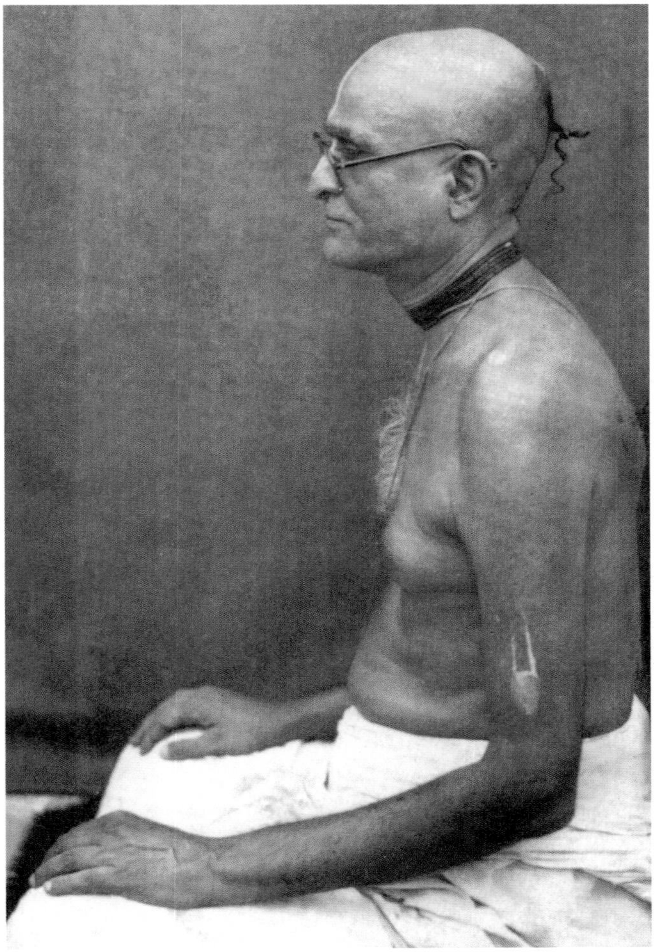

In Praise of

Śrīla Prabhupāda

The following selection is a compilation of writings from His Divine Grace Śrīla Bhakti Pramode Purī Gosvāmī Ṭhākura in remembrance of his beloved spiritual master Śrīla Prabhupāda, Śrīla Bhaktisiddhānta Sarasvatī Gosvāmī Ṭhākura.

Glorification of Śrīla Prabhupāda

By Śrīla Bhakti Pramode Purī Gosvāmī Mahārāja

Over the years, I have made several attempts to set down in writing various aspects of the transcendental life of His Divine Grace, *nitya-līlā-praviṣṭa* Om Vishnupada Śrī Śrīmad Bhaktisiddhānta Sarasvatī Gosvāmī Ṭhākura, my most worshipable spiritual master. These articles appeared in *Caitanya Vāṇī,* the monthly magazine of the Caitanya Gauḍīya Maṭha, founded by my godbrother, the late reverend Tridaṇḍi-sannyāsī Śrī Śrīmad Bhakti Dayita Mādhava Gosvāmī Mahārāja. I wanted to add to this series of articles, but since I am now 94 years old, I see that such an ambition will have to remain unfulfilled unless Śrīla Prabhupāda bestows upon me his special, causeless mercy.

After Śrīla Prabhupāda's disappearance, the editor of the weekly *Gauḍīya* magazine (who has now himself gone to the eternal abode) published a large number of valuable facts about Śrīla Prabhupāda's life in *Sarasvatī Jayaśrī*. Unfortunately, the article I composed for that volume was never published.

Our most worshipable Śrīla Prabhupāda is most dear to Śrī Kṛṣṇa. His birth and activities are all transcendental and superhuman, like those of the Lord. So, in truth, they cannot be known by the foolish, but by the surrendered souls alone—*mūḍhair avedyaṁ praṇatābhigamyam*. He reveals the secrets of His pastimes to those who are sincerely surrendered to Kṛṣṇa's lotus feet. Many fortunate devotees witnessed Śrīla Prabhupāda's divine ecstasies as he spoke about Guru, Gaurāṅga, Gāndharvikā and Giridhārī. Upon seeing the tears filling his eyes and hearing the deep spiritual emotions trembling in his voice, the devotees themselves were barely able to hold back their own tears.

Śrīla Prabhupāda was simultaneously harder than a thunderbolt and softer than a rose. He could not tolerate words that opposed or misrepresented the pure devotional doctrines taught by Śrī Caitanya Mahāprabhu and His dear associates, or those that misconstrued the proper portrayal of divine *rasa* (*rasābhāsa*). Throughout his life, he made an unflagging effort to establish consciousness in the *jiva* souls of their eternal nature as servants of Kṛṣṇa. While speaking about Kṛṣṇa, he would completely lose himself. Five books: Bhaktivinoda Ṭhākura's *Śaraṇāgati, Kalyāṇa-kalpa-taru, Gītāvalī,* and Narottama's *Prārthanā* and *Prema-bhakti-candrikā,* were especially dear to Śrīla Prabhupāda and he recited them daily.

From childhood on, his life was a glowing example of determination to serve the Holy Names and to preach their glories. He was never able to tolerate the arrogance of those who followed the path of meditation on one's own spiritual form while showing indifference to the Holy Name. Nor was he able to accept those who made an artificial effort to follow the path of *rāgānugā-bhakti* while ignoring Mahāprabhu's instructions in the *Śikṣāṣṭaka* and those of Rūpa Gosvāmī in the *Upadeśāmṛta*. After establishing in us proper foundation, he then conceded to advise us to maintain our effort to attain the supreme goal of life—love for Śrī Kṛṣṇa in the elevated, effulgent sweet mood of Vraja distributed by Śrī Caitanya Mahāprabhu. He gave most precedence to Mahāprabhu's command, "In this age of Kali, the chanting of the Holy Names is the only means (*nāma-saṅkīrtana kalau parama upāya*)."

Śrīla Prabhupāda was adorned by the four qualities mentioned in the *Śikṣāṣṭaka's tṛṇād api* verse, and with these qualities he propagated the glories of the Holy Name. He constantly warned us, his disciples, that we should not try to steal from the storehouse of religious experience and also that false renunciation is inimical to spiritual advancement. Śrīla Prabhupāda recommended appropriate renunciation or *yukta-vairāgya.*

kanaka-kāminī pratiṣṭhā-bāghinī
chāḍiyāche jāre se to vaiṣṇava

sei anāsakta sei śuddha bhakta
saṁsāra tathāya pāya parābhava

A Vaiṣṇava is one who has abandoned the tigress of desire for gold, women, and worldly prestige. He is truly detached and thus a pure devotee. In him, the bondage of *saṁsāra* is overcome. (*Vaiṣṇava ke?*)

Prabhupāda considered material prestige to be detestable, comparing it to hog stool. He never sanctioned the impersonalist philosophy or devotion adulterated by *jñāna*, *yoga*, or *karma*, as these are in opposition to pure *bhakti*. He showed indomitable enthusiasm for preaching the Holy Name and Mahāprabhu's religion of love, from the oceans to the Himalaya Mountains and beyond. As a result, the fires of the sacrifice of the Holy Name were ignited and the victory flag of the Holy Name now waves in almost every corner of the world. So many thoughtful persons from the western countries have been fortunate to accept the spiritual ways of India.

Śrīla Prabhupāda taught that every single living being is eligible to engage in the worship of the Lord. Everywhere he went, he loudly proclaimed that there is no consideration of ethnic background or race in devotional service. The essence of Śrīla Prabhupāda's teachings is to sincerely take shelter of the genuine guru and make all efforts to engage in devotional service in the association of pure devotees. I myself heard Śrīla Prabhupāda say to his disciples in regard to world peace, "Genuine peace will never be established in this world without practicing and preaching the religion of love taught by Śrī Caitanya Mahāprabhu."

When speaking about society's duty to educate its children, Prabhupāda repeated the teachings of the great soul Śrīla Bhaktivinoda Ṭhākura,

jaḍa-vidyā jata māyāra vaibhava
tomāra bhajane bādhā
moha janamiyā anitya saṁsāre
jīvake karaye gādhā

"Material knowledge is the great power of the illusory energy and an impediment to pure devotional service. It creates an illusory attachment to samsara and turns a human being into an ass."

We should therefore take shelter of the Holy Name, for transcendental knowledge (*parā vidyā*), the opposite of material knowledge, follows the Holy Name like a faithful wife. These are the words used by Mahāprabhu—*vidyā-vadhū-jīvanam*. In view of this, there is no need to attain any knowledge other than that which helps preach the glories of the Holy Name. We will never be able to remove the hatred, envy, and enmity that exist between living beings unless we stop the use of human talents, science, arts, culture, commerce, ethics, and religion as means for achieving sense gratification rather than for the highest goal of life. It is out of respect for his acheivements in this domain that the pure devotee must be given the highest seat of honor in human society.

May we follow the path established by Śrī Vyāsadeva and Śukadeva with all our being! Then only will we be able to achieve our true goal. If we disregard the scriptures that are based on the realizations of the great devotional authorities, the false and deceptive paths that we accept will lead us to take up all sorts of improper activities in the name of religion. Prabhupāda would therefore say:

pṛthivīte jata kathā dharma-nāme cale
bhāgavata kahe tāhā paripūrṇa chale

"So many things on earth are promoted in the name of religion, but the *Bhāgavatam* says that they are nothing more than deception."

We pray that Śrīla Prabhupāda's message of auspiciousness will be spread throughout the world. This will destroy the atheism that is so destructive to our planet and establish a genuine theism for the benefit of all humanity. This will bring peace and auspiciousness to all.

Aspiring for the lotus feet of Śrīla Prabhupāda,
Servant of the servant,
Śrī Bhakti Pramode Purī

His Last Instructions

"In the Caitanya-caritāmṛta, it is written that the most important instructions are the last ones—avaśeṣa ājñā balavān. In keeping with this directive, we should repeatedly examine Śrīla Prabhupāda's final instructions and make them the guiding principles of our lives, for they contain the essence of his teachings."

From Jagannātha Purī, Śrīla Prabhupāda went to the Calcutta Bagbazar Maṭha. There, on December 23, in front of an audience of devotees, Prabhupāda gave some important instructions to his initiated disciples about how to maintain their spiritual lives after his departure. On the very morning that he disappeared from this world, he ordered some of them to sing several bhajans, including Narottama Dāsa's *Śrī Rūpa-manjarī-pada* and Bhaktivinoda Ṭhākura's translation of the second verse of *Śikṣāṣṭaka*: *tũhu dayā-sāgara tārayite prāṇī, nāma aneka tuwā śikhāoāli āni* ("You are the ocean of mercy, and so You came to reveal Your numerous holy names to deliver the living beings," from *Gītāvalī*).

On hearing these songs, Śrīla Prabhupāda commented, "Ṭhākura Narottama brought Rūpa and Raghunātha's message to Bengal. It is therefore best for us to follow his teachings." With these words, he reiterated the instructions he had given his disciples on December 23, underlining their importance.

Although Śrīla Prabhupāda showed special mercy to certain of his disciples on that occasion by mentioning their names, in fact his blessings extended to every single one of them without exception, wherever they happened to be at that time. He said, "All of you should know that I give you my blessings, whether you are present here today or far away. Just remember that our only religious duty is to preach the message of the *Bhagavata* and service to the Lord."

Our most worshipable spiritual master Om Vishnupada 108 Śrīmad Bhaktisiddhānta Sarasvatī Gosvāmī Ṭhākura was like the sun in the firmament of the Gauḍīya Vaiṣṇava world. After displaying his pastimes in this world for sixty-three years, at about 5:30 A.M., on Thursday, January 1, 1937, a *kṛṣṇa caturthī*, he entered the eternal abode, joining Rādhā and Kṛṣṇa in the predawn pastimes (*niśānta-līlā*) of their eternal 24-hour cycle of activities in Vraja. At the end of every night, Rādhā and Kṛṣṇa lie intertwined in embrace, becoming as one body. It is at this moment, when their united form of Gaurasundara is eternally manifest, that Vārṣabhānavī-dayita Dāsa, their servant, joined them. This moment is considered a Wednesday by Indian calculations, according to which a new day begins with the sunrise.

Just a week prior to his leaving this world, on the morning of December 23, 1936, Śrīla Prabhupāda gave some special instructions to his disciples about the way they should carry on their *sādhana* and *bhajana*. Though they were intended for his own disciples, they are of interest for anyone who desires spiritual perfection. Only a few of Śrīla Prabhupāda's disciples are left in the world; nevertheless, they should pay special attention to these instructions and continually discuss them amongst themselves.

1. All of you please preach the message of Rūpa and Raghunātha with great enthusiasm. The ultimate object of our desires is to become specks of dust at the lotus feet of the followers of Rūpa Gosvāmī.

2. All of you remain united in submission to the Lord's form as the repository of devotion (āśraya-vigraha), seeking to satisfy the transcendental senses of the one, non-dual supreme consciousness. Make your way through this impermanent, transitory life in whatever way you can, keeping the goal of worshiping the Lord foremost in your minds. Don't abandon this goal, even in the face of hundreds of dangers, insults, or persecutions.

3. Don't lose your spirit if you see that the majority of people cannot accept the principle of selfless service to the Supreme Lord. Never abandon your bhajana, hearing and chanting kṛṣṇa-kathā, the be-all and end-all of your devotional life. Please always chant the name of the Lord, being humbler than a blade of grass and more tolerant than a tree.

4. Our true being and identity is to be the dust at the lotus feet of Śrī Rūpa Prabhu, life after life. The channel that flows from Śrīla Bhaktivinoda Ṭhākura can never be obstructed. Remember this and vow to double your efforts to fulfill Śrīla Bhaktivinoda Ṭhākura's desires. Amongst you are many capable and worthy individuals. We seek nothing for ourselves; our only motto is:

   ādadānas tṛṇaṁ dantair
   idaṁ yāce punaḥ punaḥ
   śrīmad rūpa-padāmbhoja-
   dhūliḥ syāṁ janma-janmani

   "Taking grass between my teeth, I pray repeatedly that I may become a speck of dust at Śrī Rūpa Gosvāmī's lotus feet, birth after birth." (Raghunātha Dāsa Gosvāmī, *Muktā-carita*)

5. In the material world we continuously come into contact with difficulties. There is no need for us to be bewildered by these difficulties, nor should it be our objective to remove them. Rather we should think of what will be left to be attained after all these obstacles are removed. We must learn about our eternal life while we are still in this world. Our only real obligation is to go beyond duality and to enter that realm of eternal fulfillment.

6. In this world, no person should be a special object of attraction or aversion. All arrangements we make here last only for moments. Our only unavoidable necessity is to seek out the ultimate goal of life.

7. Work together with a single purpose—to win the qualifications to serve the original repository of love for Kṛṣṇa, Śrīmatī Rādhārāṇī.

8. May the current of ideas propagated by Rūpa Gosvāmī flow throughout the world.

9. May we never under any circumstances become indifferent to the seven-tongued sacrificial flame of the Holy Name. If our attraction to the Holy Name continually increases, we will achieve all perfection.

10. Remain exclusively faithful to the followers of Rūpa Gosvāmī and preach Rūpa and Raghunātha's teachings enthusiastically and fearlessly.

Courtesy Sundar Gopal Das

Prayers to Follow These Instructions

If we wish to show our love and faith for our spiritual master, it will be by following these teachings.

Dear Śrīla Prabhupāda! These teachings spoken by you are in no way different from the Vedas. The scripture tells us: "*ājñā gurūṇāṁ hy avicaraṇīyā* – the orders of the spiritual master are not subject to question." We therefore pray for the ability to follow them to the letter, without any ulterior motive. We pray to you most humbly to take care of us eternally by bestowing upon us clear intelligence, strength of heart, and your blessings.

We pray that our commitment to these last instructions of his manifest presence in this world be unfailing. May we never interpret these words to elicit secondary meanings that allow us to engage in sense gratification, but rather, single-mindedly dedicating all our energies and working together, aim for the pleasure of "the senses of the one, non-dual Supreme Truth," making it the one and only goal of our lives. If we wish to show our love and faith for our spiritual master, it will be by following these teachings. However, rather than giving full attention to the desires of the spiritual master, we may focus on serving his body or the extensions of his body represented by temples and ashrams. If we do so, we will never be free of the pitfall of seeing the guru in purely human terms (*martyāsad-dhīḥ*). The Lord can only be seen through the path of transcendental sound (*śrutekṣita-pathaḥ*) and the spiritual master, being his manifest representative, is also perceptible through divine sound vibration.

Honoring Śrīla Prabhupāda as an Eternal Associate

"When the spiritual master leaves the world, the Lord's eternal associates give him the title *nitya-līlā-praviṣṭa,* meaning that he has gone to join them in the eternal abode. By this we should understand that if we in any way disregard this eternal associate of the Lord, especially when we remember that in the form of Nayana-maṇi Mañjarī, he [Śrīla Prabhupāda] is directly engaged in the service of Śrīmatī Rādhārāṇī, the focus of all Kṛṣṇa's love, then we should not expect the Divine Couple to take any of our efforts to display affection for them seriously. If Kṛṣṇa gets angry with someone, then the spiritual master can intervene and pacify Him. On the other hand, the Lord does not care the slightest for someone who shows disrespect to the spiritual master."

No Space for Hatred In The Heart

"How can any attachment or hatred for material objects find a place in the heart where attachment to the guru, the eternal associate of Śrīmatī Rādhārāṇī, has awakened? In such a heart, there is constant awareness of the absolute necessity of attaining the supreme goal of life, loving service to Śrī Kṛṣṇa. This alone is the ultimate purpose of life for every single living entity."

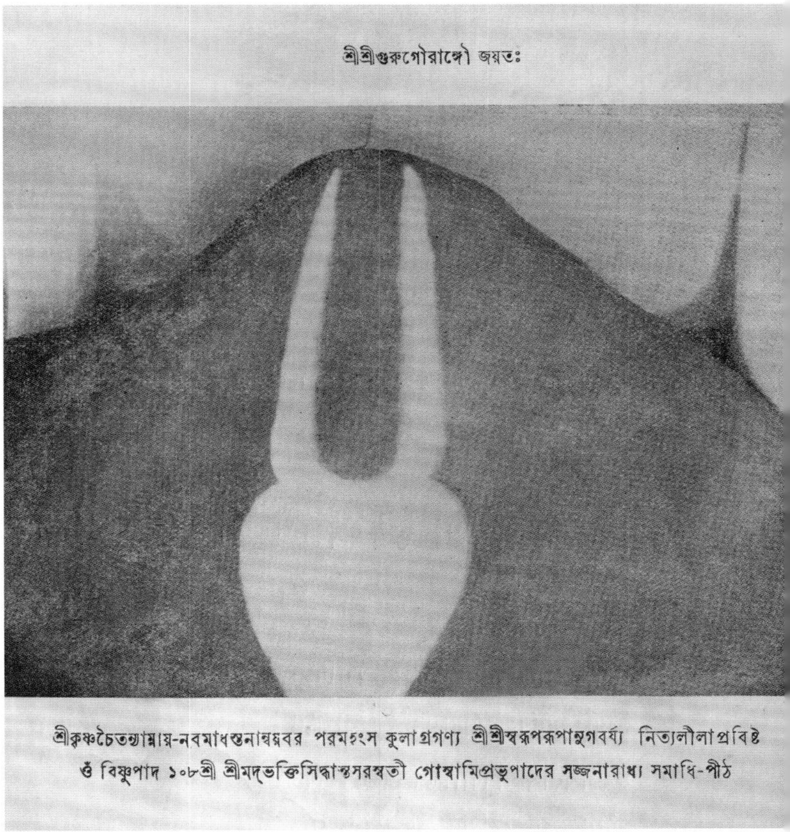

Śrīla Prabhupāda's Samādhi Pīṭha
(Courtesy of Bhaktivedanta Research Center)

Relationship with Purī Dhāma

The Name "Bimala Prasad"

Bhaktivinoda Ṭhākura decided to name his son Bimala Prasad (Vimalā-prasāda) after the goddess Vimalā, Lord Jagannātha's divine energy or Yogamāyā potency. The word *prasāda* means mercy or blessing. Without Her mercy, it is impossible for anyone to enter into His holy *dhāma* or into the mysteries of His pastimes along with His name, form, qualities, associates, and their special characteristics. Śrīla Prabhupāda was the incarnation of that mercy.

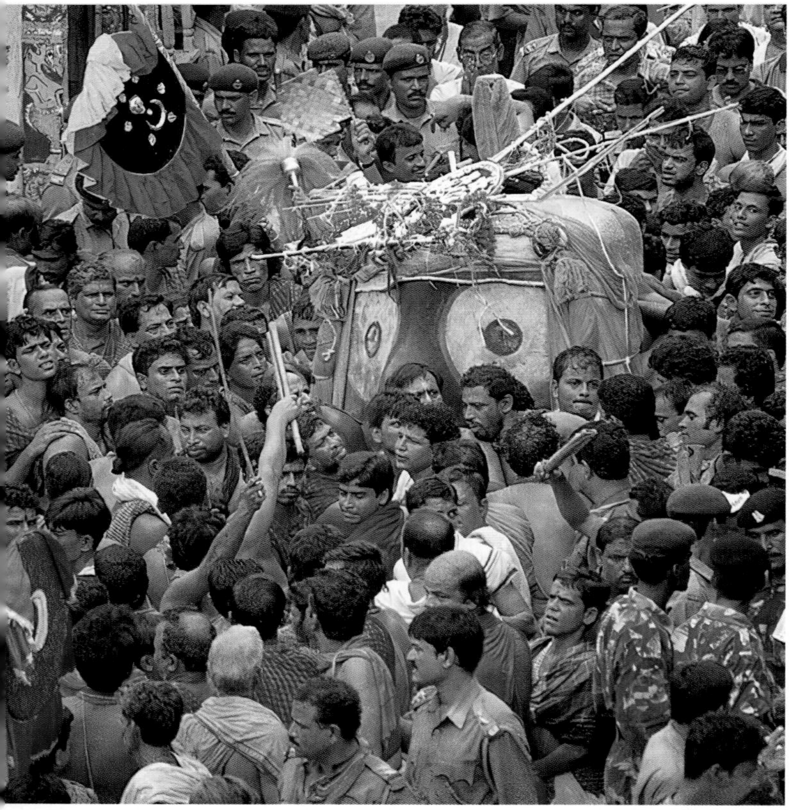

"[Ṭhākura Bhaktivinoda] recognized that my spiritual master, Śrīla Prabhupāda, had taken birth in the land of Puruṣottama, Jagannātha Purī, where the Supreme Lord Himself had come to relish the taste of love in separation, in order to fulfill His divine will. He thus recognized his appearance to be the manifestation of the blessings of Jagannātha Deva's personal energy, Vimalā Devī, who was acting to enrich the Lord's own pastimes and so named him Bimala Prasad. It is impossible for anyone to preach the divine abode, name, form, activities, and glories of the Supreme Lord without the direct blessings of His internal potency, Yogamaya—*kṛṣṇa-śakti vinā nahe tāra pravartana.*"

Attachment to Purī Dhāma

All of the unique features of Śrī Caitanya Mahāprabhu's pastimes were fully revealed in Purī Dhāma. This is why the incarnation of Gaurāṅga's mercy, Śrīla Prabhupāda, decided to begin his worldly pastimes in that holy place. Purī remained very dear to Śrīla Prabhupāda's heart throughout his life. His last visit to Purī took place not long before his disappearance. In fact, he left Śrī Purushottam Maṭha on the ocean beach in Purī on the morning of December 7, 1936—just twenty-four days prior to his disappearance.

Kurukṣetra and The Mood of Separation

When Śrīla Prabhupāda was relishing the mood of separation from the Lord, his natural feelings of ecstatic love would be observable to everyone. He particularly relished the internal significance of Lord Gaurasundara's Ratha-yātrā pastime, wherein Mahāprabhu, in the mood of Rādhārāṇī, took Purī to be Kurukṣetra and wished to carry Lord Jagannātha off to Sundarācala, which He saw as Vraja. The strong feelings and deep connection that Śrīla Prabhupāda had for this lila were particularly evident when he established an annual Ratha-yātrā festival at the Kurukṣetra Maṭha so that he could relish the same mood there.

Establishing the Birthplace of Śrīla Prabhupāda

On March 24, 1980, the cornerstone for a new temple was laid in the house in Jagannātha Purī where Śrīla Prabhupāda was born. While the foundations were being dug, the devotees were overjoyed at seeing the pure earth with the fragrance of sandalwood incense. Just as Prabhupāda was self-manifest, his birthplace is similarly so. Though many obstacles had to be overcome in order to make this temple a possibility, Prabhupāda's dear disciple Śrīmad Bhakti Dayita Mādhava Gosvāmī Mahārāja, out of his compassion for the devotees, agreed to accept the service and undertook the efforts to restore the holy site.

Now Śrīman Mahāprabhu and Jagannātha Deva, Mahāprabhu in another form, have manifested a beautiful skyscraping temple over the site of Their dear devotee's appearance. Through their blessings and the inspiration given by Śrīla Prabhupāda himself, a powerful desire to do this work manifested in the heart of Prabhupāda's intimate associate Śrīla Mādhava Gosvāmī Mahārāja. He had to overcome numerous difficulties to achieve this work, but now deities have been consecrated and their service is being carried out in this temple. He had a two-story building constructed to house the devotees before he himself went to join his spiritual master in the eternal abode. His disciples sought to fulfill his desires, and the Supreme Lord also arranged for the beautiful temple to be built where He and His manifest representative, Śrīla Prabhupāda, could be worshiped. This took place on February 5, 1982, on the holy advent anniversary of Śrīla Prabhupāda.

All glories to Lord Jagannātha, the caretaker of His devotees!

All glories to the Lord of the Gambhirā, who has taken the mood and bodily hue of the daughter of Vṛṣabhānu!

All glories to Caitanya Mahāprabhu, the Lord of Svarūpa, Rūpa, Raghunātha, and Vārṣabhānavī-dayita Dāsa!

All glories to the divine abode of Puruṣottama Dhāma!

All glories to the devotees of the Dhāma!

All glories to Śrīla Prabhupāda and all his disciples!

All glories to his divine birth, his divine works, and his divine birthplace!

Srila Prabhupada's birthplace in Sri Jagganath Puri under the care of Sree Chaitanaya Gaudiya Math. (Courtesy Sundar Gopal Das)

Śrīla Prabhupāda's Divine Qualities

Śrīla Prabhupāda had an incomparable attachment to hari-kathā, ambrosial discussions about the Lord. Hours would go by; even so, he would become irritated when his disciples indicated that prasāda had been served. He would say, "There is really a famine of hari-kathā in the world!" Sometimes he was advised by doctors not to speak, for the sake of his health. If someone asked him how he was, he would answer, "I am well, but they won't let me speak about Kṛṣṇa. That is what is making me sick."

Personification of Mahāprabhu's Message

He could be as fierce as thunder when arguing against heretical doctrines, but when relishing the flavors of pure devotion, he revealed a greater softness than that of a flower, shedding tears of ecstasy. Both these characteristics were seen in his dealings with his disciples, in which he proved his affectionate feelings for them. Śrīla Prabhupāda was the personification of Śrī Caitanya Mahāprabhu's message.

Bold & Uncompromising

Śrīla Prabhupāda, as the perfect follower of Svarūpa Dāmodara and Rūpa Gosvāmī, was similarly the personification of the orthodox Vaiṣṇava doctrine (*śuddha-bhakti-siddhānta-vāṇī*). He never compromised Mahāprabhu's teachings out of considerations for public opinion. Prabhupāda would quote *Caitanya-caritāmṛta* (3.3.23): "*nirapekṣa nahile dharma nā jāya rakṣaṇa* – No one can preserve their principles without being aloof from the opinions of the world." Those who try to preserve the principles of religion while simultaneously trying to maintain popularity with the worldly will have to show their approval for so many conflicting doctrines that the purity of the true religion will be lost. Rather than serving that pure spiritual religion, they become servants of public opinion instead. Though they may receive applause from the people at large, they cannot do them any real good.

Bolt of Lightning

When rejecting those things that oppose pure devotion, Prabhupāda could be more uncompromising than a bolt of lightning. On the other hand, when accepting those things that are favorable to pure devotional service, his heart was softer than a rose. Tears would pour from his eyes whenever he spoke on Rādhārāṇī's distress at Kṛṣṇa's leaving for Mathurā.

Follower of Pure Devotion

Our most worshipable Śrīla Prabhupāda, the best of the followers of Śrīla Rūpa Gosvāmī, would always quote the following verse from the *Bhakti-rasāmṛta-sindhu*:

anyābhilāṣitā-śūnyaṁ
jñāna-karmādy-anāvṛtam
ānukūlyena kṛṣṇānu-
śīlanaṁ bhaktir uttamā

"The highest category of devotion, or *bhakti*, is defined as the culture of a favorable attitude to Kṛṣṇa, devoid of all material desires and without any adulteration by monistic philosophy or fruitive action." (BRS 1.1.11, CC 2.19.167)

In other words, to engage in pure devotion, we must give up all activities that go against the principles of service to the Lord, including illicit sexual activity or indeed any kind of unethical conduct. Such devotional service must be unblemished by desires for sense gratification or personal salvation and must be characterized by the direct effort to please the senses of the Lord. This verse is the guiding thread of *bhakti* theology; it shows that *bhakti* is independent of the paths of knowledge, works, and yoga, all of which are permeated with selfish desire. Prabhupāda followed this thread and dedicated himself to preaching this exclusive devotion by which all illusory fulfillments are eradicated.

Attachment to the Holy Name

Our most worshipable Śrīla Prabhupāda displayed an extraordinary attachment for the chanting of the Holy Name from his very childhood. He had such spontaneous enthusiasm for both chanting and deity worship that his father, mother and other relatives were astonished. He constantly read from the songbooks of Narottama Dāsa Ṭhākura.

Natural Taste for Worshiping the Lord

As a small boy, Śrīla Prabhupāda did not show the typical childish enthusiasm for playing and sports. He considered it all to be a waste of time. His taste for worshiping the Lord and chanting His name was entirely natural. Śrīla Bhaktivinoda Ṭhākura gave Prabhupāda his blessings to go and live in Māyāpura in a place called Baraja-pota. Śrīla Prabhupāda renamed the place Vraja-pattana and later established Caitanya Maṭha there. He lived there following a strict celibate lifestyle, exemplifying the dutiful behavior of a *sādhaka* by taking the vows of *cāturmāsya* and chanting one billion Holy Names. During this time, he also wrote commentaries on *Caitanya-caritāmṛta, Śrīmad-Bhāgavatam,* Śrīla Rūpa Gosvāmī's *Upadeśāmṛta,* and Mahāprabhu's *Śikṣāṣṭaka,* as well as his book describing the relative positions of the Vaiṣṇava and the *brāhmaṇa*. This work made him the object of Mahāprabhu and Bhaktivinoda Ṭhākura's undying affection.

Śrī Caitanya Mahāprabhu (top), Śrī Nityānanda (bottom)

Living Example of Tridaṇḍi Sannyāsa

There is a Sanskrit saying that one does not become a true renunciate by simply carrying a bamboo staff (*veṇubhir na bhaved yatiḥ*): one has to exercise control over the body, mind, and words, engaging all these faculties in the service of the Lord. This is the meaning of the triple staff. This is why Nityānanda Prabhu broke Mahāprabhu's staff into three pieces in order to demonstrate that His *sannyāsa* meant such a threefold commitment to Kṛṣṇa's service. The meaning of the monastic order is a commitment to attaining the Supreme Soul; the only duty of the renunciate is to serve Lord Mukunda. A monk who does not take the vow of service is simply engaged in fraud and self-deception.

ŚRĪLA PRABHUPĀDA SET THE EXAMPLE OF ENGAGING IN THE LORD'S SERVICE FOR EACH AND EVERY ONE OF THE TWENTY-FOUR HOURS IN A DAY. BY SO DOING, HE GAVE A LIVING EXAMPLE OF WHAT IS MEANT BY TRIDAṆḌI-SANNYĀSA.

Intolerance for Rasābhāsa

Prabhupāda also loved *kīrtana*, but he hated hearing *kīrtana* that was sung by unqualified people, contained elements that went against the pure dogmas of Gauḍīya Vaishnavism, or in which there was a corrupt understanding of the divine *rasas* (*rasābhāsa*). He wrote the following verse, making it clear who was actually qualified to chant the Holy Names:

prāṇa āche jāra, sei hetu pracāra
pratiṣṭhāśā hīna kṛṣṇa-gāthā saba
śrī-dayita-dāsa kīrtanete āśa
kara uccaiḥsvare harināma raba

"O mind! This humble servant of Rādhā and Kṛṣṇa places his hopes in *kīrtana* and loudly sings the names of Lord Hari! Those who have spiritual life in abundance preach the Lord's message. Every word they speak is free from the taint of desire for personal prestige." (*Vaiṣṇava ke?*)

Taking shelter of the Lord without any desire for personal aggrandizement is what gives the devotee life. A non-devotee who has not taken shelter of the Lord may speak about Kṛṣṇa, but such topics are lifeless, as devoid of spirit as a cadaver, and are not worthy of being heard. Prabhupāda could not tolerate discussion of topics that were outside of one's range of qualification (*anadhikāra-carcā*). Constant remembrance of Lord Kṛṣṇa's lotus feet is the purifier of existence and results in devotion to the Lord. "One who chants without offenses attains love for Kṛṣṇa" (*niraparādhe laile nāma upajaya prema-dhana*). Prabhupāda was unable to tolerate those who made no effort to chant the Holy Name without offenses but made an external show of practicing devotional service while seeking profit, adoration, and prestige.

Śrīla Prabhupāda with Śrī Kuñjabihārī Vidyābhūṣaṇa

Śrīla Prabhupāda, along with Śrīpāda Kuñjabihārī Vidyābhūṣaṇa and Śrī Vinodabihārī Brahmacārī, welcome the governor of Bengal, Sir John Anderson in Māyāpura, January 1935.

Śrīla Prabhupāda's Dynamic Preaching

As Mahāprabhu's eternal associate, he naturally looked for ways to benefit all of humanity by preaching Śrī Caitanya Mahāprabhu's teachings around the world. Out of his firm faith in this principle, he demonstrated an indomitable enthusiasm for practicing and preaching Mahāprabhu's message wherever he went.

Establishment of Important Centers

Gradually Śrīla Prabhupāda and his disciples spread Mahāprabhu's gospel of pure devotional service to many places throughout India and abroad. This preaching work is still going on today. Sometimes Prabhupāda went himself; other times he sent his qualified disciples on preaching missions to distribute this message of Mahāprabhu to all and sundry."

Our most worshipable Śrīla Prabhupāda was unswervingly devoted to the chanting of the Holy Name from his childhood. While Bhaktivinoda Ṭhākura was a deputy magistrate in Serampore, Śrīla Prabhupāda was only a seventh-grade student. When he recognized Prabhupāda's enthusiasm for the worship of the Holy Name, the Ṭhākura gave him a gift of a *japa mālā* made of *tulasi* beads which he had brought back from a trip to Jagannātha Purī. Along with the *japa* beads, the Ṭhākura also initiated him in the chanting of *harināma* and the Nṛsiṁha mantra.

In 1881, when Bhaktivinoda Ṭhākura started construction on Bhakti Bhavan, his Calcutta home in the Ram Bagan neighborhood, a small Deity of Kūrma was found during the digging of its foundations. Though Śrīla Prabhupāda was only eight or nine years old at the time, when his father saw his eagerness to worship the Deity, he gave him the Kūrma mantra and taught him the related procedures. From that time on, Prabhupāda regularly engaged in the service of the Deity and also began wearing *tilaka* and following other aspects of Vaiṣṇava behavior. I myself have had the good fortune of seeing this Kūrma *śālagrāma,* which is still present at the Bhakti Bhavan building in Calcutta.

Śrīla Prabhupāda began to preach Mahāprabhu's message in 1905 when he came to live in Śrī Māyāpura. During this time, he followed in the footsteps of the Namācārya, Śrīla Haridāsa Ṭhākura, and began chanting three lakhs of Holy Names every day, taking up a vow to chant a billion (*śata-koṭi*) in all. At the same time, he took up severe ascetic practices. In 1909, he had a cottage built on the site of Candraśekhara's house where he continued his intense *bhajana*. By its side, he also had a tank excavated. He saw this pond to be a direct manifestation of Rādhā Kuṇḍa and so gave it that name.

On March 7, 1918, on the occasion of Śrī Caitanya Mahāprabhu's appearance day, Śrīla Prabhupāda took *tridaṇḍi-sannyāsa* in Śrī Māyāpura. On that same day, he consecrated the Deities of Guru-Gaurāṅga and Rādhā-Govinda at the house of Candraśekhara Ācārya and established the Śrī Caitanya Maṭha. On March 2, 1923, work began on the construction of the temple there. In the main temple room, Deities of Guru-Gaurāṅga and Gāndharvikā-Giridhārī were installed, while in the four corners the worship of the founders of the four Vaiṣṇava schools or *sampradāyas* (coming down from Lakṣmī, Brahmā, Rudra, and the four Kumāras) and their *ācāryas* (Rāmānuja, Madhva, Viṣṇusvāmī, and Nimbārka) was established.

On March 18, the cornerstone for the proposed temple at the birthplace of Caitanya Mahāprabhu was laid, and another for a smaller temple at Murāri Gupta's house. Three months later, at 10 A.M. on June 13, the four-armed form of Viṣṇu known as

Adhokṣaja, formerly worshiped by Jagannātha Miśra, was found in the ground while digging the foundations for the new Yogapīṭha temple. This *mūrti* is still worshiped there. On Ḍola Pūrṇimā, March 20, 1935, the Mahārāja of the independent state of Tripura, Sir Bir Vikram Kishor Devavarma Manikya Bahadur, came to Māyāpura on Śrīla Prabhupāda's invitation to officially open the temple doors.

Caitanya Maṭha's first branch opened in Calcutta in 1920 in a rented house at 1 Ultadanga Junction Road. The center was transferred to a newly built temple in Bagbazar in October of 1930. Gradually Śrīla Prabhupāda and his disciples spread Mahāprabhu's gospel of pure devotional service to many places throughout India and abroad. This preaching work is still going on today. Sometimes Prabhupāda went himself; other times he sent his qualified disciples on preaching missions to distribute this message of Mahāprabhu to all and sundry. He also published daily, weekly, and monthly magazines and journals in various languages, as well as many of the books written by Mahāprabhu's dear associates, the Six Gosvāmīs. Through the use of such means, which were revolutionary for the time, the movement expanded rapidly and widely.

Never Skipping the Necessary

The unique characteristic of Śrīla Prabhupāda's preaching was that even though he often spoke about the highest realms of devotional perfection, he always took care that none of his disciples got ahead of themselves and skipped necessary intermediate steps in the stage of practice to engage in *anadhikāra-carcā* ("discussion of matters for which one is not qualified").

A devotee who reverently follows the practices and regulative principles of the *vidhi-bhakti* path, and particularly takes to regular chanting of the Holy Names, receives the mercy of the Name that gradually bestows upon him the qualifications to engage in *rāgānugā bhakti*. If one does not seek the mercy of the Holy Name first, but artificially tries to appropriate the right to engage in such practices, he is like a pumpkin that ripens too quickly and bursts—he inevitably falls down. For this reason, Śrīla Prabhupāda did not artificially give *siddha-praṇālī* and instructions to remember the *aṣṭa-kālīya-līlā* to people who were not ready for it.

The Ideal Temple

Śrīla Prabhupāda established temples and *maṭhas* throughout India as centers for preaching the pure devotional service taught by Śrī Caitanya Mahāprabhu. Nevertheless, he often said that he hadn't taken birth to become a bricklayer or carpenter. The goal was not to simply build temples and install deities in order to make a living–eating, sleeping, and pleasing one's own senses. The residents of the *maṭhas* must engage in the pure devotional lifestyle and try to spread the teachings in order to please the Lord, the guru, and the Vaiṣṇavas.

Mahāprabhu told us to make our lives successful and to do good for others. No one can do good for others without leading an exemplary life himself. If the temples serve as centers for people who are leading this exemplary lifestyle and preaching Mahāprabhu's message and initiating others, then the whole world will benefit immensely.

Extensive Preaching

Prabhupāda made every effort to see that preaching went on in as much of India as possible. To this end he had books and magazines published in various different languages.

To make a business of selling books is not helpful for one's spiritual life. It is the same as making a business out of giving initiation or selling mantras and the Holy Name. Prabhupāda especially detested this kind of behavior, for the scriptures condemn teaching the scriptures in order to make money. He used every means possible, whether books, slide shows, or dioramas, to interest people in the devotional message.

Pilgrimage Sites and Establishing Preaching Centers

Śrīla Prabhupāda either went himself with his entourage or sent his disciples to most of the pilgrimage sites and major cities throughout both northern and southern India, establishing preaching centers, Deity worship, and spreading Lord Caitanya's religion of love in all these places. During the time Prabhupāda was present in this world, sixty-four *maṭhas* were established, a list of which was printed in the weekly *Gauḍīya* magazine. Today, we see that his disciples have greatly expanded the number of temples and *maṭhas* throughout India and the rest of the world.

Establishing Shrines for Mahāprabhu's Lotus Feet

Śrīla Prabhupāda also had the goal of establishing 108 or more shrines to Mahāprabhu's lotus feet in all the places that He had visited in the course of His travels throughout India. During Prabhupāda's lifetime, eight such shrines were established at Mandara, Kanai Natashala, Jajpur, Kūrmakṣetra, Siṁhācala, Kavoor, Maṅgala-giri, and Chatrabhoga. Since then, other such shrines have been placed in Maldah, Purī (Atharonala), and other places.

Parikramā

Śrīla Prabhupāda used to participate personally in the circumambulation, or *parikramā* of Vṛndāvana and Gaura Maṇḍala. He also often visited the main holy places in Purī.

He made the annual *parikramā* of Navadvīpa Dhāma an institution, which his disciples have maintained out of faithfulness to his instruction. Śrīla Prabhupāda used to say that the *Śrī-Dhāma-parikramā* gave everyone the opportunity to simultaneously engage in all five principal devotional acts (associating with devotees, chanting the Holy Name, hearing the *Bhāgavatam*, living in the Holy Dhāma, and worshiping the Deity). For this reason, we continue to perform this service annually and with great care on the days preceding Mahāprabhu's appearance day on Ḍola Pūrṇimā.

Dioramas & Exhibitions

To make an impression on the minds of the conditioned souls, Śrīla Prabhupāda established a program of transcendental diorama exhibitions illustrating the main points of Lord Caitanya's philosophy.

The Kurukṣetra Gauḍīya Exhibition (*pradarśanī*) was opened on November 4, 1928, August 21, 1933, and June 19, 1936; the Śrīdhāma Māyāpura-Navadvīpa Exhibition on February 9, 1930; the Calcutta Gauḍīya Maṭha Spiritual Exhibition (*Pāramārthika Pradarśanī*) on November 5, 1930; the Calcutta Gauḍīya Maṭha Saintly Teachings Exhibition (*Sat-śikṣā Pradarśanī*) on September 6, 1931; and the Dhaka Saintly Teachings Exhibition on January 6, 1933; the Patna Spiritual Exhibition on November 14, 1933, the Kashi Spiritual Exhibition on December 24, 1933 and the Prayag Saintly Teachings Exhibition on January 7, 1936.

Throughout The World

Though the most merciful Śrīla Prabhupāda was born in the holy land of Bhārata, he sought to establish pure devotional service and spread it throughout the world.

During his own lifetime, he sent disciples to Europe on two different occasions, despite knowing that these countries are completely lacking in any strict principles of behavior, or *sadācāra*, in the hope that they would be able to raise the victory flag of the Holy Name. From that time Mahāprabhu's name began to be heard in the West and finally, after Śrīla Prabhupāda's departure, another most worthy disciple [A.C. Bhaktivedanta Swami Mahārāja] took up the mission, and the entire western world was filled with the sounds of the Holy Name and the pure doctrines taught by Śrī Caitanya Mahāprabhu. All of Prabhupāda's disciples are overjoyed to see learned people from all over the world inquiring about the truth of spiritual life in this way.

First Five Western Disciples

Below are the names of five Western disciples who were initiated with the chanting beads of Śrīla Bhaktisiddhānta Sarasvatī Ṭhākura Prabhupāda between 1933 and 1937. The descriptions below were published in the Gauḍīya *magazine* (Volume 12, 13, and 15). *(Courtesy Bhaktivedanta Research Center and Sundar Gopal Das)*

1. Mr. Arnold Corbluth (Kṛṣṇa dāsa)

On the 1st of October 1933, a talented budding meritorious student of London University, Arnold Corbluth, was given initiation. Śrīla Prabhupāda sent the *tulasī* beads (chanted by him) and wrote the 16 names and 32 syllables of Harināma Mahā-mantra on a paper. He received initiation through Bhakti Pradīpa Tīrtha Mahārāja. He was awarded the name Kṛṣṇa Dāsa. Corbluth was wore *tulasī* neck beads around his neck and adorned long *tilaka* on his forehead. Bhakti Pradīpa Tīrtha Mahārāja read out the Mahā-mantra, written by Śrīla Prabhupāda, to Mr. Corbluth. He then paid prostrated obeisances in front of the picture of Śrīla Prabhupāda and after praying for his grace and blessings, started to chant on the beads.

2. Mrs. Hilda Korbel

An intellectual woman also took initiation in the same way and vowed to follow the rules of Vaiṣṇavism. She appreciated Śrīla Prabhupāda's greatness as well.

3. Herr Earnst Schulze (Sadānanda dāsa)

We learn about Herr Earnst Schulze from Volume 12, Issue 36 (21st April 1934) of the *Gauḍīya*.

His request to accept Bhaktisiddhānta Sarasvatī Ṭhakura Prabhupāda as his spiritual master was penned down by Svāmī Bon and sent to Calcutta Gauḍīya Maṭha. Śrīla Prabhupāda agreed to it and a letter was sent. Getting the approval from Śrīla Prabhupāda, Herr Earnst Schulze traveled from Berling to London and began residing with Śrīpad Bhakti Pradīpa Tīrtha Mahārāja and Svāmī Bon at London Gauḍīya Maṭha and listened to their lectures. By the advice of Śrīla Prabhupāda, he took shelter of *harināma*. He wore *tulasī* neck beads around his neck and puts *tilaka* on his forehead. He sincerely chanted on the *tulasī* beads on which Śrīla Prabhupāda had chanted. In 1935, when he came to India with Bhakti Hṛdaya Bon Mahārāja, he was given the name Sadānanda Dāsa by Śrīla Prabhupāda. He used to stay in Bagbazar Gauḍīya Maṭha in association of Śrīla Prabhupāda and other devotees.

4. Daisy Cecilia Bowtell (Vinode-vāṇī dāsī)

Miss D.C. Bowtell, a young English lady, was one of the listeners of Śrī A.B. Gosvāmī (later known as Bhakti Sāraṅga Gosvāmī). With heart and soul, she and Stella Harris (Viṣṇuprīya dāsī) took shelter unto the lotus feet of the Supreme Lord and his dear most associate Śrīla Prabhupāda. Subsequently, she received initiation and was named Vinode-vāṇī dāsī. The *'Nāma Mālikā'* (the chanting beads) were handed down by Śrīla Prabhupāda to A.B. Gosvāmī in 1937. Since then, she dedicated her whole life (including her own home) to the mission, which first moved to her rented flat at 46 Christ Church Avenue, Brondesbury, and in April 1961, permanently, to 27 Cranhurst Road, Cricklewood. Vinode-vāṇī dāsī never had the opportunity to visit India, but she kept in constant correspondence with her co-religionists in Bengal. She studied the sacred scriptures of Gauḍīya Vaiṣṇavism and engaged in spiritual practices together with her friend Stella Harris (Viṣṇuprīya dāsī) and others to whom she circulated the teachings of Gauḍīya Vaiṣṇavism.

5. Stella Harris (Viṣṇuprīya dāsī)

Stella Harris was a regular attendee of lectures at the Gauḍīya Mission Society and her heart was transformed hearing the lectures of A.B. Gosvāmī. She was also initiated in the same process as Vinode-vāṇī dāsī in 1937. After initiation, she was named Viṣṇuprīya dāsī. She became a dedicated member of Gauḍīya Mission and one of Vinode-vāṇī dāsī's close associates.

Śrīla Prabhupāda showered so much love and affection on all his disciples, and in turn, every disciple felt love for their gurudeva, Śrīla Prabhupāda. The depth of his care and concern for his disciples can be felt in these two letters written by Śrīla Prabhupāda to Śrīla Bhakti Sāraṅga Gosvāmī Mahārāja (referred to below as Aprākṛta Prabhu) on the 14th and the 17th of December 1936. The letters were written approximately two weeks before Śrīla Prabhupāda's physical departure.

14th December 1936

My loving affectionate Aprākṛta Prabhu,

I am very happy to read about your meeting with the king of England in the newspaper. As you know, my time has arrived for me to leave this world. In the days to come, you will face many devotional obstacles in the western world in preaching Lord Chaitanya's doctrine, but you should carry on with full enthusiasm. I understand that you are suffering a great deal with the cold climate, and I assume that you are also not able to eat properly. If I was close to you then I would have been able to serve you. Against all unfavorable conditions you are continuously serving the Lord. Consequently, there is no one beside you to look after you. Thinking of your situation, I become directionless. I humbly pray to Gaura Hari to bestow all favorable conditions unto you.

With blessings,
Śrī Siddhānta Sarasvatī

17th December 1936

My dear Aprākṛta Prabhu,

I was happy to receive your previous letter. I am eagerly waiting to hear about your meeting with Lord Jetlander (?). I am waiting to hear how the preaching is going and how it is progressing. I assume you have learnt to cook in a different way. I am sure you have created a favorable atmosphere for preaching there. Please aim to preach to maximum number of people and bring them under your preaching. For this to happen, it would be necessary to arrange a press conference with journalists. I am sure you understand. Keep in mind that you must arrange conferences in big halls and then the preaching will spread elaborately.

With blessings,
Śrī Siddhānta Sarasvatī

Sadānanda dāsa

Viṣṇupriya dāsī and Vinode-vāṇī dāsI

Preaching Abroad

In 1918, after the announcement of the formation of the Bhaktivinoda Āsana, people began coming from everywhere to gain the association of Śrīla Prabhupāda. During that time, Pūjyapāda Swami Mahārāja and all of us used to come to the lotus feet of Śrīla Prabhupāda and listen to discourses spoken on Lord Hari from Śrīla Prabhupāda's divine mouth.

It was at that time when I first met with Pūjyapāda Swami Mahārāja and received his close association. Śrīla Prabhupāda used to see Pūjyapāda Swami Mahārāja as his own intimate associate. During his student days, Pūjyapāda Swami Mahārāja was an excellent student. He was very proficient in the English language; thus it was Śrīla Prabhupāda's special desire that he would preach in the English language. Śrīla Bhaktivinoda Ṭhākura had also said that it is necessary for preaching to take place in the Western countries.

Today, seeing such a large assembly of devotees—the fruit of Pūjyapāda Swami Mahārāja's preaching efforts—my heart is totally overwhelmed by bliss. I am unable to express it in words. What bliss I am experiencing! Pūjyapāda Swami Mahārāja preached the message of Śrīla Prabhupāda in Europe, America, Germany, and various countries. All of you, the devotees of all of those countries, have come together here—this is my sight of great bliss!

You all know the life of Pūjyapāda Swami Mahārāja very well. What more will I say? Pūjyapāda Swami Mahārāja did not have wealth or manpower. Having one-pointed faith in the lotus feet of his guru, he crossed the ocean by ship. He had no idea where he would stay when he landed, where he would go. However, despite the circumstances, he never deviated from his goal. The Supreme Lord showed him the way at each and every step. When we think about this wonder, we are in awe. He had no money. He had no manpower. He had only the strength of the lotus feet of his guru, and with that strength, he went to that huge country. Sarva-śakti nāme dilā kariyā vibhāga. ["The Lord entrusted all His potency into the holy name."] Seeing how that all-powerful holy name was so widely preached and expanded just through his divine mouth, we are in awe.

(Excerpted from a translated lecture given at ISKCON Vṛndāvana on the occasion of Śrīla A.C. Bhaktivedanta Swami Prabhupāda Mahārāja's disappearance day festival, November 8, 1994 by Śrīla Bhakti Pramode Purī Gosvāmī Mahārāja.)

Bon Mahārāja and German devotees upon arriving in Bombay in September 1935. Far-right, Śrī Abhaya Caraṇāravinda Dāsa.

Śrīla Prabhupāda gave Aprākṛta Bhakti Sāraṅga Prabhu the responsibility to preach the message of Lord Caitanya in Europe and America. Prior to sending him off to London on October 23, 1936, he gave him instructions in the worship of the Gomati, Gaṇḍaki, and Govardhana *śīlās*. To bid him a glorious passage, a large public meeting was held in the Bagbazar Gauḍīya Maṭha's *kīrtana* hall (*Sārasvata-śravaṇa-sadana*). In his speech, Śrīla Prabhupāda encouraged Bhakti Sāraṅga Prabhu in his London preaching mission and gave him profuse blessings.

Śrīla Prabhupāda had previously (from March 1933 to 1936) sent his disciples Tridaṇḍi Svāmī Bhakti Pradīpa Tīrtha and Bhakti Hridaya Bon Mahārāja to London and Germany with the goal of holding public meetings to preach Mahāprabhu's message. He kept in touch with them by airmail, regularly sending them articles and preaching advice. Through this effort, many highly educated and respectable people had the opportunity to hear about Mahāprabhu. With Prabhupāda's approval, these two preachers established the London Gauḍīya Mission Society and the London Gauḍīya Maṭha. Lord Zetland was made chairman of the Mission Society and he led weekly discussions of Śrīla Prabhupāda's epistles on the special characteristics of Lord Caitanya's message.

Prabhupāda also sent missionaries to Rangoon in Burma (now Myanmar). In 1936, the Rangoon preaching center was opened and deities were installed there. Unfortunately, the political climate in Burma then was such that people were unable to appreciate Mahāprabhu's religion of love and the center was closed not long afterward.

Rarity of Human Life

labdhvā sudurlabham idaṁ bahu-sambhavānte
mānuṣyam arthadam anityam apīha dhīraḥ
tūrṇaṁ yateta na pated anumṛtyu yāvat
niḥśreyasāya viṣayaḥ khalu sarvataḥ syāt

"After many, many births, one is finally born in a most rare and valuable human body. Although it may be temporary, it provides an opportunity to attain the supreme goal. Therefore, the wise individual should immediately take up the effort to find that which provides the supreme good in all times and circumstances, and not give it up right to the moment of death." (SB 11.9.29)

The most compassionate Śrīla Prabhupāda often quoted this verse to stress the rarity of human life and the necessity of engaging in the worship of the Lord without delay. In his comments on this verse, he wrote, "The conditioned soul is subject to repeated rebirths in which he may sometimes become a god, sometimes a human, or even an animal, a tree, or some other immovable entity. These various external sheaths give the being differing identities according to which they engage in sense gratification and other activities appropriate to that species. The specificity of the human form of life, however, is that it allows one to learn about and experience the truth. It is thus an extremely important stop on the soul's voyage from species to species, for elsewhere such experience and understanding of the truth about reality are beyond reach.

"At the same time, the human body is not everlasting. The embodied soul that resides within that body has an extraordinary opportunity to achieve something of ultimate value. While in this body, he can consider what is the supreme good for himself. Before death strikes him down, it is imperative that he learn what that supreme good is. He must distance himself from all the apparent benefits related to the impermanent body and seek the joy that comes from his eternal duty of service to the supreme truth. This is most important for one who wishes to achieve that which is of eternal benefit to him. Those who have use of their intelligence should think this matter over.

"The human being's use of time should be directed to the most important things, namely the service of the Supreme Lord. We can establish our ultimate good by following those who are committed to serving the Lord and do not waste their time in the trivial pursuit of flickering sense pleasures. The human being's only duty is understanding what is his ultimate good; when assessing which of our duties are more or less important, we should place this priority at the top of the list. *Bhakti*, the true end of repeated births and deaths, arises through association with devotees. Without *bhakti*, the living being is so afflicted by the three kinds of material suffering that he either becomes a *māyāvādī* out of the desire for personal salvation or a fruitive worker out of a desire for sense gratification."

Uniting People in Chanting the Lord's Glories

Śrīla Prabhupāda often spoke of the inner identity of the two aspects of devotion known as the *Bhāgavata* and the *Pañcarātra* paths. The *Pañcarātra* path refers specifically to the worship of deities, the construction of temples, and other related activities that cannot be carried out uninterruptedly. This is not true of the *Bhāgavata* path consisting of hearing, chanting, and remembering the Lord's names, forms, and activities. However, Prabhupāda showed how the two were harmonious on the transcendental plane. He never promoted the building of temples and monasteries for the simple purpose of having opulent Deity worship for beginners in devotional service, the *kaniṣṭha adhikārīs*. Rather, he saw them as an institution for the worship of the Holy Name, in accordance with the various scriptural statements defining *saṅkīrtana* as the uniting of many people in the chanting of the Lord's glories (*bahubhir militvā yat kīrtanaṁ tad eva saṅkīrtanam*), for the congregational chanting of the Lord's names is the supreme religious activity of the age–*paraṁ vijayate śrī-kṛṣṇa-saṅkīrtanam*—and has the power to clear the mind of all impurities, *ceto-darpaṇa-mārjanam*.

For Prabhupāda, the first verse of Mahāprabhu's *Śikṣāṣṭakam* described the seven flames of the divine sacrifice of the Holy Name. He saw the value of constructing *maṭhas* and *mandiras* to the extent in which they facilitated the performance of this sacrifice; otherwise, a temple without the "deity" of the Holy Name was really empty and without any opulence whatsoever. Prabhupāda would say, "We didn't come into this world to become bricklayers or carpenters; we are simply peons carrying the message of Lord Caitanya."

Thus, though Śrīla Prabhupāda established monasteries, built temples, and instituted the practice of deity worship and festivals, their underlying purpose was the preaching of *Bhāgavata-dharma*. This was the way in which he harmonized the *Pañcarātra* and *Bhāgavata* paths of devotion.

Genuine Bhajana

Our most worshipable Śrīla Prabhupāda never said that deity worship was the ultimate devotional activity nor that the other aspects of devotional service were epitomized by the activity of *arcana*. Rather, he said the following:

"The worship of the deity is generally in the category of worship in awe and reverence. The consciousness that one has is of offering respect with various elements to the worshipable Lord in the consciousness of His having materialized a form. Even though devotees engaged in the *rāgānugā* path may have dimmed the harsh sunlight of awe and reverence, no one can deny that it bears no comparison to the superiority of the cooling moon-rays of the mood of divine sweetness. Deity worship is never quite free of bodily consciousness, whether it is that of the gross or subtle identification. In the world of genuine *bhajana*, the practitioner engages in direct service to the Supreme Lord in a spiritual body. Being entirely free of any material identifications, all the senses of the truly devoted practitioner of *bhajana* are perceived as being non-material; they are engaged as in a service state beyond the mental platform and beyond time due to proximity with the non-dual supreme substance."

"WE DIDN'T COME INTO THIS WORLD TO BECOME BRICKLAYERS OR CARPENTERS; WE ARE SIMPLY PEONS CARRYING THE MESSAGE OF LORD CAITANYA."

THE DIVINE PRINTING PRESS

ŚRĪLA PRABHUPĀDA CALLED THE PRINTING PRESS THE "BIG DRUM" (BṚHAT MṚDAṄGA). HOWEVER, THE SOUND OF THE CLAY MṚDAṄGA ONLY CARRIES A SHORT DISTANCE, WHEREAS THE REACH OF THE PRINTING PRESS HAS NO LIMIT; THUS, THE WORSHIP OF KṚṢṆA'S SAṄKĪRTANA SO DEAR TO MAHĀPRABHU CAN BE MORE PERFECTLY CARRIED OUT.

Preaching the Mission of Bhaktivinoda Ṭhākura

Nevertheless, Śrīla Prabhupāda said that his main mission in life was to preach the books and message of Bhaktivinoda Ṭhākura. He considered Bhaktivinoda to be the manifest representative of Śrīmatī Rādhārāṇī.

He had a saying, "bābā bādhā rādhā," which means "thinking of him as a father is an obstacle to attaining Rādhārāṇī." Throughout his career, Śrīla Prabhupāda nearly always named the deities he installed in his temples vinoda, such as Vinodānanda, Vinoda-prāṇa, etc.

Bhaktivinoda Ṭhākura's Words of Affection

The Ṭhākura also showed his particular affection for Śrīla Prabhupāda when he wrote:

sarasvatī kṛṣṇa-priyā kṛṣṇa-bhakti tāra hiyā
vinodera sei se vaibhava

"Sarasvatī is dear to Kṛṣṇa; his heart is filled with devotion for Kṛṣṇa. He is the manifestation of Bhaktivinoda's opulence."

Bhakti Bhavan

In 1885, Śrīla Bhaktivinoda Ṭhākura established the Vaiṣṇava Depository in his Calcutta home, Bhakti Bhavan, for the purpose of disseminating *bhakti* literature. Śrīla Prabhupāda gained experience in printing and publishing in those days. He was engaged in proofreading and later writing articles for *Sajjana-toṣaṇī*, the monthly magazine edited by his father, Bhaktivinoda Ṭhākura.

The Printing Press

The first steps that Śrīla Prabhupāda took to establish Śrī Caitanya Mahāprabhu's mission were to open a printing press in Calcutta called the Bhāgavata Press and begin publishing books on pure devotion. Up to that point he had not opened temples or established deity worship anywhere. He had learned from Bhaktivinoda Ṭhākura to engage in the service of the *śrauta-vāṇī*, that is, the Divine Word or Logos emanating from the disciplic succession.

During this time Śrīla Prabhupāda accompanied his father on a tour of various places associated with Mahāprabhu's pastimes and companions, such as Kulina-grāma and Sapta-grāma. Śrīla Prabhupāda's life is thus a perfect example of Prahlāda Mahārāja's instruction in the *Bhāgavata* for everyone to start practicing the *Bhāgavata-dharma* in childhood.

Indescribable Service

Between them, Śrīla Bhaktivinoda Ṭhākura and Śrīla Prabhupāda wrote more than a hundred books on devotional subjects, including translations and commentaries on the *Bhagavad-gītā*, *Śrīmad-Bhāgavatam*, *Caitanya-caritāmṛta*, *Caitanya-bhāgavata*,

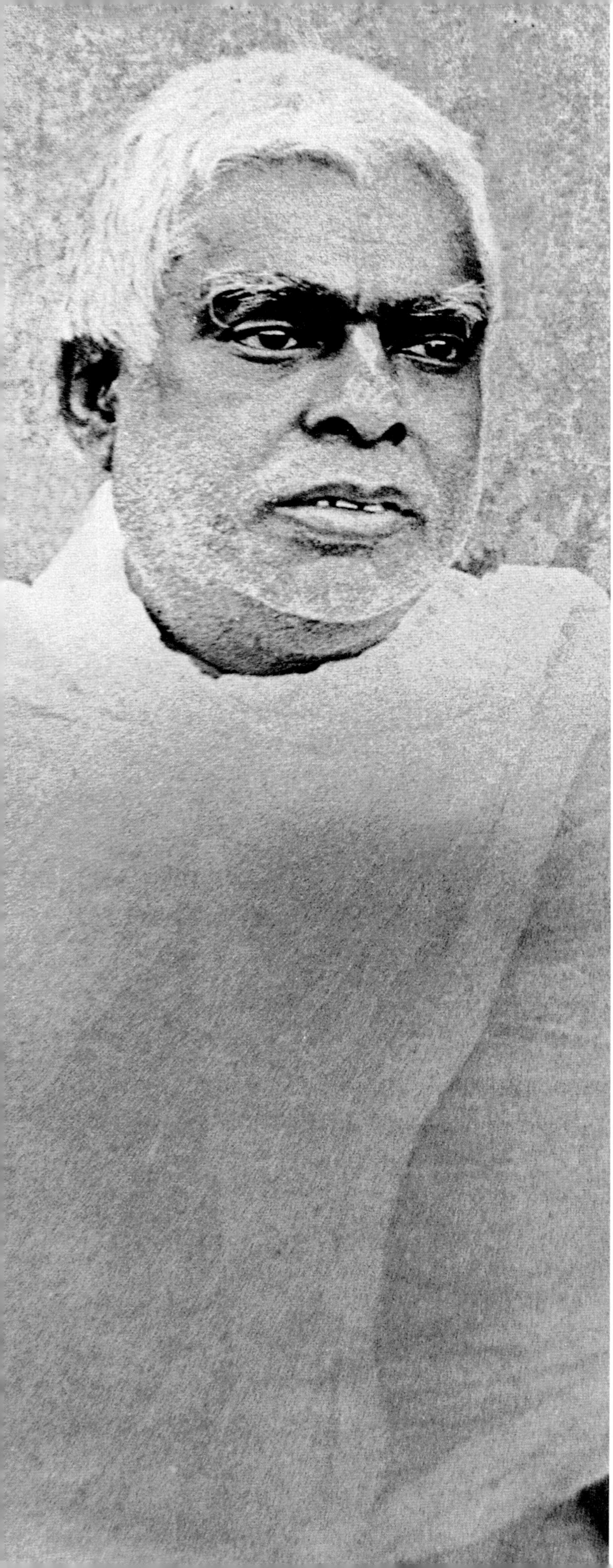

etc. By doing so, they performed an indescribable service for Gauḍīya Vaiṣṇava society.

Today, those who are free from prejudice, who recognize and approve the truth and good qualities in others, lament the absence of these two great ācāryas, what to speak of their disciples and grand-disciples. Those who follow the teachings and example of these two great ācāryas sense their absence sorely. Nevertheless, those who truly feel their separation are fairly rare, for it is beyond the capacity of those who wish to equate materialistic activities with the spiritual to understand the contribution they made–namely their propagation and bestowal of pure devotional service consisting of the culture of those activities that are pleasing to Kṛṣṇa, without any desire for liberation or sense gratification.

It is far beyond my finite capacities to adequately describe all the wonderful things that I heard and witnessed of Śrīla Prabhupāda's glories during my personal association with him. I saw that he would not tolerate even the slightest disrespect to the names of Lord Kṛṣṇa, to His devotees, to His deity form, or to His person.

Victory Flag of Non-Sectarian Religion

Śrīla Prabhupāda told his disciples, "May Bhaktivinoda Ṭhākura's songs and transcendental literature, which contain the same deep purport as those of Narottama Dāsa Ṭhākura, be distributed in abundance throughout Bengal, Orissa and Assam. May intelligent people all over the world recognize the glories of *Jaiva-dharma* and *Caitanya-śikṣāmṛta*. May they carry aloft the victory flag of non-sectarian religion and recognize that Śrī Kṛṣṇa Caitanya, the Holy Name and the *Śrīmad-Bhāgavatam* are one and the same. May this transcendental institution of the followers of Rūpa Gosvāmī be forever engaged in Śrī Caitanya Mahāprabhu's service. The Gauḍīya Maṭha's supreme motto is found in Mahāprabhu's *Śikṣāṣṭakam*: *paraṁ vijayate śrī-kṛṣṇa-saṅkīrtanam*. The only thing we desire in our lives is the dust of the lotus feet of Rūpa Gosvāmī, who made the desires of Lord Caitanya a reality on this earth."

Śrīla Prabhupāda's Dedication to the Holy Name

"May we never under any circumstances become indifferent to the seven-tongued sacrificial flame of the Holy Name. If our attraction to it remains ever-increasing, we will achieve all perfection."

-Śrīla Prabhupāda

During the time he was present on this earth, our most worshipable Śrīla Prabhupāda wrote many letters to his disciples. In most of these, he gave instructions about the chanting of the Holy Names–nāma-bhajana. A number of these letters were collected and published in three volumes as Śrīla Prabhupādera Patrāvalī. We have collected some of Prabhupāda's instructions on chanting from all these handwritten letters. Śrīla Prabhupāda mercifully wrote, "The Holy Name alone is our life and soul." Mahāprabhu stated that the nine principal types of devotional activities quickly give rise to prema, but among them, the chanting of the Holy Name is the most powerful. The proviso to avoid committing offenses to the Name is of course there. Prabhupāda would often remind us that the Name quickly bears fruit if we chant humbly, being tolerant of the vicissitudes that face us in life, without desiring any honor for ourselves and always being prepared to honor all others.

"All auspiciousness comes from the regular chanting of a fixed number of Holy Names. It gives me great joy to know that you have understood this. Do not let up simply because various mundane thoughts disturb you while you are chanting the Holy Name. Such useless thoughts will gradually disappear as a result of chanting, so don't become agitated on account of them."

"You cannot get the results of chanting prematurely. When you have a great deal of attraction for the Holy Name, the allure of mundane thoughts will diminish. If we do not have great enthusiasm for chanting, how will we ever get rid of such thoughts? If we serve the Holy Name with our bodies, minds and souls, then the Named will reveal His all-auspicious form to us." (Vol. I, p. 3)

"I am overjoyed to hear that your enthusiasm for chanting is increasing. As our contaminations are removed by the chanting, the Lord's form, qualities and pastimes will be revealed to us in the Holy Name."

"Only the Holy Name reveals the spiritual form of the living being and then causes him to be attracted to Kṛṣṇa's form. Only the Holy Name reveals the spiritual qualities of the living being and then causes him to be attracted to Kṛṣṇa's qualities. Only the Holy Name reveals the spiritual activities of the living being and then causes him to be attracted to Kṛṣṇa's pastimes." (Vol. I, p. 4-5)

"By service to the Holy Name we do not only mean the chanting of the Holy Name; it also includes the other duties of the chanter. If we serve the Holy Name in body, mind and soul, then the direction of that service spontaneously manifests like the sun in the clear sky of the chanter's heart." (Vol. I, p. 4-5)

"What is the nature of the Holy Name? Eventually all these understandings spontaneously appear in the heart of one who chants the Holy Name. The true nature of *harināma* is revealed through listening to, reading, and studying the scriptures. It is unnecessary to write anything further on this subject. All these things will be revealed to you through chanting." (Vol. I, p. 4-5)

"If you wish to give up offenses while chanting, then just go on chanting constantly and the offenses will stop. Śrīman Mahāprabhu gave all His powers to Rūpa Gosvāmī. So pray to Śrī Rūpa and his followers and beg them to bestow Mahāprabhu's mercy upon you. You should especially pray to the personified Name to make you worthy of serving Him. Through the Lord's name, the Lord of the Name (*Nāma-prabhu*) will take up residence in your heart." (Vol. I, p. 6)

"The Lord does not accept any offering given by someone who does not chant a lakh of Holy Names every single day." (Vol. I, p. 9)

"Make an effort to increase the number of rounds you chant until you reach 64. If you subsequently decrease your number below that, you are considered 'fallen'. So take care to chant without fail." (Vol. I, p. 68)

"Of all the means of avoiding the association of the unholy, the best is to increase the amount of japa that you are doing; so take care to do this. If you chant a lakh every single day, then offenders to the Holy Name will not be able to create a disruption in your spiritual life. Make sure that you set aside the time needed to chant a lakh of Names every day." (Vol. I, p. 53)

"CONTINUE TO INCREASE MY ETERNAL ECSTASY BY TAKING THE NAME OFFENSELESSLY." (VOL. I, P. 10)

"The Lord and His name are one and the same entity. For those who continue to make the distinction between the Lord and His name, it is absolutely necessary to associate with and serve those devotees who are expert in *bhajana*, for only in this way will the contaminations be removed from their hearts." (Vol. I, p. 61-62)

"The Lord and His name are one and the same entity. Chanting the Holy Name and having a direct vision of the Supreme Lord may appear to be two different things, but in actuality they are one. Liberated souls consider the Holy Name to be their object of worship. Study holy literatures like *Caitanya-bhāgavata*, *Caitanya-caritāmṛta*, Narottama's *Prārthanā* and *Prema-bhakti-candrikā*, and Bhaktivinoda's *Kalyāṇa-kalpa-taru*. You should know that the true fruit of meditation and deity worship is the chanting of Kṛṣṇa's name." (Vol. II, p. 3)

"Even if you have little taste for it, if you continue to chant the Holy Names with respect, then you will be able to learn that both Mahāprabhu and Kṛṣṇa are not different from Their names. Before everything else, worship the spiritual master, then Gaura and then Kṛṣṇa. Chant the Holy Names according to a fixed number. Gaurahari and Rādhā-Kṛṣṇa are the same entity; one should not make any distinction between Them. Gaura is Kṛṣṇa. As you get to know Them, as you realize this, you will receive Their blessings. Nothing can compare with the mercy of Lord Gaurasundara. There is no limit to the sweetness of Lord Kṛṣṇacandra." (Vol. II, p. 9)

"Do not be preoccupied with the end result of chanting. Rather, chant Kṛṣṇa's name constantly with patience and forbearance. The Lord will surely not sit silently and do nothing. Gaurahari will certainly reward every practitioner according to the nature of his practice. Service to the Lord is called *bhakti*. You can also know that uttering the name of the Lord is devotion. As you run your hands over the *japa-mālā*, think that you are touching Lord Gaurasundara's lotus feet. That is the way you should chant." (Vol. II, p. 10)

"Read the *Caitanya-caritāmṛta* with understanding and chant the Holy Name without offenses." (Vol. II, p. 12)

"The living entities who render service to Hari, Guru and the Vaiṣṇavas will be released from repeated birth and death; those who do not will be swallowed up by material life. Chant the Holy Name with faith constantly. Study the *Upadeśāmṛta* and *Caitanya-caritāmṛta* and try to understand their deep inner meaning. The Lord is supremely merciful; one day or another, He will surely give you His blessings." (Vol. II, p. 14)

"Serve the Holy Name with a special faith; then everything will be successful. Bless us that we may be able to chant the Name free from offenses." (Vol. II, p. 24)

"Always be detached and chant the Holy Names without offenses. Always study holy literatures like *Caitanya-bhāgavata, Caitanya-caritāmṛta, Prārthanā* and *Prema-bhakti-candrikā*, and *Kalyāṇa-kalpa-taru*. If you do so, all auspiciousness will come." (Vol. II, p. 25)

"If you chant Kṛṣṇa's name, all bad association will disappear like the morning mist." (Vol. II, p. 27)

"We will engage in service to the Holy Dhāma of Māyāpura by announcing the marketplace of the Holy Name, and not by chanting in seclusion. Do not disrupt the service of Māyāpura by selfishly engaging in *nirjana-bhajana*." (Vol. II, p.51)

"Remember Bhaktivinoda Ṭhākura's words, `I cannot find the strength in myself alone' (*ekākī āmāya nāhi pāi bala*) and work cooperatively to complete the sacrifice to the Holy Name in the way that I desire. Those who have responsibility for the performance of this sacrifice must cultivate the virtue of making friendship with everyone, that is, of winning the hearts and minds of all the Vaiṣṇavas and engaging them in the service of the Lord." (Vol. II, p.53)

"PRAY TO THE HOLY NAME AS YOU CHANT; THEN THE HOLY NAME WILL BLESS YOU." (VOL. II, P. 17)

"We beg everyone for their blessings that, in the spirit of Gaurasundara's teaching to be more humble than the straw, more tolerant than the tree, respectful to all and asking no respect for ourselves, we may follow His method of chanting the Holy Names. We also pray that we may hold the shoes of those who chant in this way on our foreheads out of respect, and so be empowered to purify the world of all the distasteful refuse of temporary and useless things that have been foisted on it by the sense enjoyers, the *karmīs, jñānīs* and others who lack discrimination, who torture our eyes and render useless our ability to see." (Vol. II, p. 87-88)

"Every one of the senses is engaged in protecting the body as a whole, and if they are reluctant to do so, the entire body is to some extent adversely affected. In the same way, every individual must serve the society as a whole, otherwise it will experience some degree of loss. In view of this, all those who seek the good of human society have a duty to engage in simultaneously serving the Vaiṣṇavas, showing compassion to the living beings, and chanting the Holy Name. Anything that is favorable to this principle should be accepted, and whatever goes against it must be rejected." (Vol. I, p. 11)

"We should constantly pray to the Holy Name for His mercy. One who is still in a contaminated state should not engage in *smaraṇa* of the daily cycle of the Lord's pastimes (*aṣṭa-kālīya-līlā*). When we engage in chanting the Holy Names, we are simultaneously engaged in hearing and the opportunity for remembering is included in that. One should not engage in such meditation on false premises."(Vol. II, p. 118-119)

"Those engaged in chanting the Holy Name experience a state of astonishing rapture when they reach the advanced stage." (Vol. III, p. 86)

"If you establish centers in England with deities of Jagannātha and Śrīman Mahāprabhu, offer Indian-style preparations and distribute the maha prasad, then the English will gradually develop a sympathy for India and faith in devotional practices, with the result that they will contribute to the Lord's service. I pray for the day when the people of that country will sing the names of Gaura and honor the transcendental prasad from the temple with a spiritual attitude; then they will understand true spiritual life and cultivate Kṛṣṇa consciousness." (Vol. II, p. 141, dated May 27, 1934)

Heartfelt Prayers to His Divine Grace

On the day before you departed from this world, you made me so fortunate by placing your lotus feet on my chest. May those feet, as cooling as a million moons, remain there eternally. May I worship them always in my heart. Though I am completely unworthy, I beg of you that you bestow this causeless mercy on me.

My most worshipable Gurudeva, Śrīla Prabhupāda, did not see the faults in anyone; he was most compassionate. We who aspire to become the servants of his servants and to partake of the remnants of his plate pray to him with all the sincerity at our command that by his causeless mercy he will give us the worthiness to serve him. We pray to him to please make our hearts simple and free from deception; may he forgive us of our offenses, and consider us the servants of his servants, birth after birth. May he free us from the attractions and aversions of this world and keep us fixed in service to his lotus feet.

In conclusion, we offer our heartfelt prayers to the lotus feet of our most worshipable Śrīla Prabhupāda: "O master! Please be merciful to us and gradually lead us from the *vidhi-mārga* to the *rāgānugā* path by giving us ever increasing enthusiasm for the worship of the Holy Names, in the way that you have instructed us. Then we will be able to very quickly win the right to enter into the most secret realms of the mystic service of the Lord. We are the least of the servants of your servants; knowing this, Rādhā-Madana-mohana, Govinda, and Gopīnātha will be merciful to us and enrich our understanding of the *sambandha, abhidheya,* and *prayojana-tattvas.* Then they will give us entry into their loving service and make our lives completely perfect. We will never make a pretense of being advanced *rasika* devotees in order to win profit, adoration, and prestige because we know that such falsehood will only lead us inevitably down to hell. Therefore, the most intelligent thing to do is to follow the example of Śrī Caitanya Mahāprabhu and worship Kṛṣṇa's holy name in the spirit of separation. Through the mercy of the Holy Name we will have the good fortune of attaining all perfection in spiritual life."

O Śrīla Prabhupāda, you are the true shelter of those who know no other resort. For someone as worthless as me, there is no salvation other than your causeless mercy. You instructed me privately in the mantra, told me to chant the Holy Names without offenses, and to keep my mantra secret–but I have not been able to follow these instructions properly. There is no *puraścaraṇa* other than service to the spiritual master; without such service, there can be no perfection of the mantra; the deity of the mantra does not give His blessing or reveal Himself. Without having properly served my spiritual master and thus developed the power of the mantra, I have initiated so many unqualified people and thus committed offenses.

kṛṣṇa āmāya pāle rākhe jāne sarva-kāla
ātma-nivedana-dainye ghucāya jañjāla

"A surrendered devotee knows that Kṛṣṇa protects him at all times. By giving himself to Kṛṣṇa in humility, he is free from all life's difficulties."

The spiritual master is also the manifestation of Kṛṣṇa Himself, and so he too acts as the protector and maintainer of his disciple. I therefore pray to my spiritual master that I may always think of him as my worshipable deity, and that by his grace I may always worship the fearless, ambrosial feet of Śrī Guru-Gaurāṅga-Gāndharvikā-Giridhārī. O Gurudeva! Do not deprive me of your mercy! Protect and maintain me always; free me of all impurities; forgive all my offenses and any mistakes or errors I have made. Give this most unfortunate soul a permanent place at your lotus feet. Make me the servant of your servants. Give me the capacity to serve you and make this life of mine successful.

AN OFFERING OF LOVE AND SEPARATION

[Selections from a humble offering by Śrīla Bhakti Pramode Purī Gosvāmī Mahārāja on his spiritual master Oṁ Viṣṇupāda 108 Śrī Śrīmad Bhaktisiddhānta Sarasvatī Gosvāmī Ṭhākura's 34th disappearance day.]

adoṣa-daraśī prabho patita-uddhāra
mo-sama patita lāgi haiyā udaya
golokera dhana preme karite vistāra
sahile kata nā kaṣṭa ohe dayāmaya (6)

O Prabhu! You see no fault in others and are the savior of the fallen. You appeared in this world for the sake of unredeemable souls like myself. O compassionate one, you underwent so much difficulty in order to spread the wealth of divine love of Goloka far and wide.

mūrtimatī gaura-kṛpā-śakti hao tumi
śrī-gaura-audārya-guṇe tāi guṇī hai'
prakāśile gaura-gāthā haiyā udyamī
ahaitukī kṛpā tava hena dekhi nāi (9)

You are the embodiment of Gaurāṅga's compassionate energy; you possess His quality of benevolence. You made great efforts to explain Mahāprabhu to everyone; I have never seen causeless mercy such as yours anywhere.

pṛthivī byāpiyā habe nāmera pracāra
ei gaura-mano'bhīṣṭa karile pūraṇa
patita-pāvana nāma sārthaka tomāra
sāgara-pāreo nāma kaile vitaraṇa (17)

Through you, Mahāprabhu's wish that the glories of the Holy Name be spread throughout the world became a reality. You sent preachers of the Holy Name across the ocean; thus your title *patita-pāvana* ("savior of the fallen") is most appropriate.

antarīkṣa hate prabho śakti sañcāriyā
rakṣa rakṣa jīva-gaṇe e ghora saṅkaṭe
kṛṣṇa-sevonumukha kara śuddha-buddhi diyā
svarūpera udbodhana kara niṣkapaṭe (21)

O Prabhu, from your place in the spiritual sky, give us the energy to save the deluded souls in this terrible time. Make us favorable to Kṛṣṇa's service by giving us pure intelligence; awaken knowledge of our true identity.

aprakaṭeo prakaṭa tumi cira-kāla
antarera vyathā tāi nivedi tomāre
sahite nāro to santānera cakṣu-jala
doṣa kṣami o caraṇe rākha dayā kare (32)

Even after your disappearance from this world, you are always present. So I am telling you of the pain that I feel within me. You cannot stand to see all your children's tears, so please give me a place by your side, forgiving me of all my faults.

prakaṭa-kāle o snehe hai ni vañcita
ajñāna adhama jāni kariyācho dayā
ekhano jānaha prabho tomāri āśrita
māgiche kātare tava śrī-caraṇa-chāyā (33)

When you were with us, you never held back your affection for me. Even though I am ignorant and lowly, you did not hesitate to show your compassion to me. Even now, I am still under your shelter alone and beg to remain in the cooling shade of your lotus feet.

(śrī) rūpa-pada-dhuli jena janme janme hai
baliyā kata-i dainya karecha prārthanā
śiṣyero svarūpa prabho jānāyecho sei
anya kāmya nāhi rūpa-ānugatya vinā (34)

You yourself humbly prayed to remain a speck of dust at Śrī Rūpa Gosvāmī's lotus feet. By so doing, you taught us about the true identity of your disciples as well. There is nothing more desirable than to follow in the path of Rūpa Gosvāmī.

ei kṛpā kara prabho ohe dayāmaya
rūpa-raghunātha-pade jena thāke mati
lakṣa-nāma japa tava upadeśa haya
sadā jena sei nāma-jape bāṛe rati (35)

O most merciful master! Bless us that we too may always remain fixed at the feet of Śrī Rūpa and Raghunātha. You instructed us to chant a lakh of Holy Names every day, so I pray that I may always have the enthusiasm to do my *japa* according to this command.

bhakativinoda dhārā ruddha nāhi habe
tāṅra manobhīṣṭa sabe sādha sābadhāne
ei icchā tava prabho apūrṇa nā rabe
gāhibe tāṅhāra jaya sakala bhuvane (37)

You also said that the stream of devotion coming from Bhaktivinoda Ṭhākura shall never be dammed up and that we should dedicate ourselves to realizing his mission. O Master! This desire will not go unfulfilled; the entire world will sing his victory!

lupta-tīrthoddhāra, bhakti-śāstra prakāśana
śrī-mūrtira sevā, vaiṣṇavācāra pracāra
saba kailā jāhe sampradāya-saṁrakṣaṇa
sadācārya-varya tumi pūjya sabākāra (39)

You are the most worshipable example of what an *ācārya* should be, preserving the teachings of the disciplic succession in reestablishing the holy places, publishing devotional literature, establishing the worship of the deities, and preaching the standards of pure and saintly behavior.

svayaṁ sevya kṛṣṇa dhari sevaka mūrati
āpani ācari sevā jīvere śikhān
tāi jāni tumi kṛṣṇa-priyatama ati
bhṛtya-bhṛtya bali pada-tale deha sthāna (40)

The Supreme Lord Kṛṣṇa takes the form of a servant, teaching the conditioned souls by his own example. You know this and so you are dearest to Kṛṣṇa; and therefore I pray that you consider me the servant of your servants and give me a place at your lotus feet.

śrī rādhā-nayana-maṇi kṛṣṇa-dāsa rūpe
ātmā-paricaya dāne tomāra ullāsa
tava dāsa-dāsa yogya kari laha more
sevā adhikāra diyā rākha nija-pāśa (41)

You joyfully revealed that you are the servant of Kṛṣṇa, the cynosure of Rādhārāṇī's eyes—Nayana-maṇi. Please make me worthy to be the servant of your servant and, giving me the right to serve the Divine Couple, keep me always by your side.

tumi more hāte dhare cālāiyā lao
tabe ta supatha dhari vrajera patha pāṇ
dayāmaya dīna-bandhu patita-pāvana
e adhame āra nāhi chāṛibā kakhana

Take me by the hand and lead me on the right path, so that I may find my way to Vṛndāvana. You are most merciful; you are the friend of the destitute, the purifier of the sinful. Never leave this lowly creature.

śaraṇa lainu tava caraṇa-kamale
e dāsere kara dayā āpanāra bale

I have taken shelter at your lotus feet. Now I ask you to bless me and call me your own.

bhavadīya cira-dāsānudāsa srī-bhakti-pramoda-purī

The servant of your servant, Śrī Bhakti Pramode Purī

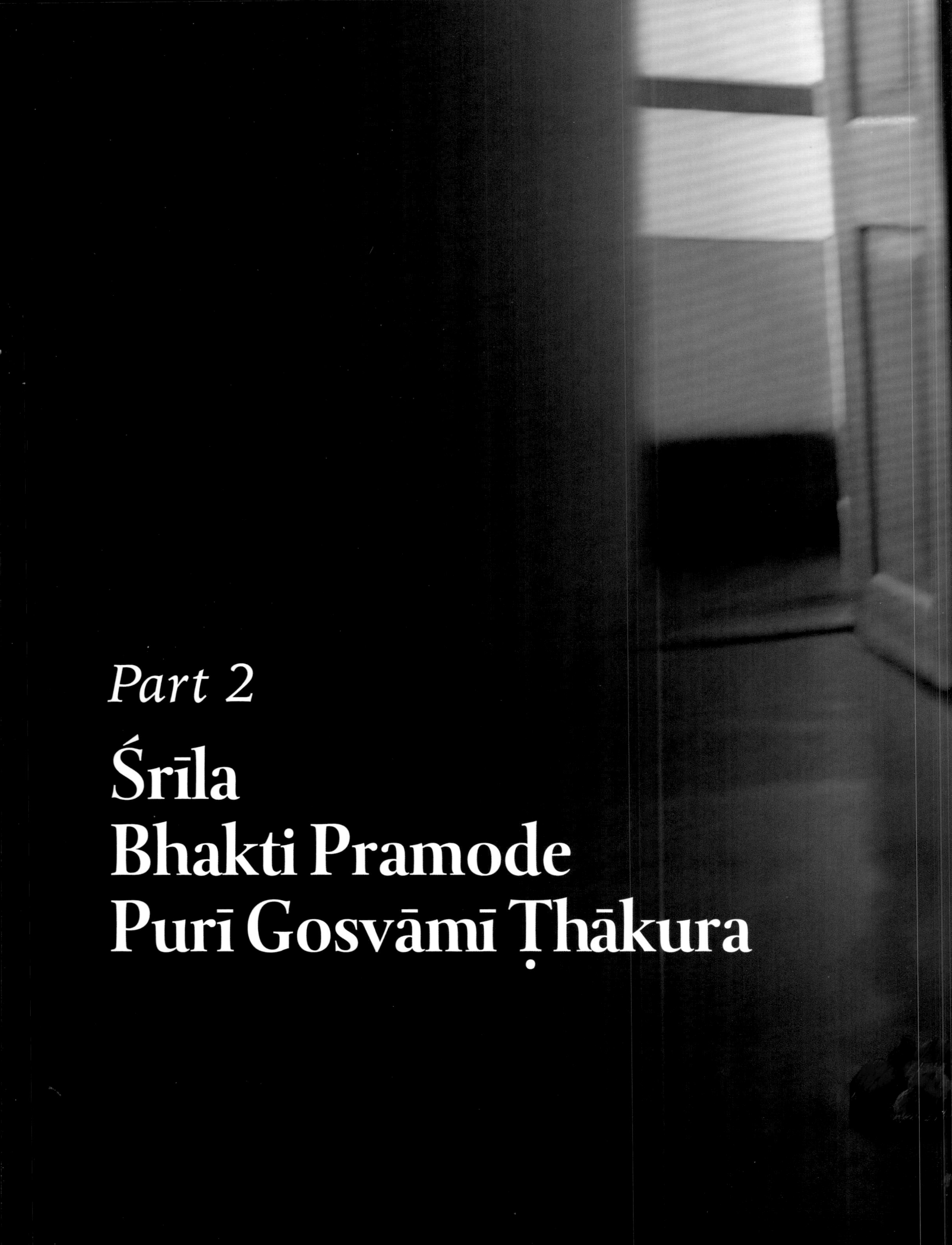

Part 2

Śrīla Bhakti Pramode Purī Gosvāmī Ṭhākura

A Brief Autobiography of Śrīla Bhakti Pramode Purī Gosvāmī Mahārāja

A Humble Submission - My Life Story

I pay my prostrated obeisances to Śrī Guru-Gaurāṅga, Gāndharvikā-Giridhari, and Gopīnātha and beg them for their causeless mercy. It is the twilight of my life, and I have completed my one hundredth year. My hands are arthritic, my memory is failing, and I am no longer able to discuss anything in a sequential manner. Even so, I make this humble submission at the feet of my Guru, the Vaiṣṇavas, and the Lord. I hope that you will find the kindness within you to forgive me for my shortcomings.

guru-vaiṣṇava-bhagavān tinera smaraṇ
tinera smaraṇa hay vighna vināśan
anāyāse hay nija vāñchita-pūraṇ

"I meditate on my guru, the Vaiṣṇavas, and the Lord, for by remembering them, all obstacles are destroyed and one easily attains the fulfillment of all desires." (*Caitanya-caritāmṛta* 1.1.20-1)

I have been inspired by the example of Kṛṣṇadāsa Kavirāja Gosvāmī to make this effort to tell my story. In the *Bhāgavata*, there is a verse:

sṛṣṭvā purāṇi vividhāny ajayātma-śaktyā
vṛkṣān sarīsṛpa-paśūn khaga-dandaśūkān
tais tair atuṣṭa-hṛdayaḥ puruṣaṁ vidhāya
brahmāloka-dhiṣaṇaṁ mudam āpa devaḥ

"With the help of His *māyā* potency, the Supreme Lord created this visible world with its trees, serpents, animals, birds, and other creatures, but his heart remained dissatisfied. Then He created man, who alone possesses the intelligence to see Brahman, and He was delighted." (*Śrīmad-Bhāgavatam* 11.9.28)

Kṛṣṇadāsa Kavirāja Gosvāmī has written the following verses in the *Caitanya-caritāmṛta*:

tār madhye sthāvar jaṅgama—dui bheda
jaṅgame tiryak-jala-sthalacara vibheda
tār madhye manuṣya-jāti ati alpatara
tār madhye mleccha, pulinda, bauddha, śabara
veda-niṣṭha-madhye ardheka veda mukhe māne
veda-niṣiddha pāpa kare, dharma nāhi gaṇe
dharmācāri-madhye bahu ta 'karma-niṣṭha'
koṭi-karma-niṣṭha-madhye eka jñānī' śreṣṭha
koṭi-jñāni-madhye haya eka jana mukta
koṭi-mukta-madhye 'durlabha' eka kṛṣṇa-bhakta

"There are two divisions of living entities—those that can move and those that cannot. Among those that move, there are birds, aquatics, and animals. Among these, the human beings are very small in number and include non-Vedic peoples such as Muslims, tribals, Buddhists, and outcastes. Of those who are followers of the Vedic principles (and thus considered civilized), half give them only lip service and engage in sinful activities which are forbidden by the scriptures and give no importance to true religion. Most of the remainder are involved in fruitive activities and a single wise man is rare among them. Out of many millions of such wise men, one may actually become liberated, and out of many millions of such liberated persons, a pure devotee of Lord Kṛṣṇa is still more difficult to find." (*Caitanya-caritāmṛta* 2.16.144-8)

Another scriptural statement explains how the *jīva* wanders through 8,400,000 species of life:

jalajā nava-lakṣāṇi sthāvarā lakṣa-viṁśati
kṛmayo rudra-saṅkhyakāḥ pakṣiṇāṁ daśa-lakṣaṇam
triṁśal-lakṣāṇi paśavaḥ catur-lakṣāṇi mānuṣāḥ

"There are 900,000 species living in the water. There are also 2,000,000 non-moving living entities (*sthāvara*) such as trees and plants. There are also 1,100,000 species of insects and reptiles, and another 1,000,000 species of birds. There are 3,000,000 varieties of animals, and 400,000 types of human beings."

labdhvā sudurlabham idaṁ bahu-sambhavānte
mānuṣyam arthadam anityam apīha dhīraḥ
tūrṇaṁ yateta na pated anumṛtyu yāvan
niḥśreyasāya viṣayaḥ khalu sarvataḥ syāt

"After many, many births, one finally is born in a most rare and valuable human body which provides an opportunity to attain the supreme goal, but is nevertheless temporary. Therefore, the wise individual should immediately take up the effort to find that which provides the supreme good in all times and circumstances, and not give it up right to the very moment of his death." (*Śrīmad-Bhāgavatam* 11.9.29)

Sense enjoyments are available in the other species of life, but only in this human body are we able to achieve the supreme good. Śrīla Bhaktivinoda Ṭhākura has sung as follows in his song *Jīva jāgo*:

emana durlabha mānava-deha
pāiyā ki karo bhāvanā keha
ebe nā bhajile yaśodā-sūta
carame paṛibe lāje

"You have attained such a rare gift, the human body, but does any one of you think of its purpose? If you do not worship the son of Yaśodā now, you will feel shame at the time of death."

Elsewhere, he wrote another song:

jīvana-samāpti-kāle karibo bhajana
ebe kari gṛha-sukha
kakhano e kathā nāhi bale vijña jana
e deha patanonmukha

"'I will wait until the end of my life before worshiping the Lord. For the moment, I intend to enjoy life.' An intelligent person never says anything like this because he knows that the body can fall at any moment."

āji vā śatek varṣe avaśya maraṇa
niścinta nā thāko bhāi
jata śīghra pāro, bhajo śrī kṛṣṇa caraṇa
jīvanera ṭhika nāi

"Whether today or in a hundred years, death is inevitable. Don't think that you can give up concentrating on this problem, my brother. Worship Kṛṣṇa's feet as soon as you can, for life offers no guarantees."

saṁsāra nirvāha kari jābo āmi vṛndāvana
ṛṇa-traya śodhibāre karitechi sujatana
āśāra nāhi prayojana
emana durāśā vaśe jābe prāṇa avaśeṣe

nā hañbe dīna-bandhu caraṇe sevana
jadi sumaṅgala cāo sadā kṛṣṇa-nāma gāo
gṛhe thāko vane thāko ithe tarka akāraṇa

"'I will go to Vṛndāvana after dealing with my family responsibilities—I am taking care to repay my threefold debt.' There is no need to aspire in this way, for your life will be wasted in trying to fulfill such distracting obligations. You will never serve the feet of the only friend of the fallen. If you wish true auspiciousness, then sing Kṛṣṇa's names constantly, regardless of your station in life. Nothing is gained by arguing the superiority of householder or renounced life."

And once again, here is another of his compositions:

janama maraṇa jarā je saṁsāre āche bharā
tāhe kibā āche bolo sāra

"Birth, death, and old age are inevitable in this life. Can you tell me what is permanent in this world?"

dhana jana parivāra keha nahe kabhu kāra
kāle mitra akāle apara
jāhā dharibāre cāi tāhe nāhi thāke bhāi
anitya samasta vinaśvara

"None of this—your possessions, friends and family—is really yours. They are friends during good times, strangers in bad. Nothing that we want to hold on to will remain, my brother; this world is temporary and bound for destruction."

āyu ati alpa-dina krame tāhā haya kṣīṇa
śamanera nikaṭa darśana
roga śoka anibāra citta kare chāra-khāra
bāndhava-viyoga durghaṭana

"Your life is extremely short, and with every day, your death comes closer into sight. Diseases and distress constantly shatter the mind, what to speak of the loss of family and friends and other mishaps."

bhāla kare dekho bhāi amiśra ānanda nāi
je ānanda duḥkhera kāraṇa
se sukhera tare tabe kena māyāra dāsa habe
hārāibe paramārtha dhana?

"Brother! Examine the matter carefully. There is no such thing as unadulterated happiness. Indeed, joy is the cause of unhappiness. So why then make such efforts for this incomplete happiness, becoming the servant of illusion and losing the treasure of the supreme spiritual good?"

And there are so many other songs written by the *mahājanas* on the same theme. They have written these songs for the benefit of the conditioned souls, placing them on guard so that they may ultimately be delivered. All of these followers of Śrī Caitanya Mahāprabhu have designated the worship of Kṛṣṇa's lotus feet as the only source of any true benefit in life. All of the books they authored, whether *Caitanya-bhāgavata*, *Caitanya-caritāmṛta*, or the *Sandarbhas* and other Gosvāmī writings, should be constantly discussed in the association of devotees.

Śrīla Prabhupāda repeatedly quoted the following verse from Śrīla Bhaktivinoda Ṭhākura's writings:

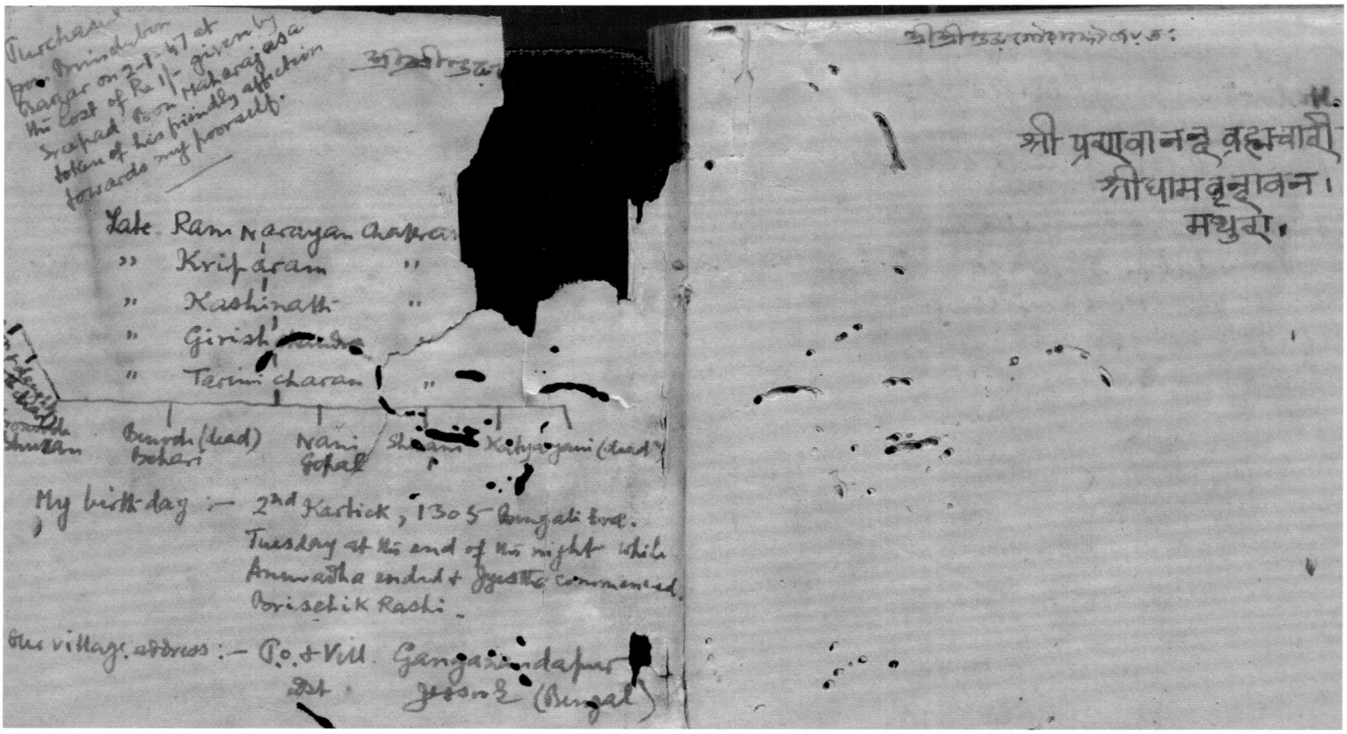

The inside of Srila Bhakti Pramode Purī Maharaja's journal where he writes he writes details of his birth and family tree.

durlabha mānava janma labhiyā saṁsāre
kṛṣṇa nā bhajinu duḥkha kahibo kāhāre
saṁsāra saṁsāra kare miche gela kāla
lābha nā hañla kichu ghaṭila jañjāla

"Though I attained a human birth in this world, I never worshiped Kṛṣṇa. Whom shall I tell of my distress? All I have done is remain absorbed in family life and hard work, wasting my time in this way. I have gained nothing, indeed, and now the calamity has arrived."

All of Bhaktivinoda Ṭhākura's writings, such as *Śaraṇāgati*, *Kalyāṇa-kalpa-taru*, *Gītāvalī* and *Gītamālā*, as well as Narottama's *Prārthanā* and *Prema-bhakti-candrikā* were constantly on Śrīla Prabhupāda's lips. All of Śrīla Bhaktivinoda Ṭhākura's writings, *Jaiva Dharma*, *Caitanya Śikṣāmṛta*, *Harināma Cintāmaṇi*, *Bhajana Rahasya*, etc., are imbued with a deep understanding of the essence of all the scriptures.

sādhu-saṅge kṛṣṇa-nāma ei mātra cāi
saṁsāra jinite āra kono vastu nāi

"All I want is association with sadhus and the holy name of Kṛṣṇa. I need nothing else in order to conquer the world of birth and death."

Now, after first remembering the lotus feet of my most worshipable spiritual master, Nitya-līlā-praviṣṭa Oṁ Viṣṇupāda 108 Śrī Bhaktisiddhānta Sarasvatī Ṭhākura Prabhupāda, and offering them unlimited prostrated obeisances, I will say a few words about my life.

A Few Words About My Life

I was born in Jessore district, in a small town called Ganganandapur on the east banks of the Kapotakha River. This place is now in Bangladesh, but it is not more than about 80 kilometers from Calcutta. There were many educated and cultured people living there at that time. We lived on the south side of the village, which consisted predominantly of *brāhmaṇa* families, but I was born in a poorer household. My father's name was Tarini Charan Chakravarti and my mother's, Ram Rangini Devi. I had a paternal uncle named Priyanath Chakravarti. On my mother's side, I also had an accomplished uncle who had earned three master's degrees, in Bengali, Sanskrit, and mathematics. He also had numerous traditional titles for studies in Sanskrit grammar and poetry, Sāṅkhya philosophy, the Vedas and Vedānta, etc. He was thus a great scholar. He taught at a high school in Śrīdhāma Māyāpura, including some time at the Ṭhākura Bhaktivinoda Institute.

Prior to my birth, my parents had lost a four-year-old daughter and a one-year-old son. Our neighbors in the village were a family of Vedic *brāhmaṇas* who had established a temple of Buḍo Śiva. My mother went faithfully to worship this Śiva deity and one day was told in a dream about my birth and that of my younger brother. She used to tell us that we were born as a result of Śiva's blessings, his *vara-putras*. According to the custom of the time, my nurse "purchased" me from my mother for only three cowries, so I was given the name Tin Koṛi. People used to call me Tinu. I could never understand the value of a life that could be sold for such a pittance. Anyway, now that I have such a big title, "Founder-President," people find it amusing. From the time that I was a baby, I was always overjoyed whenever I heard singing or music being played. For this reason, my father gave me the name Pramode Bhushan.

From my father, I heard that in the distant past the king of Bengal, Ādiśura, brought five Vedic *brāhmaṇas* from Kanyākubja to settle his land. Their names were Dakṣa, Bhaṭṭa Nārāyaṇa, Śrī Harṣa, Candora, and Vedagarbha. Our family was descended from Śrī Harsa. One of my older godbrothers, the revered Bhakti Hṛdaya Bon Mahārāja, was also descended from the same forefather. Bon Mahārāja, however, was a *kulīna-brāhmaṇa*. His family name was Mukhopādhyāya. The custom of separating *brāhmaṇas* into these higher and lower categories began under the Sena king Ballāla Sena. The nine characteristics with which the higher class or *kulīna-brāhmaṇa* were supposedly endowed are given as follows:

ācāro niyamo vidyā pratiṣṭhā tīrtha-darśanam
niṣṭhā vṛttis tapo dānaṁ navadhā kula-lakṣaṇam

"There are nine ways of judging a family: by its treatment of others, the rules it keeps, its learning, its social position, whether or not its members have performed pilgrimage, its

steadfastness, the way it makes its money, and whether its members perform austerities or give charity."

We were *śrotrīya-brāhmaṇas*, which means that we were Vedādhyāyīs, or versed in the Vedas. This is a lower ranking in the caste system than *kulīna-brāhmaṇa*. I would think that in the *Caitanya-caritāmṛta* story about Sākṣī Gopāla, of the two *brāhmaṇas* who went on pilgrimage to Vṛndāvana, the older one was likely a *kulīna-brāhmaṇa*, the younger one a *śrotrīya*. In the Smṛti scriptures it is said that if a girl from a *śrotrīya* family marries into a *kulīna* family, then the latter becomes glorious. But if a *kulīna* girl marries a *śrotrīya* man, the *kulīna* family is ruined. In those days, people were still extremely influenced by false pride based on family, caste, and lineage.

Eventually, by the Lord's will, I started to get my first understanding of Gauḍīya Vaishnavism, Śrīla Prabhupāda, and Bhaktivinoda Ṭhākura as a result of going to the Madana-mohana temple on the north side of the village with Bhaktiratna Ṭhākura and conversing with him. Prior to that, I had a superficial understanding of who Caitanya Mahāprabhu was. I would sit down next to Bhaktiratna Ṭhākura and study the writings of Bhaktivinoda Ṭhākura, Kṛṣṇadāsa Kavirājā Gosvāmī, or other Vaiṣṇava *mahājanas*. In this way, I gained a great deal of valuable knowledge about the Gauḍīya Vaiṣṇava religious path that Śrīman Mahāprabhu taught and practiced. My narrow understanding of His teachings was completely eradicated. Mahāprabhu said,

nīca-jāti nahe kṛṣṇa-bhajane ayogya
sat-kula-vipra nahe bhajanera yogya
jei bhaje sei baṛa, abhakta—hīna, chāra
kṛṣṇa-bhajane nāhi jāti-kulādi-vicāra

"A person born in a low caste is not unfit for discharging devotional service to Kṛṣṇa, nor is one fit for devotional service simply because he is born in a high-caste *brāhmaṇa* family. Anyone who takes to devotional service is exalted, whereas a non-devotee is always condemned and abominable. In the discharge of devotional service to the Lord, there is no consideration of caste or social status." (*Caitanya-caritāmṛta* 1.4.66-7)

And about Haridāsa Ṭhākura it is said,

jāti kula saba nirarthaka bujhāite
janmilena nīca-kule prabhura ājñāte

"He took birth in a low-caste family by the Lord's order in order to show that caste and social status are all irrelevant." (*Caitanya-bhāgavata* 1.16.237)

The meaning of these verses is that one's only duty is to take shelter of the feet of a genuine spiritual master and engage in the worship of Lord Hari while following the Vaiṣṇava regulative principles, or *sadācāra*. During this time, I also understood how important it was to make an intense study of the scriptures in the association of advanced devotees. Thenceforward, I began to desire to understand more fully what constitutes service to Guru-Gaurāṅga, Rādhā-Gopinātha, and Madana-mohana; in other words, what is the distinction between the object of worship, the worshiper, and the act of worshiping. At this very same temple (Ṭhākura Bāṛī), I had the fortune to receive a great amount of affection from the aunt of my now departed godbrother Bhakti Vivek Bhāratī Mahārāja. Almost everyone who visited the temple used to call her "Mother" and this was appropriate because she was truly filled with motherly affection for everyone.

Both Bhaktiratna Ṭhākura and the temple's Mātā Ṭhākurani were mantra disciples of Bagnapara's Bipin Bihari Gosvāmī. The Gosvāmī Prabhu had authorized Mātā Ṭhākurani to engage in the worship of the Lord in His *śālagrāma-śīlā* form. At first I was astonished by this because I had never seen her actually touch the Deity, only cook His *bhoga*, which was the rule to which I was accustomed from my family upbringing. You can read about these rules in the Vaiṣṇava rule book (Smṛti) *Hari-bhakti-vilāsa*.

Lord Kṛṣṇa says in the *Bhagavad-gītā*,

yaḥ śāstra-vidhim utsṛjya vartate kāma-kārataḥ
na sa siddhim avāpnoti na sukhaṁ na paraṁ gatim

"A person who transgresses the scriptural injunctions and acts whimsically can never attain perfection, nor happiness, nor the supreme destination." (*Gītā* 16.23)

The basic point is that even if a person accumulates all kinds of empiric knowledge, if he does not learn how to act from the holy scriptures, he will end up in hell. The entire human race will go down to destruction if it disregards the words of the Lord and neglects the rules He has set forth. And the conclusion of all holy scriptures is that devotion alone is the path of ultimate auspiciousness.

tasmāc chāstraṁ pramāṇaṁ te kāryākārya-vyavasthitau
jñātvā śāstra-vidhānoktaṁ karma kartum ihārhasi

"One should understand what is duty and what is not duty on the basis of scriptural evidence. Now that you know what is prescribed in the scripture, you should act accordingly." (*Gītā* 16.24)

So the conclusion is,

sādhu-saṅge kṛṣṇa-nāma ei mātra cāi
saṁsāra jinite ār kono vastu nāi

"All I desire is the Holy Name in the association of devotees. I need nothing else in order to conquer the material nature."

Bhaktiratna Ṭhākura

Devotional association, the name of Kṛṣṇa, hearing the *Bhāgavata*, residence in Mathura, and worshiping the deity form of the Lord in full faith—these are the principle practices on the devotional path.

sakala-sādhana-śreṣṭha ei pañca aṅga
kṛṣṇa-prema janmāya ei pāñcera alpa saṅga

"Superior to all other forms of devotional practice are these five limbs. Even slight contact with any of these five brings about love for Kṛṣṇa." (*Caitanya-caritāmṛta* 2.22.126)

So, I was fortunate enough to have received this wonderful opportunity to associate with devotees and hear Hari-kathā from my very childhood. As a result, I never deviated from the ideal behavior for a student. Śrīla Bhaktivinoda Ṭhākura has written,

paṛe likhe lok kṛṣṇa-bhakti labhibāre
tā yadi nā hañla tabe vidyā ki kare?

"The purpose of studying is to attain devotion to Kṛṣṇa. If that result is not achieved, then what is the use of knowledge?"

I remember some of the events of my student life. A college professor, Mahitosh Ray-Chaudhury (M.A., B.L.), who also edited a magazine, was particularly affectionate to me. A very old Deity of Kṛṣṇa named Shyama Raya had been worshiped in his home for generations. His younger brother Paritosh Kumar Ray-Chaudhury was a classmate of mine throughout childhood. It seems to me that at this time my friendship with him and my interest in the Ṭhākura Bāṛī became stronger and, as a result, I was lucky to rejoice in saintly company even more.

The northern section of our village was called Meṭho Pāṛā and was home to a community of non-Hindus. One day, these people decided to ritually slaughter a cow (*korbānī*) on some Hindu's property. When word got out, it was not long before an atmosphere of tension spread through the town. Some of the townspeople approached the District Magistrate, who then got involved in order to prevent a possible riot. The D.M. at that time was a great devotee named Upendra Mohan Sengupta, who had founded the Śāstra-dharma Pracāraka Samiti on Chowringhee

Road in Calcutta. His two nephews were named Abani Ranjan and Nalini Ranjan Sengupta. My friend Paritosh knew and respected them both a great deal. He thus knew the District Magistrate personally and called him Na' Kaka, or "uncle." When he came to Meṭho Pāṛā, Paritosh took me to see him. We entered the beautiful tent inside which he was seated and when Paritosh paid his obeisances, I did likewise. As a result of this contact, I became involved with the Śāstra-dharma Pracāraka Samiti. I don't remember whether I ever actually heard Upendra Mohan Sengupta talk about Kṛṣṇa, but I recall that just by seeing him, my heart was filled with a sense of purity. Afterwards, Paritosh and I went on occasion to the Śāstra-dharma Pracāraka Samiti and listened to *sādhus* speak *hari-kathā*.

Dr. Nalini Ranjan Sengupta Dharmaratna's older brother Abani Ranjan was a high school vice-principal at the time. Later, he became an inspector and so came to supervise the Minor Exams at our school at the end of the year. Paritosh and I were chosen by him to sit in the Scholarship Exam. Though we passed, we both missed getting scholarships by a slight margin. Later, however, through the graces of a distant uncle, Khagendra Nath Chakravarti, who had been first in the university matriculation exams, I was enrolled in a high school in Baruipur on the Diamond Harbour railway line. But I had no idea where Paritosh had been enrolled for high school.

Arrangements were made for me to stay in the neighboring village, Shason, in the house of the zamindar family of Nani Gopal, Nanda Gopal, and Saroj Kumar Chattopadhyaya. At the time, the youngest of these brothers, Saroj Babu, was studying at Calcutta's Presidency College where my uncle Khagen had also been admitted. At my uncle's behest, Saroj Babu engaged me as a tutor for their sister. Meanwhile, at Baruipur High School, the secretary Durgadasa Ray Chaudhury heard about my shortage of funds and arranged for me to study without any tuition fees. The following year, my brother Vinode Vihari also passed his Minor Exam.

By the Lord's grace, everyone was happy with my studies and conduct. After my brother Vinode Vihari had passed his Minors, he came and joined me in Baruipur, staying with me in the same *brāhmaṇa* household in Shason. At my pleading, the school secretary agreed to allow him to also study without paying any tuition. By the Lord's grace, no one had cause to complain about his studies or conduct. I think that when I was promoted from the third class to the second, Binu passed from the fourth to the third.

Everyone at the school and in Shason village highly praised us both. At this time, however, our father fell extremely ill. When we got the news, I told Binu, who took a great deal of convincing, to remain in Shason while I returned alone to Ganganandapur to see him. Binu was overcome with tears at my departure. In the meantime, a terrifying epidemic of Asian cholera struck Shason. The house in which we were staying was not far from the local crematorium and it seemed as though the area was constantly under a cloud of smoke from the funeral pyres. The sounds of mourning filled the sky. When I arrived at home, I found that my father was indeed ill, but according to my mother his situation was improving. Not long afterward, however, my brother arrived there in an extremely disheartened and sickly state. The situation in Shason had deteriorated terribly and he himself had started to experience stomach cramps. Since school was about to start, I started off on the return journey early the next morning while he remained in Ganganandapur.

My Khuro Mahashaya (father's younger brother) loved all three of us brothers very much and so did everything possible to have my brother Binu treated; even so, he died that same evening. I received a letter from my father telling me to come back home immediately. In his letter my father had not mentioned my brother's death at all, but only said that my mother was very ill. All the money that I had left, however, was Rs. 1.25, which was insufficient for a train ticket home. I bought a pomegranate and then went to the station, where I told the station master that my mother was very ill and that I had to return to see her but could not afford the fare. With tears streaming from my eyes I begged him to arrange for me to travel for free as I was a poor, helpless student. He was kind enough to assist me and so I managed to get home. When I arrived, however, I saw from the bathing ghat the white shrouds of a new bier at the cremation grounds further down the riverbank. Because of my father's letter, I thought that my mother had died, so I was very surprised when I heard her cry out, "Binu! Look, your brother has come. Come out and say hello."

She was so overcome with emotion that she jumped down from the four-foot high veranda. My heart still skips a beat when I remember her state on that day. It defies description. I returned to the cremation grounds to pay my last respects to my younger brother, but my heart was extremely heavy. I was inconsolable.

Everyone at the school and in Shason village felt great pain on hearing the news of my brother's death. It was the very day on which he was to be promoted from the fourth form to the third. I was completely overcome with grief when, in the school assembly, I accepted a silver medal and some books from the principal which had been intended as prizes for him. The thunderbolt of anguish broke my heart and torrents of tears blocked out all light from my eyes. From that day, my life changed completely. I did very well on my matriculation exams, placing first in Bengali, for which I received a gold medal and some valuable books as prizes on graduation day.

As a next step, it was my intention to study for an I.A. in literature and philosophy. However, everyone unanimously decided for me that I should study for the I.A.S. in science, as I would be able to make use of Saroj Babu's books and as it made more sense for my future economic prospects. I was enrolled in Calcutta's Bangavasi College, but because of the daily traveling and other reasons, my studies suffered and I did not do well on my exams. In the meantime, my family's poverty-stricken condition had me worried. Since my childhood, I had always wanted to lighten my father's burden but had been helpless to do or say anything to help relieve that relentless poverty. Now that I was grown up, the situation was different. By the will of God, even though I was still quite young, I had the opportunity to get a good job with the Calcutta Port Commission and so I decided to temporarily quit college. Saroj Babu had a house on Malsa Lane in Bow Bazaar where I stayed. I did my own cooking and went to work.

While living there, I became a subscriber to *Gauḍīya* magazine and the *Śrīmad-Bhāgavatam*, which was coming out in installments. I would see devotees

from Śrīla Prabhupāda's mission almost every day, especially Kīrtanānanda Brahmacārī. Gradually, as my material situation improved, I got my own lodgings on Akhil Mistri Lane and arranged for my mother and younger sister to come there and live with me. Every day after work, I would come home and then head for 1 Ultadanga Junction Road, where I would listen to my worshipable Śrīla Prabhupāda himself lecture on the Vaiṣṇava scriptures. But I have forgotten to mention something important in this connection. Even while living in my home village, when I was learning about Śrīman Mahāprabhu at the Ṭhākura Bāṛī, I had already accepted my worshipable Śrīla Prabhupāda as guru. I already recognized and felt deeply the absolute need to take shelter of a realized soul as soon as possible.

Afterwards, I frequently went to visit him at his *bhajana kuṭīra* at Vrajapattana in Śrī Māyāpura. I recognized him to be one of the Lord's eternal associates who had taken on the extremely difficult task of chanting a billion names while strictly observing celibacy, all for the intention of saving the world. I can still remember the three or four times I saw him while he was observing this sacrifice and how I would contemplate his effulgence in a state of astonishment. I heard that the *tulasī-mālā* on which Śrīla Prabhupāda performed this billion-name sacrifice had been chanted on by Śrīla Bhaktivinoda Ṭhākura, who then gave it to him with his blessings. I remember also taking Mahāprabhu's *prasad* on one occasion underneath a bel tree filled with fruits which stood behind the Yogapīṭha temple Bhaktivinoda Ṭhākura had established.

My spiritual master, my most worshipable Śrīla Prabhupāda, gave me initiation in the Holy Name and the mantra on Janmāṣṭamī, 1923, at the center on Ultadanga Junction Road. At that time, Śrīla Prabhupāda said to me, "Your name is Pramode Bhushan ("decorated with delights"), but it is not proper to have material delights as a decoration. So I am giving you the name Praṇavānanda Brahmacārī." Prabhupāda addressed me with the polite pronoun *āpani*, which gave me some pain, but later I heard from my godbrothers that Śrīla Prabhupāda was following in the footsteps of Mahāprabhu, who had revealed the true transcendental identity of the soul:

nāhaṁ vipro na ca nara-patir nāpi vaiśyo na śūdro
nāhaṁ varṇī na ca gṛha-patir no vanastho yatir vākintu
prodyan-nikhila-paramānanda-pūrnāmṛtābdher
gopī-bhartuḥ pada-kamalayor dāsa-dāsānudāsaḥ

"I am not a *brāhmaṇa*, nor am I a *kṣatriya*; I am not a *vaiśya* nor a *śudra*. I am not a *brahmacārī*, nor a householder, not a *vānaprastha*, nor a *sannyāsī*. But since Lord Śrī Kṛṣṇa, the maintainer of the *gopis* and the overflowing ocean of nectar, is the only source of universal, transcendental bliss, I claim to be a servant to the servant of the servant of His lotus feet." (*Caitanya-caritāmṛta* 2.13.8, *Padyāvalī* 74)

Śrīla Prabhupāda addressed all his disciples and everyone else as *āpani*. For some reason, he called a few disciples *tumi*—namely Param ā nanda Prabhu, Vinoda Bihārī Dāsa Brahmacārī, Narahari Dāsa Brahmacārī, Vaiṣṇava Dāsa Bābājī, and some others. And, it is true that Vinoda Bihārī Prabhu and Narahari Prabhu were the very life of the Māyāpura ashram. They deservedly received unlimited affection from Śrīla Prabhupāda as the devotees' hearts would be filled with joy at their sweet, affectionate behavior towards them. I don't know whether I ever encountered such unprepossessing, sincerely affectionate treatment from anyone in my entire life. If anyone ever paid prostrated obeisances to Śrīla Prabhupāda, he would pay his obeisances in return and say, *dāso'smi*—"I am a servant."

My worshipable Śrīla Prabhupāda had said that he was going to give me *sannyāsa* at the time of the opening of the Tridaṇḍī Gauḍīya Maṭha in Bhuvaneshwar (July 3, 1933). However, before that could happen, Prabhupāda displayed one of his divine pastimes by saying, "You know, Praṇavānanda is always calling for his mother, saying 'Ma! Ma!" [editor's note: Śrīla Prabhupāda often joked with Praṇavānanda Prabhu with great love and affection]. So, it was my misfortune not to be able to take *sannyāsa* directly from Śrīla Prabhupāda himself. Even so, his mercy is unlimited and I was blessed to receive the *sannyāsa-mantra* directly from his holy lips in a dream. I immediately wrote it down in my diary and later on, after Śrīla Prabhupāda's disappearance, I had the good fortune to take *sannyāsa* from my junior godbrother Śrīmad Bhakti Gaurava Vaikhānasa Mahārāja in

Śrī Śrī Māyāpura-candro Vijayatetamām

Śrī Śrī Navadvīpa-dhāma-Pracāriṇī-sabhāyāḥ "Śrī Śrī Gaurāśīrvāda-patram"

This excerpt from the Gauḍīya (Volume 4, Issue 28, 6 March 1926) outlines the Gaurāśīrvāda Certificate that was awarded to Pramoda Bhuṣaṇa by Śrīla Bhaktisiddhānta Sarasvatī Ṭhakura Prabhupāda.

"vaiṣṇavaitihya-vāde ca pratna-tattva-gaveṣaṇe |
vaiṣṇava-bruva-duṣṭānāṁ bhrānta-mata-nirāsane ||

[For his research in Vaiṣṇava history, philosophy, and ancient truths and for his refutation of the misguided doctrines propounded by wicked so-called Vaiṣṇavas…]

paramo bhagavad-bhaktaḥ śrīmān pramoda-bhūṣaṇaḥ |
cakravarti-samākhyo'sau pāṇḍityaṁ sama-darśayat ||

[...unto the supreme devotee of Bhagavān, Śrīmān Pramoda Bhuṣaṇa, who aptly carries the title Cakravarti, owing to his scholarship and equanimous vision…]

pradadāti mudā tasmai dhāma-pracāriṇī sabhā |
pratna-vidyālaṅkāreti sad-upādhiṁ sadātmane ||

[...the Śrī Dhāma Pracāriṇī Sabhā is delighted to bestow upon this noble soul the fitting title of "Pratna-Vidyālaṅkara"...]

śāke samudra-vedebha-niśākaramite śubhe |
phālguna-pūrṇimāyāṁ hi śrī gaura-janma-vāsare ||

[...in the auspicious Śāka year of 1332, on the Phālguna full moon day, the day of Śrī Gaura's birth…]

gaṅgā-pūrva-taṭa-śrī navadvīpa-sthale pare |
śrī māyāpura-dhāma-stha-puṇya-yogapīṭhottame ||"

[...on the eastern bank of the Ganges, in Śrī Navadvīpa, in Śrī Māyāpura Dhāma, at the sacred, exalted site of Yogapīṭha.]

(Svāḥ) ["Signed"] Śrī Bhaktisiddhānta Sarasvatī
Kāryādhyakṣa ["Secretary"]
(Svāḥ) Bhakti Vijñāna Āśrama
Sabhāpati ["Chairman"]

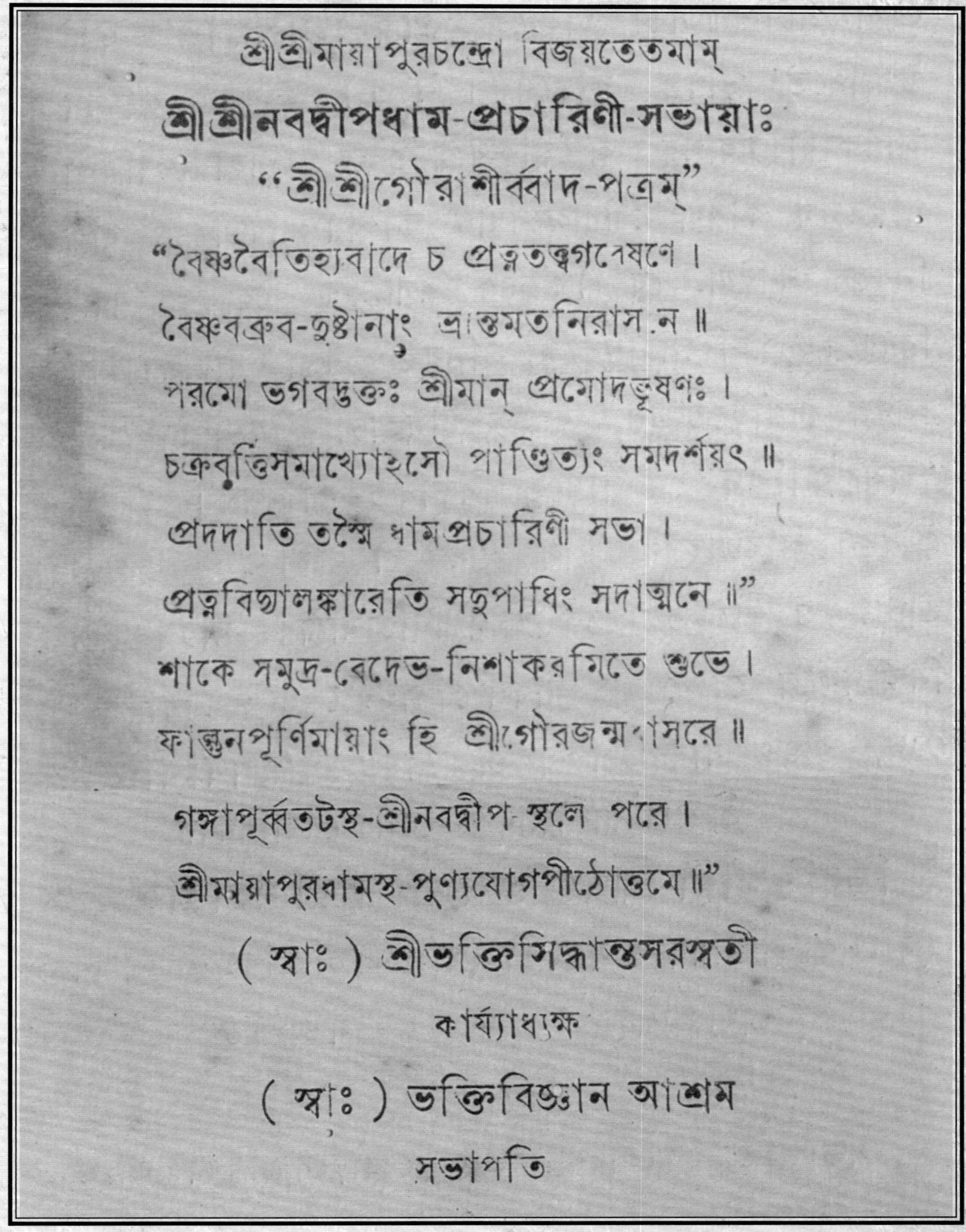

শ্রীশ্রীমায়াপুরচন্দ্রো বিজয়তেতমাম্

শ্রীশ্রীনবদ্বীপধাম-প্রচারিণী-সভায়াঃ

"শ্রীশ্রীগৌরাশীর্ব্বাদ-পত্রম্"

"বৈষ্ণবৈতিহ্যবাদে চ প্রত্নতত্ত্বগবেষণে ।
বৈষ্ণবব্রুব-দুষ্টানাং ভ্রান্তমতনিরাসনে ॥
পরমো ভগবদ্ভক্তঃ শ্রীমান্ প্রমোদভূষণঃ ।
চক্রবর্ত্তিসমাখ্যোঽসৌ পাণ্ডিত্যং সমদর্শয়ৎ ॥
প্রদদাতি তস্মৈ ধামপ্রচারিণী সভা ।
প্রত্নবিদ্যালঙ্কারেতি সদুপাধিং সদাত্মনে ॥"
শাকে সমুদ্র-বেদেভ-নিশাকরমিতে শুভে ।
ফাল্গুনপূর্ণিমায়াং হি শ্রীগৌরজন্মবাসরে ॥
গঙ্গাপূর্ব্বতটস্থ-শ্রীনবদ্বীপ-স্থলে পরে ।
শ্রীমায়াপুরধামস্থ-পুণ্যযোগপীঠোত্তমে ॥"

(স্বাঃ) শ্রীভক্তিসিদ্ধান্তসরস্বতী
কার্য্যাধ্যক্ষ

(স্বাঃ) ভক্তিবিজ্ঞান আশ্রম
সভাপতি

Gaur Ashirvad Certificate (Courtesy Bhaktivedanta Research Center) front of the Gaura-Gadādhara deities established by Mahāprabhu's associate Dvija Vāṇīnātha at Campāhāṭi in Rudradvīpa, i.e., the Gaura Gadādhara Gauḍīya Maṭha. The most revered Vaikhānasa Mahārāja and another godbrother, Ananda-līlāmaya-vigraha Dāsa, put a great deal of effort into the ceremony, and on March 3, 1947, which was the Māghī Pūrṇimā, I was given the name Śrīmad Bhakti Pramode Purī. Satīśa Prabhu also helped by cutting the bamboo and making my *daṇḍa*. Later on, at his special request, I gave him the *bābājī* dress in Śrīla Prabhupāda's name. His name is now Nayanānanda Dāsa Bābājī Mahārāja.

There is one incident which I will never forget. A few days prior to his disappearance, Śrīla Prabhupāda was sitting alone in his easy chair and I took the opportunity to place both of his feet on my chest and make some heartfelt prayers to him. Śrīla Prabhupāda mercifully looked at me with moist eyes and blessed me. When my most worshipable spiritual master returned from Purī, he displayed a pastime of being gravely ill. He took to his bed, but even in that condition he gave us all instructions in a feeble voice.

In those days I always carried paper and pen with me wherever I went. I was just about to write down what Śrīla Prabhupāda said when Sundarānanda Prabhu came in, and so I handed the pen and paper to him because he could write more quickly. So it was he who noted everything that Prabhupāda said. Afterwards, he showed these notes to Śrīla Prabhupāda, who approved them. Other than that which he said about Kṛṣṇa, much of what Śrīla Prabhupāda had said has been somewhat twisted and transformed. These last words have been printed elsewhere.

Thanks to Kuñja Dā, several *brahmacārīs*, of whom I was one, took turns serving Śrīla Prabhupāda in his last days. On December 31, 1936, my turn happened to end a few moments before Śrīla Prabhupāda left this world. I was handing the fan and oxygen funnel to Kṛṣṇānanda Brahmacārī when Prabhupāda called out, "Who is there?" I answered, "Prabhu, it is I, Pranāvānanda." My lord Śrīla Prabhupāda said in a very weak voice, "Oh, oh, Praṇavānanda Prabhu." I immediately asked him, "Prabhu, how are you feeling?" Then my lord and master said feebly, "And... and... Kṛṣṇa... Kṛṣṇa..." I handed over the fan and oxygen funnel to Kṛṣṇānanda Prabhu and went and sat down by the door. I was thinking, "What will happen to us all after Śrīla Prabhupāda leaves?" At that very instant, Kṛṣṇānanda Prabhu came to me and said, "Praṇava, come quickly. It's over!" The sound of crying and lamentation spread out in every direction; it was a fearful sound that permeated the ether. It seemed as if the world was covered with darkness.

The most amazing thing was that every clock in the *maṭha* stopped at this exact moment. It is beyond comprehension. It was as though the clocks were telling us that he had gone to a place beyond time, where the ravages of time could do no damage.

My lord and master is the spiritual master of the entire world. He is capable of delivering the unlimited universes. Therefore I respectfully say to all of you, as his initiated children, that I am not your guru. Only Śrīla Prabhupāda is your spiritual master and protector. I am one insignificant servant of his servant's servant. I am nothing but their slave and assistant. Only the Jagad Guru Śrīla Prabhupāda can maintain and deliver you. Therefore everyone that Bodhāyana Mahārāja requests me to accept, whether they are white or black, of high or low social status, rich or poor, I offer up to the feet of my own master, Śrīla Prabhupāda. Whenever I give initiation to anyone, I always tell them to closely follow the disciplic succession, the *Bhāgavata-paramparā.*

I would like to say a few more words about following in the *Bhāgavata-paramparā* as taught by Śrīla Prabhupāda. Śrīla Vedavyāsa, the incarnation of the Supreme Lord's potencies, came to his Śamyaprāsa ashram on the banks of the Sarasvatī River and began to think deeply.

durbhagāṁś ca janān vīkṣya munir divyena cakṣuṣā
sarva-varṇāśramāṇāṁ yad dadhyau hitam amogha-dṛk

"Through his transcendental powers, the great sage, who was equipped with unfailing vision, perceived the unfortunate condition of the people and began to contemplate how to achieve the welfare of people in all statuses and orders of life." (*Śrīmad-Bhāgavatam* 1.4.31)

Vyāsa was especially disturbed by their misfortune. He could understand that by the influence of time, all the religious practices and duties would be destroyed. As a result, he very cleverly wrote down the Vedas, the Upaniṣads, the *Brahma-sūtra*, the *Mahābhārata* and the other Purāṇas, separating them according to appropriate classifications. Even so, he was not entirely satisfied and he soon realized the reason for it:

kiṁ vā bhāgavatā dharmā na prāyeṇa nirūpitāḥ
priyāḥ paramahaṁsānāṁ ta eva hy acyuta-priyāḥ

"Perhaps the reason for my dissatisfaction is that I did not sufficiently describe the religion of devotion to the Supreme Lord, which is dear to both the perfect beings and the infallible Lord." (*Śrīmad-Bhāgavatam* 1.4.31)

Vyasa continued to wonder why he had been unable to find complete peace of mind when at that exact moment, Nārada Ṛṣi happened upon the scene. He began to instruct Vedavyāsa, telling him to compose the *Śrīmad-Bhāgavatam,* the ripened fruit of the tree of Vedic knowledge, in which the spotless religion devoid of all false goals would be embodied. It is non-different from the Lord Himself and is the only bestower of pure auspiciousness. He taught him the four verses known as the *Catuḥślokī-bhāgavata,* which encapsulate its essence. He brought about the dawning of the sun-like *Bhāgavatam,* which is full of the nectarean pastimes of Lord Śrī Kṛṣṇa and the destroyer of all sinful propensities. This is the very same religion of devotion to the Supreme Lord, the *Bhāgavata-dharma* which the Supreme Lord Himself had instructed to the four-faced Brahmā, which was later spoken by Śukadeva Gosvāmī, and which in the course of time was spread throughout the world in four streams, the Nimbārka, Rāmānuja, Viṣṇusvāmī and Madhva *sampradāyas*—the original founders of which are respectively the Four Kumāras, Lakṣmī, Rudra, and Brahmā. The Supreme Lord Śrī Caitanya Mahāprabhu himself accepted the authenticity of these four streams of the *Bhāgavata-dharma* and we, who are His spiritual heirs, identify ourselves as members of the Brahma-Mādhva-Gauḍīya line. According to the Purāṇas, any mantra which is not received in disciplic succession has no value—*sampradāya-vihīnā ye mantrās te niṣphalā matāḥ*.

From the scriptures we find that the Supreme Lord is not dependent on others. In the *Caitanya-caritāmṛta* it is written,

prabhu kahe—īśvara haya parama svatantra
īśvarera kṛpā nahe veda-paratantra

"Śrī Caitanya Mahāprabhu said, 'God is the supreme independent. Therefore the mercy of the Supreme Personality of Godhead is not subject to any Vedic rules or regulations.'" (*Caitanya-caritāmṛta* 2.10.137)

If Śaṅkara can be ordered by the Supreme Lord to start a new *sampradāya* in order to teach an unholy scripture for the deception of those with a demonic mentality, then some other powerful devotees may also make some minor or superficial changes to external features of the religion at the Lord's behest. For example, Śyāmānanda Prabhu implemented a unique *tilaka* marking on the order of Śrīmatī Rādhārāṇī Herself, but there is no question that he slighted his guru Hṛdaya Caitanya, who never wore this specific marking. None of Mahāprabhu's associates, nor any of His *nitya-siddha* companions whom He sends into this world, are conditioned souls, dependent on matter. So, if out of foolishness or ignorance anyone ascribes flaws to the teachings which come down in disciplic succession from them, their only profit will be an untimely death.

kālena naṣṭā pralaye vāṇīyaṁ veda-saṁjñitā
mayādau brahmaṇe proktā yasyāṁ dharmo mad-ātmakaḥ
tena proktā sva-putrāya manave ...
yābhir bhūtāni bhidyante bhūtānāṁ patayas tathā
evaṁ prakṛti-vaicitryād bhidyante martayo nèṇām
pāramparyeṇa keṣāṁcit pāṣaṇḍa-matayo'pare

> "This teaching known as the Vedic knowledge was lost in the course of time during the universal dissolution. Then at the time of creation, I instructed the same teachings of the *Bhāgavata* religion to Brahmā. He then transmitted them to his son Manu, etc.... All living beings are distinguished from each other by the material qualities of goodness, passion, and ignorance, as are their forefathers. In the same way, human beings have come to differ according to their nature and their opinions. Some of them have even come to possess atheistic views as a result of the improper transmission of knowledge." (*Śrīmad-Bhāgavatam* 11.14.3-7)

This teaching was given by Śrī Kṛṣṇa to Uddhava: "I first taught this knowledge to Brahmā. It contains the religion of all living beings—the *jaiva-dharma*, which in essence is pure devotion to My original form. These Vedic teachings are eternal. Though apparently lost at the time of the annihilation of the universe, I instruct Brahmā in this knowledge whenever creation takes place again. He in turn teaches it to his son Manu, who instructs the gods, the sages and seers, and human beings, so that everyone has the opportunity to learn about this religion of devotion to the Supreme Lord. All creatures and their forefathers have different natures according to the three modes of goodness, passion and ignorance, and according to the mixtures of these material qualities they are each different from the other. According to their different natures, they have widely differing perceptions of the world and so explain it differently. O Uddhava! Those who have heard this message explained in direct disciplic succession from Brahmā accept the purest doctrine. All the rest get involved in a wide variety

of differences of opinion until finally they become subservient to some atheistic doctrine."

From this account, it is clear that the Brāhma-sampradāya exists since the beginning of creation. This disciplic succession has preserved the pure, eternal message of devotion to the Supreme Lord, also known as the Vedic knowledge or *Bhāgavata-dharma*. Those who accept Śrī Caitanya Mahāprabhu's religious school but secretly reject the perfect channel of its *guru-paramparā* are Kali's emissaries—what else can we conclude?

Jīva Gosvāmī first establishes that *āpta-vākya*, or authoritative testimony, is the best source of knowledge. Then, after showing that other Purāṇas do not exclusively teach the supreme religion, he establishes beyond argument that the *Śrīmad-Bhāgavatam* is the best source of such authoritative testimony. Jīva Gosvāmī also names the scriptures quoted by Madhvācārya, who is the *tattva-guru* of Vijayadhvaja, Brahmaṇya Tīrtha, Vyāsa Tīrtha, and other *ācāryas* of the *sampradāya* which descends from Brahmā, Nārada, Vyāsa, and Śukadeva as authoritative on the same basis as the *Śrīmad-Bhāgavatam*.

From the statements in all these scriptures, it is clear that the Brāhma-sampradāya is the disciplic succession accepted by the servants of Lord Śrī Caitanya Mahāprabhu. Kavi Karṇapūra Gosvāmī has strengthened this claim in his *Gaura-gaṇoddeśa-dīpikā,* where he has recited the entire disciplic line. The same line has been confirmed by the commentator on the *Vedānta-sūtra,* Baladeva Vidyābhūṣaṇa. Anyone who doubts this disciplic connection is the worst enemy of Śrī Kṛṣṇa Caitanya's followers. Can there be any doubt of this?

It is clearly seen in the *Śrīmad-Bhāgavatam* that Śukrācārya's disciple Bali Mahārāja did not attain his status as a *mahājana,* or great spiritual leader, from his guru, but from the king of the Lord's devotees, Prahlāda Mahārāja. So the *Bhāgavata's* conclusion is that the *Bhāgavata-paramparā* is the true bestower of the supreme good because it is free of all deception—it is completely free of any cheating proclivity. The story of Gokarṇa is told in the *Padma Purāṇa's Bhāgavata-māhātmya.* Gokarṇa was not Dhundhukari's mantra disciple but he took instruction in the *Bhāgavata* from him. It was as a result of these teachings that he achieved *svarūpa-siddhi,* or the perfection of achieving his eternal identity. Pariksit also considered Śukadeva Gosvāmī to be his guru in the *Bhāgavata-dharma,* even though he was not his *mantra-śiṣya.* It was the teaching he received from Śukadeva which resulted in his achieving spiritual perfection. So it is advised to abandon the superficial argumentative mentality and to examine the matter with a little finer or subtler vision. If one does so, he will understand that the *Bhāgavata-paramparā* is the most important vehicle of divine transmission, for it is through this succession that the teachings of the *Bhāgavata-dharma,* given by the Supreme Lord Himself, become alive and vibrant in our hearts. So, may the storm caused by unorthodox doctrines be pacified and the disciplic succession taught by Śrīla Prabhupāda, the *Bhāgavata-paramparā,* be ever victorious.

Now there is one other thing that needs to be said about another area of controversy. I think that something briefly needs to be said about some aspects of the teachings of Rūpa Gosvāmī. Śrīnātha Cakravartī writes, summarizing Mahāprabhu's teaching in one verse:

ārādhyo bhagavān vrajeśa-tanayas
tad-dhāma vṛndavanaṁ
ramya kācid upāsanā vraja-vadhū-vargeṇa yā kalpitā
śrīmad-bhāgavatam pramāṇam amalaṁ
premān pum-artho mahān
śrī-caitanya-mahāprabhor matam idaṁ
tatrādaro naḥ paraḥ

"The ultimate object of worship is the son of the king of Vraja, Kṛṣṇa, and Vṛndāvana is His abode, as worshipable as He. The supreme form of worship is that which was devised by the wives of Vraja. The best scriptural evidence of this is to be found in the spotless Purāṇa known as the *Bhāgavatam*. The ultimate goal of human life is love for the Supreme Lord. These five things constitute Śrī Caitanya Mahāprabhu's teaching, for which I have the highest respect. I do not have the same regard for other doctrines."

Śrī Kṛṣṇa of Vṛndāvana is the eternal object of our worship. The wives of the cowherds in Vraja worshiped Kṛṣṇa on the *rāga-mārga,* or path of passionate devotion. This particular path has been called *ramaṇīya* in this verse, which means "particularly attractive," or the best. But this kind of worship depends on one's qualifications, for it is said in the *Caitanya-caritāmṛta*:

iṣṭe svārasikī rāgaḥ paramāviṣṭatā bhavet
tanmayī yā bhaved bhaktiḥ sātra rāgātmikoditā

"The natural impulse to serve the object of worship in extreme absorption is called *rāga,* or passion. If one's devotion to Kṛṣṇa is essentially passionate according to this definition, it is called *rāgātmikā bhakti.*" (*Caitanya-caritāmṛta* 2.22.150, quoting BRS i.2.272)

This verse is broken down as follows by Śrīla Prabhupāda in his *Anubhāṣya*: *Rāga* is defined here as being *paramāviṣṭatā* or "the impulse to engage in service with complete absorption." That is further modified by the adjective *svārasikī,* indicating "according to one's own particular spiritual taste" and further, "with a naturally occurring, deep enthusiasm or thirst" for the *iṣṭa,* or "desired object." If this devotion is *tan-mayī,* referring back to the word *rāga,* or "essentially of the nature of passion." then *atra,* "here in the scriptures dealing

with pure devotional service," it goes by the name of *rāgātmikā bhakti*.

The kind of natural passionate devotion described in this verse is found in the eternal associates of Kṛṣṇa in Vraja. Devotion which follows in the footsteps of this passionate mood is called *rāga-svarūpā bhakti*, or the devotion which identifies with the passionate mood of Vraja. The worship of Kṛṣṇa according to *rāga-svarūpā bhakti* is said to be superior to all other modes of worship. When the Lord is worshiped according to the *vidhi-mārga*, then one's affection towards Him becomes inhibited, and such an enfeebled love is not pleasing to Him.

It is only through the Holy Name that one develops the qualifications necessary to enter into the stream of devotion in the spirit taught by Rūpa Gosvāmī. Śrīla Bhaktivinoda Ṭhākura has stated this most wonderfully in the song *Kṛṣṇa-nām dhare kata bal?*—"How much power is contained in Kṛṣṇa's name?"

īṣat vikaśi punaḥ dekhāya nija rūpa guṇa
citta hari laya kṛṣṇa pāśa
pūrṇa vikaśita hañā vraje more jāya lañā
dekhāya more svarūpa-vilās

"When the Name is even slightly revealed, it shows me my own spiritual form and characteristics. It steals my mind and takes it to Kṛṣṇa's side. When the Name is fully revealed, it takes me directly to Vraja, where it shows me my personal role in the eternal pastimes."

The Lord has placed all His potencies into His own names. Thus, by taking exclusive shelter of this all-powerful Holy Name, we can obtain the good fortune to leave the *vidhi-mārga* behind and enter into the path of passionate devotion. Śrīman Mahāprabhu told us that in this matter the *Śrīmad-Bhāgavatam* is the best source of evidence, as the supreme form of spiritual sound, or *śabda-brahma*. According to the supreme source of evidence, the *Śrīmad-Bhāgavatam*, simply by performing the activities of hearing and chanting, *śravaṇa-kīrtana*, the good fortune arises by which we enter into the supreme goal, the *paramārtha*. The *Bhāgavatam* is the Supreme Lord's body, as is stated in the following verse from the *Padma Purāṇa*. In other words, the *Bhāgavatam* is the embodiment of the transcendental Lord.

pādau yadīyau prathama-dvitīyau
tṛtīya-tūryau kathitau yad-ūrū
nābhis tathā pañcama eva ṣaṣṭho
bhujāntaraṁ dor-yugalaṁ tathānyau
kaṇṭhas tu rājan navamo yadīyo
mukhāravindaṁ daśamaḥ praphullam
ekādaśo yasya lalāṭa-paṭṭaṁ
śiro'pi tu dvādaśa eva bhāti
tam ādidevaṁ karuṇā-nidhānaṁ
tamāla-varṇaṁ suhitāvatāram
apāra-saṁsāra-samudra-setuṁ
bhajāmahe bhāgavata-svarūpam

"I worship the original Lord, the fountainhead of compassion, whose color is like that of a *tamāla* tree. He incarnates in the form of the *Bhāgavata*, the bridge which spans across the limitless ocean of birth and death, for the benefit of the entire world. The first and second cantos are said to be His feet; the third and fourth, His thighs. The fifth canto is His belly and the sixth His chest. The seventh and eighth cantos are His arms and the ninth his neck. The tenth canto is His ever smiling, blooming lotus face. The eleventh canto is His forehead and the twelfth, the crown of His head."

The equivalent of the Rāsa-sthalī in Mahāprabhu's *līlā* is Śrīvās Āṅgana, which Śrīla Prabhupāda used to call "the site of the sacrifice of the Holy Name." The Supreme Lord Śrī Kṛṣṇa Caitanya there lit the flame of the Holy Name's sacrificial fire; if we can throw ourselves as an offering into the seven flames of that sacrificial fire, we will become qualified to receive the seven benefits of the sacrificial act. These seven results are cited in the verse *ceto-darpaṇa-marjanam*. Once we thus gain those qualifications, we will be able to enter into the site of the *rāsa* dance in Vṛndāvana and participate in the *līlā* which is going on there. In other words, without the mercy of the Nāma-Brahma, we will never gain the qualifications necessary to enter into the Rāsa-sthali in Vṛndāvana.

The proof of this is once again found in the *Bhāgavatam*:

kṛṣṇa-varṇaṁ tviṣākṛṣṇaṁ sāṅgopāṅgāstra-pārṣadam
yajñaiḥ saṅkīrtana-prāyair yajanti hi su-medhasaḥ

"The most intelligent worship Lord Kṛṣṇa, whose color will not be black, who is accompanied by His associates, primarily through the performance of the *saṅkīrtana-yajña*." (*Śrīmad-Bhāgavatam* 11.5.32)

So, within the book *Bhāgavatam*, which is the spotless testimony and the sound incarnation of the Lord, we find this verse which tells us that in the Age of Kali, Kṛṣṇa will always be uttering the two syllables Kṛṣ-ṇa (*kṛṣṇa-varṇaṁ*); His bodily hue (*tviṣā*) will not be black (*akṛṣṇaṁ*), in other words, golden. He will be surrounded by His *sāṅga*, *upāṅga*, *astra*, and *pārṣada*—the other members of the Pañca Tattva. The intelligent persons in this age of darkness will worship Him through the performance of the sacrifice of the Holy Name.

This verse completely describes the incarnation of Śrī Caitanya Mahāprabhu and the sacrifice of the Holy Name which he instituted. Thus, if one abandons useless arguments and simply takes up this path, he will certainly attain all good fortune. I have full faith in all the devotees. I wanted to say a great deal more about the *Bhāgavatam*, but I am obliged to stop here.

I pay my prostrated obeisances to all of Śrīla Prabhupāda's followers whether still living or passed away—the founders and *ācāryas* of all the different monasteries and temples as well as his other servants. May they continue to give their blessings and forgive the shortcomings of an old and sickly man like myself. I am in so many ways indebted to my godbrother Śrīla Bhakti Dayita Mādhava Gosvāmī Mahārāja and his disciples, headed by Śrīla Bhakti Ballabha Tīrtha Mahārāja. I stayed in his *maṭha* for 33 years, during which time I was fortunate to have the opportunity to visit nearly all of India's holy sites. I once again give greetings to and pay my prostrated obeisances to all my godbrothers, whether living or gone to join the eternal pastimes, and to my disciples and servants. May they bless me with their causeless mercy.

Today, at the twilight of my life, I simply remember Śrīla Bhaktivinoda Ṭhākura's morning prayer, *Udila aruṇa pūraba bhāge*:

ebe nā bhajile yaśodā sūta
carame paṛibe lāje

"If you do not now worship the son of Yaśodā, you will feel shame at the time of death."

It is true that I have not been able to do any *hari-bhajana* in this life, and so today I am very much ashamed. I humbly beg to all the devotees of Śrī Caitanya Mahāprabhu that they grant me the following boon: that in the little time I have left, I may worship the Lord and behave courteously to all.

The servant of the servant of
Vārṣabhānavī-dayita Dāsa,
Śrī Bhakti Pramode Purī

A Century of Devotion

An excerpt from the biography of Śrīla Bhakti Pramode Purī Gosvāmī Mahārāja

A Field Trip to Māyāpura

Having consoled Mā Rāma-raṅginī Devī and other family members, Śrī Pramode Bhushan returned to Shason village. From time to time, Pramode Bhushan, along with his schoolmate Śrī Paritosh Kumar, participated in a religious assembly referred to as Shastra Dharma Prachar Sabha, organized by the followers of Śrī Rāmānuja in Kolkata. Paritosh Kumar was related to the organizer of the Shastra Dharma Prachar Sabha. Pramode Bhushan, on the other hand, had gleaned the essence of pure devotional service from the writings of Śrīla Bhaktivinoda Ṭhākura and so found himself losing interest in the Shastra Dharma Prachar Sabha, wondering, "Where will I find the teachings of pure devotion? Who will educate me in the teachings of *bhakti-dharma*?"

In 1915, Pramode Bhushan proposed to his classmates that they go on a field trip. Naturally, a debate took place about where they should go. Considering him a genius, his classmates agreed to go wherever Pramode Bhushan chose. Pramode Bhushan explained the purpose and successful outcome of travel or pilgrimage, dismissing the idea of going to some modern park, as there is only temporary mundane thrills to be had in such places. "Anyone can be given the gross objects of this world," he explained, "but to obtain that great treasure that trivializes all tempting gross material objects, to attain that which inspires learned persons to give up the cultivation of mundane knowledge and even ignore the affection of their parents and loved ones, should be everyone's aim.

"The great devotee Prahlāda is the prime example of this. He gave up his attachment for gross royal opulence and abandoned the teachers who were appointed by his demoniac father Hiraṇyakaśipu, who was envious of Lord Hari. At the same time, he imparted to us valuable instructions by ignoring his father's affection.

"On the other hand, the devotee Dhruva Mahārāja set the ideal example of how, upon attaining the priceless spiritual wealth, one can easily give up gross and tempting objects of this material world, understanding them to be most insignificant. Initially, in order to occupy the throne of his father, Dhruva Mahārāja engaged in severe penance within the forest with the desire to receive a boon from the Supreme Lord. Being pleased by his austerity, the Supreme Lord appeared before him. Dhruva Mahārāja then realized that the achievement of his father's throne is completely insignificant in comparison to the achievement of the lotus feet of the Supreme Lord. Based on this realization, he desired the favor of the Supreme Lord rather than his father's royal throne."

In this way, he put forward various arguments to establish the genuine delight to be found in a rural and spiritual environment. Drawing on the inspiration he received from Bhaktiratna Ṭhākura, Pramode Bhushan begun to extol the glories of Śrīdhāma Māyāpura. He opened up to his classmates about the glories of Śrīdhāma Māyāpura as the birthplace of Śrī Caitanya Mahāprabhu, the deliverer of the fallen souls of Kali-yuga. Not only that, but he shed light on the magnanimous nature of Mahāprabhu as described by Śrīla Bhaktivinoda Ṭhākura, adding, "There is no place equal to Māyāpura within the three worlds."

He continued to explain the glories of Śrīdhāma Navadvīpa and Māyāpura: "The Supreme Lord, Śrī Caitanya Mahāprabhu, appeared in 1486 in Śrīdhāma Māyāpura, which is very near our school. That holy place had been lost to time. However, the abode of the Supreme Lord is actually eternal. In order to prove this fact, Śrīla Bhaktivinoda Ṭhākura, who revived the lineage of pure devotion, rediscovered the Supreme Lord's lost birthplace. If we visit that place and relish the Supreme Lord's magnanimous pastimes, then we will certainly have a good time."

Pramode Bhushan's classmates were excited to go to Māyāpura. The morning of their excursion, they took a train together, under Pramode Bhushan's leadership, and arrived at Dhubulia station, where they disembarked and continued on to Māyāpura by bullock cart. Back then, there was only a dirt road going to Māyāpura, and the area was filled with dense forests, so not many people lived nearby. Pramode Bhushan's classmates were a little disappointed once they realized this, but they did not say anything. Still, they were surprised by their friend's choice, wondering why he would bring them to this jungle region when there are so many more convenient places to go on a tour. And the fact was, Pramode Bhushan himself did not know much about this place either, although it was he who had led them there.

With Pramode Bhushan in the lead, the group of friends arrived in Māyāpura at noon. Suddenly, there before their eyes was the birthplace of Śrīman Mahāprabhu, just as described in Śrīla Bhaktivinoda Ṭhākura's books. As soon as Pramode Bhushan saw Mahāprabhu's appearance place, his heart filled with infinite bliss. A stream of tears began to flow from his eyes. His voice choked with emotion, he turned to his friends and said, "This place is supremely sanctified and the most exalted holy place in the whole world. We are indeed all glorious and supremely fortunate for having been able to see and touch this transcendental place today."

Then Pramode Bhushan, followed by his friends, offered their devotion-filled obeisance to Lord Gaurahari and His associates, falling flat on the ground. Then they decided to go across the Ganges to its western bank and visit different places in Navadvīpa. They crossed the Ganges and began to wander about nearby Ranirchara.

The Departure of Śrīla Gaura-kiśora dāsa Bābājī Mahārāja

They arrived at a spot in Ranirchara where they saw several *bābājīs* quarreling among themselves over the body of another *bābājī*—arguing about whether the body should be placed into *samādhi* or dragged through the streets of Navadvīpa and Māyāpura. As the quarrel peaked, a few *bābājīs* angrily left. A few moments later, Pramode Bhushan saw an effulgent personality dressed in white. When this effulgent personality entered the scene, along with some police inspectors, the whole atmosphere quieted down. He spoke in a grave and steady tone: "I am the only disciple of my spiritual master. The way you are all quarreling over his transcendental body proves that none of you want to serve him. Instead, you aim to do some business with this body in order to fulfill your own self-interest. I am extremely sad to see this behavior. I will take this body away and place my *gurudeva* in *samādhi* in a proper place. I will not allow any of you to even *touch* this transcendental body."

This was the body of the exalted Śrīla Gaura-kiśora dāsa Bābājī Mahārāja, the crest-jewel of the entire Vaiṣṇava community (*paramahaṁsa kula-cūḍāmaṇi*). Śrī Pramode Bhushan would later learn that Śrīla Bhaktivinoda Ṭhākura had greatly respected Śrīla Gaura-kiśora dāsa Bābājī Mahārāja and so had instructed his son Śrī Bimalā Prasāda to take Vaiṣṇava initiation from him. When Bimalā Prasāda first approached Śrīla Gaura-kiśora dāsa Bābājī Mahārāja for initiation, Śrīla Gaura-kiśora dāsa Bābājī Mahārāja said, "Oh, I need to first ask Nityānanda Prabhu. If He orders me, then I can give you initiation." After some days Bimalā Prasāda returned and again requested Śrīla Gaura-kiśora dāsa Bābājī Mahārāja for initiation, asking him what Nityānanda Prabhu had replied. Śrīla Gaura-kiśora dāsa Bābājī Mahārāja said, "Oh, I forgot to ask Nityānanda Prabhu."

Bimalā Prasāda approached Śrīla Gaura-kiśora dāsa Bābājī Mahārāja several times, but each time, Śrīla Gaura-kiśora dāsa Bābājī Mahārāja told him either he had forgotten to ask Nityānanda Prabhu or that he did not give anyone initiation. In this way, Śrīla Gaura-kiśora dāsa Bābājī Mahārāja was testing Bimalā Prasāda's tolerance. Finally, one day, Bimalā Prasāda again came and begged for initiation and Śrīla Gaura-kiśora dāsa Bābājī Mahāraja replied, "Lord Nityānanda has given me permission to fulfill your desire." This is how Bimalā Prasāda received initiation from Śrīla Gaura-kiśora dāsa Bābājī Mahārāja.

Śrīla Gaura-kiśora dāsa Bābājī Mahārāja used to listen to *Śrīmad-Bhāgavatam* discourses at Śrīla Bhaktivinoda Ṭhākura's Svānanda Sukhada Kuñja, in Godrumadvīpa, Nadiyā. Śrīla Bhaktivinoda Ṭhākura's *puṣpa-samādhi*—the remnants of his divine body after his cremation—is established where he used to sit to give discourses. Beside this is a small temple commemorating the place where Śrīla Gaura-kiśora dāsa Bābājī Mahārāja sat to listen to these *Śrīmad-Bhāgavatam* discourses and chant the holy names.

As we know, humility is the ornament of a Vaiṣṇava. Before his departure from this world, the humble Śrīla Gaura-kiśora dāsa Bābājī Mahāraja had stated that he wanted his body to be tied to a bullock cart with ropes and dragged through the streets of Navadvīpa. His body, he said, should be pulled until it broke into the dust and become part of the holy dust of the *Dhāma*. Bimalā Prasāda was the only disciple Śrīla Gaura-kiśora dāsa Bābājī Mahārāja ever initiated. Although his spiritual master had expressed such sentiments before leaving his body, Bimalā Prasāda would not allow his spiritual master's body to be dragged in such a way by people dressed as devotees but whose actual motive was to make money from both the spectacle and the remains of Śrīla Gaura-kiśora dāsa Bābājī Mahārāja's body.[1]

When Pramode Bhushan saw Bimalā Prasāda, he thought, "I heard from Bhaktiratna Ṭhākura about a great Vaiṣṇava named Bimalā Prasāda. Maybe this is the same person. When I am ready to accept a spiritual master, I wish for him to be my guru."

Pramode Bhushan and his classmates watched as the effulgent Bimalā Prasāda spoke with determination: "Only one who has not had any unlawful connection with a woman in the last year may touch this transcendental body." Nobody stepped forward. Then Bimalā Prasāda again said, "That person who has not indulged in sex in the last six months will be qualified to touch this body." Still no one stepped forward.

Hearing Bimalā Prasāda's challenge, one of the police officer asked, "What if someone has had illicit relations with a woman but still tries to claim the body? How will you know if he is telling the truth?" Bimalā Prasāda replied, "If someone lies, he will immediately receive a reaction for the lie. Wait and see."

Then for a third time Bimalā Prasāda repeated the condition for touching his guru's transcendental body, this time reducing the period of abstinence from the last six months to the last three months and then to one month, one week, three days, and, finally, to the night before. Still, no one came forward to claim the body. The policemen were astonished, and simply gazed at the brightly shining saint. Then, with the policemen's consent, Bimala Prasad lifted his guru's transcendental body and carried it away from the quarreling *bābājīs*. He then proceeded to the place chosen for his guru's *samādhi*, in Ranirchara, Navadvīpa.[2] Pramode Bhushan and his schoolmates witnessed this transcendental pastime, and it left Pramode Bhushan wanting to know the identity of the effulgent personality.

Having completed the *samādhi* arrangements, Bimalā Prasāda returned to Māyāpura, to the present-day location of Śrī Caitanya Maṭha, and resumed chanting the Hare Kṛṣṇa *mahā-mantra* on his prayer beads. It was late in the afternoon. Pramode Bhushan and his friends began heading back to Shason village. They crossed the Ganges and walked along its eastern bank. As they passed Śrī Caitanya Mahāprabhu's birthplace, they came upon an enchanting, peaceful spot. By way of fate and good fortune, Pramode Bhushan and his friends again had *darśana* of that effulgent personality. This time, Pramode Bhushan could not restrain himself. He approached the saint and asked, "May I know your name?"

The saint replied, "Yes, certainly. I am a fallen servant of Bhagavān named Bimalā Prasāda."

Hearing this, Pramode Bhushan felt completely blessed and fell to the ground to offer his obeisance at Bimalā Prasāda's feet. Pramode Bhushan then said, "I have heard so much about you from my neighbor, Śrīla Bhaktiratna Thākura. He gave me many books of Śrīla Bhaktivinoda Ṭhākura to study. That is how I came to know of Śrīdhāma Māyāpura and that is why I have come to have *darśana* of Māyāpura with my school friends. It is my supreme fortune to have obtained your *darśana*. From the moment I saw you, a revolution started in my mind. I first saw you fearlessly defending the body of the departed *bābājī*, who was your *gurudeva*."

Bimalā Prasāda smiled. "Tell me your name," he said. Pramode Bhushan introduced himself and his friends. Bimalā Prasāda then said, "That *bābājī* who departed his body today in Navadvīpa was my most

1 Even my spiritual master, Śrīla Bhakti Pramode Purī Gosvāmī Ṭhākura, expressed that he wanted his body to be put into *samādhi* in the ocean at Purī. He wanted that all the aquatic creatures could eat his body. But his disciples, following Bimalā Prasāda's example, did not do this. Instead, we placed him in a *samādhi* in Māyāpura-Dhāma. Some years before speaking of the ocean at Purī, my spiritual master said he would like to be placed in *samādhi* in Māyāpura-Dhāma because his *gurudeva* and all his godbrothers also had their *samādhis* there. However, toward the last months of his life, and out of his humility, he mentioned placing his body in the ocean so the fish could feed off his body.

2 The Gaṅgā often changes her course over time. Eventually, as the Gaṅgā again changed course, Śrīla Gaura-kiśora dāsa Bābājī Mahārāja's *samādhi* was almost flooded. At that time, Bimalā Prasāda, by then known as Śrīla Prabhupāda Bhaktisiddhānta Sarasvatī Gosvāmī Ṭhākura, moved his guru's *samādhi* to the campus of Śrī Caitanya Maṭha, in Māyāpura.

worshipful spiritual master, Paramahaṁsa-kūla-cuḍāmaṇi Śrīla Gaura-kiśora dāsa Bābājī Mahārāja. His body is transcendental. I pray for the dust of his lotus feet birth after birth. Śrīla Bhaktivinoda Ṭhākura is my instructing spiritual master and guide. It is by his mercy that I obtained my *gurudeva*."

Pramode Bhushan was stunned upon Bimalā Prasāda's grave and sweet words. He realized that this meeting was the mercy of Śrīla Bhaktivinoda Ṭhākura. "You have sent me to a great personality who is very dear to you," he thought. Thus he praised Śrīla Bhaktivinoda Ṭhākura in his mind and repeatedly resolved to accept Śrī Bimalā Prasāda as his spiritual master. That evening Pramode Bhushan and his friends returned to Shason village.

Pramode Bhushan Transformed

Receiving the *darśana* of Śrīla Bimalā Prasāda in Śrīdhāma Māyāpura and witnessing his captivating specialities, his sweet language, his lion-like roaring at miscreants, and his extraordinary personality, Pramode Bhushan kept thinking of that divine personality and his words all the time. Although he had returned to Shason village with his friends, he had left his mind at the lotus feet of that incomparable divine personality, Śrīla Bimalā Prasāda, in Śrī Māyāpura.

Pramode Bhushan's friends and teachers began to notice, much to their astonishment, a marked change in Pramode Bhushan's behavior. It seemed he was pondering something deeply. His teachers thought perhaps he was worried about his upcoming matriculation examination. Pramode Bhushan was the crest-jewel among the students, so the other students could not understand why their friend had suddenly become indifferent after returning from Śrī Māyāpura. They too thought he was anxious about the matriculation exam and still grieving the sudden death of his brother. Even the members of the Śrī Durgadāsa Rāya Chaudhurī family, in whose home Pramode Bhushan lived, noticed his change of heart.

Soon enough, the day to sit the matriculation exam arrived. After the exam, everyone, including Pramode Bhushan's teachers, classmates, neighbors from both Ganganandapur and Shason village, and relatives, awaited the results. To everyone's surprise, Pramode Bhushan scored such wonderful results that the school management awarded him a gold medal. No one in the history of the school had scored so high. His classmates and neighbors then arranged a cultural program, during which they lavishly praised Pramode Bhushan's intelligence and gifted him with various novels written by the literary stalwarts of Bengal.

This marked the end of Pramode Bhushan's school life at Shason village, but instead of being happy to return to Ganganandapur, Pramode Bhushan meditated constantly on going back to Śrīdhāma Māyāpura.

In 1916, at the insistence of neighbors and family friends, Tāriṇī-caraṇa Cakravartī had Pramode Bhushan enrolled in the science division at Bangabasi College, in Kolkata. Seeing Pramode Bhushan's matriculation exam results, the administration and professors at Bangabasi College were proud to have him as their student. They relaxed some of the admission rules for him and made some additional arrangements to accommodate him, so that this genius student would

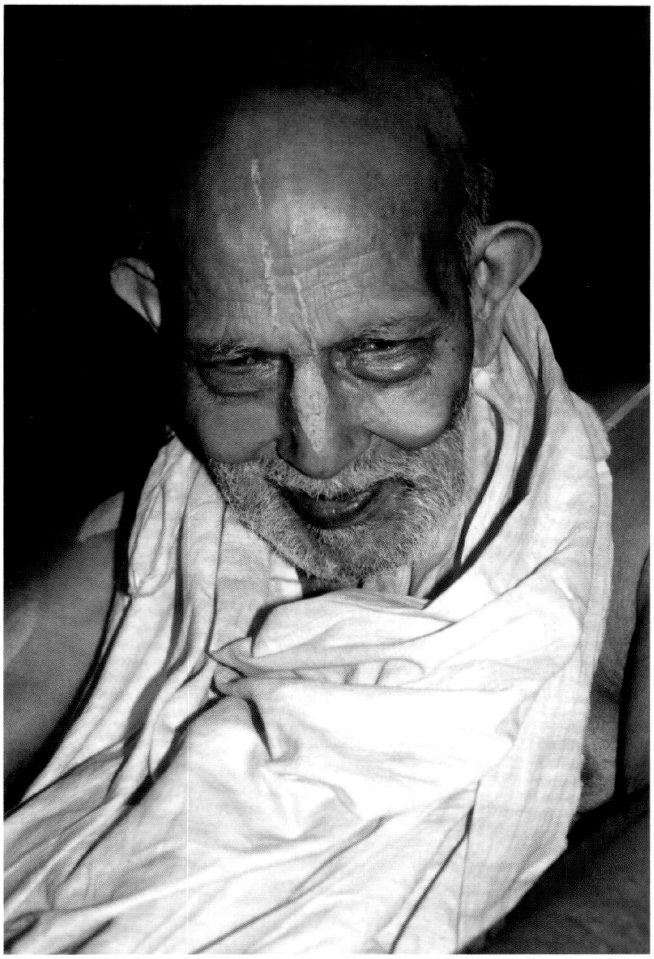

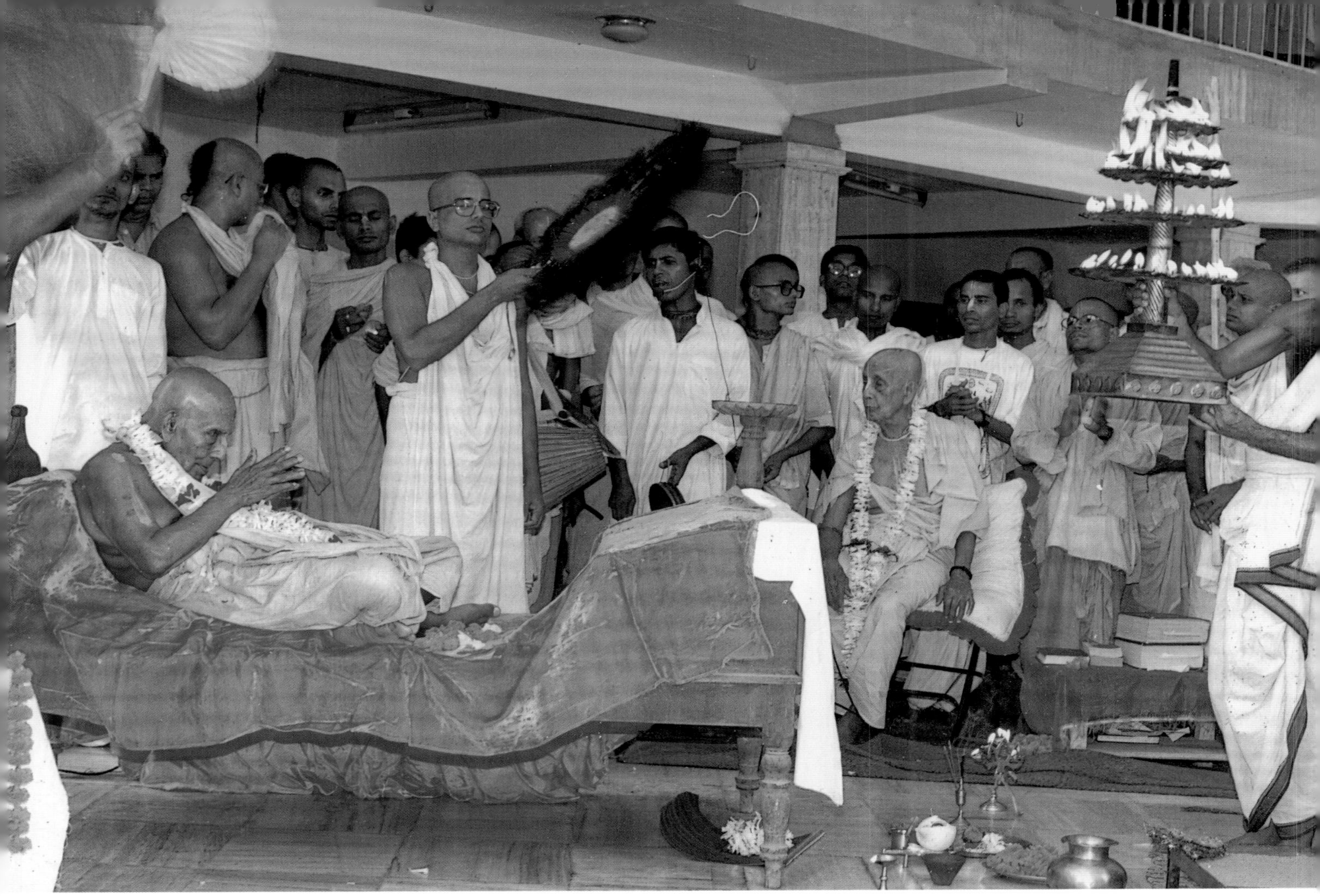

not leave and go to another college, as they were sure he would elevate the reputation of the college.

However, because of his father's financial constraints, Pramode Bhushan could not afford to rent a room in Kolkata. So, to avoid causing his father any strain, Pramode Bhushan continued his studies from the house of Durgadāsa Rāya Chaudhurī in Shason village. The members of the Chaudhurī family would say, "We have been blessed by the presence of such a great personality. Pramode Bhushan tolerates all manner of difficulty in our house to pursue his higher studies." Some of the members of that household now live in the upper-class Salt Lake area of Kolkata.

It was about two kilometers from Shason village to the local train station, then about an hour and a half journey by train to Kolkata's Sealdah station. Pramode Bhushan attended classes every day except Sunday. His professors gave him special treatment, understanding that an eighteen-year-old boy was pursuing his higher education despite so much inconvenience. Despite the long commute, Pramode Bhushan's attendance was perfect. He was a diligent student, yet remained indifferent. Sometimes he discussed spiritual matters. His conduct was completely different from the other students in this regard, and his nature wholly distinctive.

His peers were amazed that he would walk two kilometers to get to the train station, ride an hour and a half on the train, and then walk again, from Sealdah station to Bangabasi College. Clearly, this required extraordinary patience and tolerance on his part. If not for the direct favor of the Supreme Lord, it would have been impossible for such a young person to travel every day in such a manner without it affecting the quality of his studies. Perhaps Pramode Bhushan enacted such a pastime just to prove that everything is possible by the Lord's mercy.

One day, one of Pramode Bhushan's classes ran longer than usual and the students were not dismissed until evening. After giving his full attention to the class for longer than usual and then trying to memorize the lesson, Pramode Bhushan fell asleep on the train back to Shason village. When he woke up, he saw that he had gone way past his stop. The other passengers started telling him he ought to be concerned about ghosts. Some of them were helpful and suggested that he get off at the next station, take shelter at a house near the station, and return to Shason village the next morning. However, the pull of the Chaudhurī family's affection for him was strong, particularly that of the elder matriarch of the house, so Pramode Bhushan ignored everyone's advice and, getting off the train at the next stop, returned to Shason village by foot in the dead of night. While walking, he kept repeating to himself a phrase he had read in one of his textbooks: "When God is with you, there will only be victory." When he arrived home, the elderly lady of the house was standing at the door, lantern in hand, eagerly awaiting his return. By the Lord's mercy, he had returned safely.

A Second Meeting with Bimalā Prasāda

It was now 1917, and almost two years had passed since Pramode Bhushan had started college. One day, Pramode Bhushan told the students of his science class about his unforgettable experience in Śrī Māyāpura with his classmates from Shason village. His description was so enticing that a few of his classmates decided they would also like to visit Śrīdhāma Māyāpura under his guidance. The college would be closed for one week, from December 25 until the January 1, so the group decided to go to Māyāpura on December 25. Instantly, the memory of meeting with Śrī Bimalā Prasāda and witnessing his extraordinary beauty, tenderness and charismatic personality flooded back to Pramode Bhushan's mind like the recollection of a dream.

The morning of December 25, Pramode Bhushan and his friends arrived at Sealdah station. From there they traveled by train to Dhubulia, where they disembarked and took a bullock cart, arriving in Māyāpura at what would later become Śrī Caitanya Maṭha. Pramode Bhushan paid the cart driver and quickly went ahead to meet Śrī Bimalā Prasāda. When he could not find him where he had last met him, he wondered if he had relocated somewhere else.

Fortunately, Pramode Bhushan encountered two other individuals. It occurred to him that they either lived there or were frequent visitors. Pramode Bhushan humbly approached them and asked, "In 1915, I met a wonderful, sweet-spoken, grave personality here and spoke with him briefly. His name was Bimalā Prasāda. Do you know where he is now?"

Hearing Pramode Bhushan's sincere inquiry, they said, "Do you really want to see him? If you do, then come with us. At present, he is at the birthplace of Mahāprabhu. We are also going there to discuss something with him."

Pramode Bhushan turned to his friends and said, "Now we will go with them to meet a great personality." His friends agreed, and they walked together to Mahāprabhu's birth site. There, they saw the same red building that was there during their prior visit in 1915. With mixed feelings of great joy and some nervous excitement, Pramode Bhushan entered the red building with his friends and the two men he had just met.

There was Śrī Bimalā Prasāda Prabhu, his lotus petal-like eyes closed, as he remained deeply absorbed in chanting the holy names of Lord Hari. The two men who had led Pramode Bhushan and his schoolmates there offered their respectful obeisance to Śrī Bimalā Prasāda Prabhu by falling flat on the ground as soon as they saw him. Pramode Bhushan followed their example. Hearing the movement of people in the room, Śrī Bimalā Prasāda opened his eyes and addressed them.

"Kuñja Bābu, when did you come? Paramānanda, where did you go?" Then he turned to Pramode Bhushan and said, "You took a long time to come back. Are you keeping well?" Pramode Bhushan was incredibly surprised that Śrī Bimalā Prasāda had recognized him and continued to converse with him as though they were very close. Pramode Bhushan was deeply moved by this behavior of Śrī Bimalā Prasāda and felt a great attraction to him. Śrī Bimalā Prasāda then addressed Paramānanda, "It is already past noon. Go and arrange *prasāda* for them."

Paramānanda Prabhu escorted Pramode Bhushan and his friends out behind the red building and sat them beneath the large bael tree there. A short while later, an elderly lady brought pots full of rice, dal, and vegetables. Paramānanda Prabhu brought leaf plates for them and the elderly lady began to serve them the *prasāda*. This elderly lady was none other than Śrīla Bimalā Prasāda's mother, Bhagavatī Devī.

Paramānanda Prabhu asked Pramode Bhushan, "Do you know who this is? She is the mother of our Śrī Bimalā Prasāda Prabhu. Her name is Bhagavatī Devī." While honoring *prasāda*, Pramode Bhushan thought, "Yes, she is the goddess Bhagavatī! She is the embodiment of compassion and devotion. Out of compassion, Bhakti Devī has assumed a form and appeared before us."

After honoring the *prasāda* with great satisfaction, they returned to Śrī Bimalā Prasāda. There, they saw Kuñja Bābu sitting with Śrī Bimalā Prasāda, discussing something. Kuñja Bābu repeatedly said, "Your priceless instructions should be preached throughout the world. If you simply live here like this in Māyāpura, then many pious and educated persons will be deprived of hearing your message. Therefore, if you permit me, I can make arrangements for your stay some place in Kolkata."

Hearing this, Śrī Bimalā Prasāda Prabhu replied, "Whatever God decides will happen. Pray to Śrīman Mahāprabhu. His wish is my wish; I have no independent desire of my own."

The more Pramode Bhushan heard these transcendental topics, the more captivated he became. He contemplated, "If he really goes to Kolkata, I will move there as soon as I've completed my studies in about eighteen months. I will rent a room, get a job there, and associate with this great personality every day. If I live in Kolkata, I will be able to associate with this divine personality and, once I get a job, my father's financial difficulties will be reduced."

After a lengthy discussion with Kuñja Bābu, Śrī Bimalā Prasāda Prabhu addressed Pramode Bhushan, "If you find time, please visit me. I have many things to discuss with you. It is possible that, under the supervision of Kuñja Bābu, I will reside in Kolkata for some time in order to preach the teachings of Śrīman Mahāprabhu."

At that, Pramode Bhushan offered his obeisance to Śrī Bimalā Prasāda Prabhu and, with utmost faith and devotion, begged his blessings to soon see him again. With folded hands, Śrī Bimalā Prasāda Prabhu said, "*Kṛṣṇe matir astu* – May your mind be fixed in Kṛṣṇa." Taking this blessing upon his head, Pramode Bhushan then visited the other important places in the compound with his friends. Pramode Bhushan then sought the blessings of Mother Bhagavatī Devī and took his friends to see the other holy sites in Māyāpura. They spent the night there and, the next day, returned to Sealdah station via Dhubulia, and from there to their respective homes.

A Visit Home to Jessore

The next day, Pramode Bhushan was preparing to return to Jessore. As he was leaving, the elderly lady of the house said, "My dear child, you just came back last night, and already you are leaving again?"

Pramode Bhushana gently replied, "I am on holiday from my college. I have not seen my mother for a long time, and ever since my brother died of cholera, my mother worries about me. So, I would like to go home to pacify her and see what the situation is at home with my own eyes. Our college will remain closed until January 1. Don't worry about me. I will be back on the night of December 31."

With these words, Pramode Bhushan gently removed the tethers of the elderly woman's affection for him and set out for Ganganandapur. At Baruipur railway station, Pramode Bhushan boarded his train, taking a corner seat. As the train began to move, he went back to Māyāpura in his mind. There was Bimalā Prasāda with his lotus-like eyes. He heard his humble, grave voice, and relished again the *prasāda* he had been served by Bhagavatī Devī. He thought, "When will I overcome the illusion of family attachment, and the bondage of mundane education, and be able to dedicate my whole life to the service of Śrī Bimalā Prasāda Prabhu? When will that auspicious day come in my life?" As he contemplated these matters, the train reached the Jessore station. Pramode Bhushan got off the train and proceeded to his village. Everyone in the village was asking him, "When did you come? How long will you stay? When will you return to Kolkata?"

পুরোহিত দর্পণ

Pramode Bhushan replied in a detached mood, "I just arrived today. About going to Kolkata, only God knows." The villagers could not understand why Pramode Bhushan appeared to be so indifferent. They thought that perhaps he was still grieving his brother's death. In fact, however, his mind was totally absorbed in remembering the lotus feet of Śrī Bimalā Prasāda Prabhu.

Attaining Śrīla Bhaktiratna Ṭhākura's Mercy

After exchanging greetings with everyone at home, Pramode Bhushan went to the Datta house, where he found Śrī Bhaktiratna Ṭhākura Mahāśaya in his bedroom, studying a few of the books written by Śrīla Bhaktivinoda Ṭhākura. He had just completed his service to Śrī Śrī Rādhā Madana-mohana for the day. As soon as he saw Pramode Bhushan, he inquired cheerfully, "My dear son, have you read the books Śrīla Bhaktivinoda Ṭhākura wrote that I gave you?"

Pramode Bhushan softly replied, "I have read them all. The songs in *Śaraṇāgati* are so easily understood, so instructive, that I wasn't satiated by reading them only once, so I've been reading them again and again."

He then reported, "I took my college friends to visit Māyāpura, Śrī Kṛṣṇa Caitanya Mahāprabhu's birthplace, which Śrīla Bhaktivinoda Ṭhākura discovered. I've actually gone twice in two years. There I had the *darśana* of a divine personality, Bimalā Prasāda Prabhu, who is highly respected by all. When I went back two years later, he still remembered me. He spoke with me too."

After hearing the details of Pramode Bhushan's Māyāpura visit, Śrī Bhaktiratna Ṭhākura Mahāśaya said, "My dear son, you are really very fortunate! Our Bimalā Prasāda is truly a divine personality. For

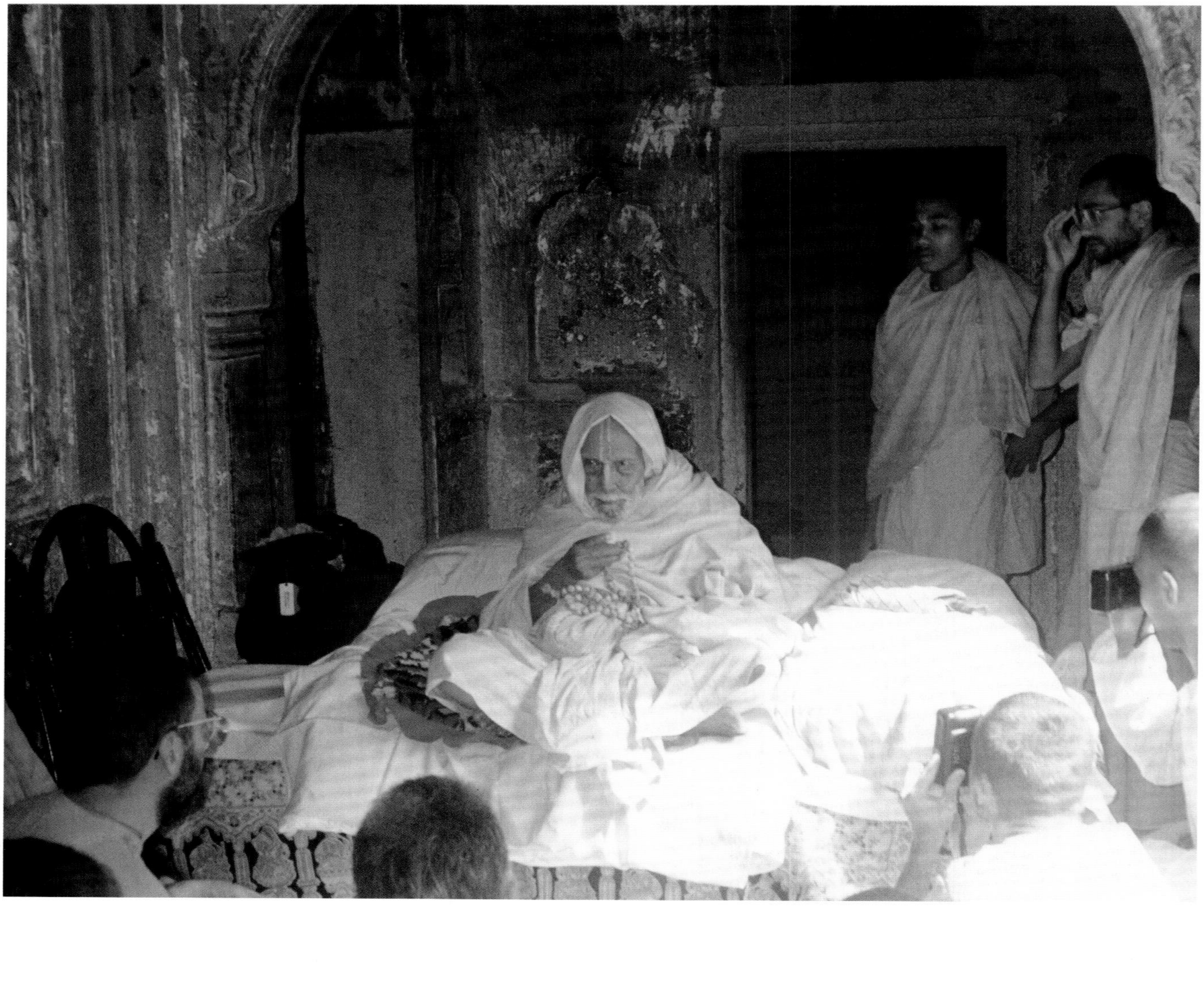

the past nine years he has sat on the same *āsana* and chanted three hundred thousand names of the Lord daily on his *tulasī* beads, following in the footsteps of Śrīla Haridāsa Ṭhākura. This is not possible for an ordinary person. This Bimalā Prasāda has received the blessings of Śrīla Bhaktivinoda Ṭhākura and is an ambassador from Goloka, sent by Śrīman Mahāprabhu. Seeing the pathetic condition of the people of Kali-yuga, Mahāprabhu and His associates have sent Bimalā Prasāda to deliver all the living entities. You are indeed fortunate. Bimalā Prasāda still remembered you two years later and spoke with you. I have no words to describe how lucky you are. As long as you are here, son, please come and see me every day. But when will you go to Kolkata? And what will you do there?"

Pramode Bhushan replied, "I have to complete my studies and find a job. I must do something to reduce my family's financial burden. My father, mother, sister and younger brother, Nani Gopāla, are depending on me; my father's current monthly earnings are hardly enough to maintain the family. When I heard that Bimalā Prasāda Prabhu will soon be moving to Kolkata with his disciple Kuñjabihārī Vidyābhūṣaṇa to preach the message of Lord Caitanya, I realized that if I got a job in Kolkata I could hear *hari-kathā* from Bimalā Prasāda Prabhu every day."

Śrī Bhaktiratna Ṭhākura Mahāśaya said, "My dear Pramode Bhushan, Kṛṣṇa alone is taking care of everyone and maintaining each of us. If Kṛṣṇa saves someone, who can kill him? And if Kṛṣṇa kills someone, who can save him? Hiraṇyakaśipu was a powerful king whose son was the great devotee Prahlāda. The king was very proud and denied God's existence. He sent Prahlāda to study under the care of the two sons of Śukrācārya, Ṣaṇḍa and Amarka, and repeatedly ordered them to make sure his son never met any devotees of Viṣṇu or heard anything about Viṣṇu. When Prahlāda came home after completing his semester, his father addressed him affectionately and asked what he had learned so far. Prahlāda spoke about devotional service—the teachings he had learned while in the womb of his mother, Kayādu, for ten thousand years, hearing from Śrī Nārada Muni.

"When Hiraṇyakaśipu heard Prahlāda speak like this, his affection for his son evaporated. He began to devise various ways to kill Prahlāda. But even after many attempts and after exhausting all possible means, Hiraṇyakaśipu could not touch or remove even a single hair on Prahlāda's head. More recently, during Mahāprabhu's time, we see what happened to Nāmācarya Haridāsa Ṭhākura. Although the Kazi's followers beat Haridāsa Ṭhākura in twenty-two marketplaces, he felt no pain. The Supreme Lord directs and maintains the whole universe. He holds His devotees in His own heart and protects them from all kinds of dangers in this material world. These pastimes are enacted to demonstrate this fact. Lord Kṛṣṇa instructed Arjuna in the *Bhagavad-gītā* (9.22) as follows:

ananyāś cintayanto māṁ
ye janāḥ paryupāsate
teṣāṁ nityābhiyuktānāṁ
yoga-kṣemaṁ vahāmy aham

'For those who constantly meditate upon Me and are always engaged in My service, I satisfy all their needs and protect what they have.'

"My dear Pramode Bhushan, please understand that Kṛṣṇa alone is your maintainer. In this regard, I would like to narrate a short history. Śrī Kṛṣṇa's instructions appear in the form of the *Gītā Upaniṣad*. No one can change the instructions in the *Gītā*. If someone changes the instructions, he will see the result of such an action in his life.

"There was a pious *brāhmaṇa* in Jagannātha Purī who used to read the *Gītā* every day. His name was Arjuna Miśra, but he was known as the Gītā Pāṇḍā. Once, Gītā Pāṇḍā doubted this very *ananyāś cintayanto māṁ* verse from *Gītā*. Gītā Pāṇḍā wondered in particular about the phrase *'yoga-kṣemaṁ vahāmy aham.'* How is it possible that the Lord brings all one's necessities Himself? Rather, he thought, it should say *dadāmy aham,* indicating that the Lord *provides* the requirements through someone else and not that He Himself actually carries them to the devotee.

"After a lot of deliberation, Gītā Pāṇḍā replaced *vahāmy aham* with *dadāmy aham* in his own *Bhagavad-gītā*. Then he went out to beg alms, as was his daily custom. However, that day no one gave him any alms. Exhausted, he fell asleep beneath a tree.

"Usually, he was home by midday, and his wife would cook his lunch with the grains and vegetables he had been given. But on this day, while Gītā Pāṇḍā was out begging, two small boys—one black and one white—carried a huge basket of groceries, including fruits and vegetables, to the *brāhmaṇa's* home and gave them to Gītā Pāṇḍā's wife. While they were speaking, Gītā Pāṇḍā's wife saw blood dripping from the dark-complexioned boy's back. 'How did you get that cut?' she asked. The boy said, 'Your husband asked us to bring these two baskets of groceries to your home, and when we refused, he whipped me.' The lady's heart filled with sympathy, and saddened by her husband's behavior, she asked the boys to sit and wait. She would quickly cook a meal with the ingredients they had brought, offer it to the Lord, and give them the *prasāda*. After feeding the boys, she sat to wait for her husband.

"But on this day, Gītā Pāṇḍā did not arrive home until sunset. He was still empty-handed, and he looked depressed. As soon as he entered his home, he said, '*Brāhmaṇa,* today I was not able to collect any alms. Everybody refused me. I don't know why.'

"Gītā Pāṇḍā's wife was surprised by this. 'How is this possible? How come? You sent two boys here with all kinds of ingredients—more than you usually bring. I already cooked and fed those boys. I even let them rest in our bedroom. So, what are you talking about?'

"Gītā Pāṇḍā was astonished and exclaimed, 'Where are those boys? Let me see them.' So he and his wife entered their bedroom, but nobody was there. Then the *brāhmaṇa* said, 'You whipped that black boy!' Gītā Pāṇḍā suddenly remembered how, in the morning, he had crossed out the words *'vahāmy aham'* in the *Gītā*. He went to his book and opened it to that page. There he saw that the phrase was no longer crossed out. Then he understood that the two boys had been Kṛṣṇa and Balarāma. 'Because I had changed the words in the *Gītā*, I could not collect alms today, so both Kṛṣṇa and Balarāma personally brought food to our home.'

"The *brāhmaṇa* told his wife, 'When I crossed out the words in the *Gītā*, it became a cut on the black boy's back.' Then Gītā Pāṇḍā, with eyes full of tears, said, '*Brāhmaṇa*! You are most fortunate. You fed the Lord with your own two hands. Those two boys were Kṛṣṇa and Balarāma. I now realize my mistake. I should never cut or change words in the *Bhagavad-gītā*. Whatever is written in the *Gītā* is the absolute truth.'

"In this way," Śrī Bhaktiratna Ṭhākura Mahāśaya said, "we must believe that Kṛṣṇa is the maintainer and protector. Don't be too attached to your family."

Pramode Bhushan was an intelligent person and sincerely surrendered to the Supreme Lord. On hearing Śrī Bhaktiratna Ṭhākura Mahāśaya's transcendental message, he made up his mind that during his free time, in-between studies, he would stop just idly chatting with friends and instead engage in the service of the Supreme Lord with utmost devotion until the last day of his life.

From that time on, Pramode Bhushan's mood of rendering service to Śrī Śrī Rādhā-Madana-mohana blossomed even further. To enhance Pramode Bhushan's faith and devotion for the Supreme Lord and His devotees, Śrī Bhaktiratna Ṭhākura gave him a few more books by Śrīla Bhaktivinoda Ṭhākura to study, and made a daily habit of glorifying the transcendental qualities of

Śrī Bimalā Prasāda. Gradually, the propensity to seek material happiness and prosperity disappeared from Pramode Bhushan's mind and instead he felt inspired to dedicate his life to the service of Śrī Madana-mohana and His intimate devotee, Śrīla Bimalā Prasāda.

The Beginning of the End of Material Bondage

Pramode Bhushan had seemed distant for quite some time. His family members, especially his mother, Rāma-raṅgiṇī Devī, could not understand his mood. One day, as Pramode Bhushan returned to his father's house from Śrī Rādhā-Madana-mohana's temple, his mother asked him, "Did something happen to you?"

Pramode Bhushan answered with a simple "No."

Rāma-raṅgiṇī Devī said, "You came home for vacation, but you are spending more time at that Rādhā-Madana-mohana temple than in your own home?"

Humbly, Pramode Bhushan explained, "I like Śrī Bhaktiratna Ṭhākura's association and the service of his family deity."

His mother replied, "But by looking at you, I can tell that you are suffering some pangs of separation."

Pramode Bhushan replied, "Yes, both times I went to Māyāpura, I met a divine personality there. I feel pain in my heart—the pain of separation from him—and my heart is also feeling the thorn of separation from the service of Śrī Rādhā-Madana-mohana. I don't want to waste my human form of life. I want to make this life, which is rare even for the *devas* and *devīs*, successful by remaining in the association of that wonderful person I met in Māyāpura. I wish to spend the rest of my life in his service. When I look at the faces of my family, I realize you each have so many hopes and expectations of me. The Supreme Lord has not made us financially prosperous, and so we are always having to depend on others. Whatever Father earns each month is insufficient to maintain the family. So, I am thinking of completing my studies soon, then trying to find a job to ease his burden. In a few years, I will have to sit for the final exam of my bachelor's degree in science. But with all these thoughts I have, I don't know how I will perform and what results I will get. At present, I am very fond of reading religious literature. Whenever I come here, I rush to the Madana-mohana temple to get the association of Śrī Bhaktiratna Ṭhākura. He has given me a few books written by his godbrother, Śrīla Saccidānanda Bhaktivinoda Ṭhākura. After reading them, the goals of the material world seem so temporary and insignificant. I do not know what will happen in the future, but I will try my best to bring joy to your hearts and smiles to your faces. Mother, please bless me so I may win the battle against Māyā and engage myself in the eternal service of the Supreme Lord in Goloka Vṛndāvana, the eternal residence of all living entities. I will have to go back to Kolkata in a few days, and I am already feeling pain at the prospect of being not being able to continue my service to Madana-mohana here in Ganganandapur. Since you are my mother, you can understand my state of mind.

Mother, I will try to finish this mundane education as soon as possible."

Mother Rāma-raṅgiṇī Devī was shocked to hear all this and began to think that her son was not planning to stay with them for long. She embraced Pramode Bhushan tightly to her chest. Tears in her eyes, she was breathing heavily. She said, "My dear Tinu, don't leave me and go away forever. Wherever you go, stay in touch with me. You are my hope for the future." Then, wiping her tears, she returned to her household duties, her mind filled with anxiety.

Seeing how unhappy he had made her, Pramode Bhushan's mind began to roil. "What should I do now?" he asked himself. "What is right? What is wrong?" Confused, he finally went to the Rādhā-Madana-mohana temple and related the conversation to Śrī Bhaktiratna Ṭhākura, who said, "My dear Pramode Bhushan, it's already late afternoon. You had better take care of the Lord's evening services. We will discuss all this later."

As the *ārati* went on, everything in the world seemed uncertain to Pramode Bhushan. He already felt that studying for a material degree was a waste of his valuable time, which he could put to better use in the eternal service of the Supreme Lord. Yet how to help his family? Conflicting thoughts flooded his mind.

One evening, he again approached Śrī Bhaktiratna Ṭhākura to reveal his mind and ask for direction. Śrī Bhaktiratna Ṭhākura said, "Pramode, your confusion about your best way forward is appropriate. Both Śrīla Bhaktivinoda Ṭhākura Mahāśaya and his dear son Bimalā Prasāda pursued higher education to serve the Supreme Lord better. Instead of using their material education for sense gratification, they used it to give the Supreme Lord pleasure, and, in this way they made their material education grandly successful. It is a fact that everything in this material world is temporary and full of uncertainties, but if you neglect your studies, how will you comprehend the transcendental literature Śrīla Bhaktivinoda Ṭhākura wrote? So continue your college education. If you remain uneducated, the respected and influential persons of the material world will show no interest in your words. I feel that very soon you will be presented with a lot of responsibility in the Lord's service. The fact you felt cold and suffered a fever for forgetting to offer the deity a blanket and your detachment from your schooling are signs of what is to come. Nowadays, ordinary students get their college degrees and then establish themselves in society in some superficial way. They read and pay special attention to acquiring general knowledge so they can enjoy unrestricted sense gratification. In your case, I can see it is quite the opposite."

Śrīla Bhaktiratna Ṭhākura then quoted a verse from the *Caitanya-bhāgavata* (Ādi-khaṇḍa 12.49):

paḍe kene loka? kṛṣṇa bhakti jānibāre
se yadi nāhila tabe vidyāya ki kare

> "Why do people study? People study in order to know about devotion to Krsna. If this purpose is not accomplished, then what is the use of education?"

Śrīla Bhaktiratna Ṭhākura continued, "Śrī Caitanya Mahāprabhu gave us this instruction. So complete your college education properly. When the time is right, Śrī Caitanya Mahāprabhu will certainly engage you in His service very nicely under the guidance of Śrī Bimalā Prasāda. Śrīla Raghunātha dāsa Gosvāmī, one of the Six Gosvāmīs of Vṛndāvana, met Śrī Caitanya Mahāprabhu at Śāntipura. There, he disclosed his intention to renounce family life and exhibited his detachment from his father's great wealth. Śrī Caitanya Mahāprabu said to him:

sthira hañā ghare yāo, nā hao bātula
krame krame pāya loka bhava-sindhu-kūla

markaṭa-vairāgya nā kara loka dekhāñā
yathā-yogya viṣaya bhuñja' anāsakta hañā

antare niṣṭhā kara, bāhye loka-vyavahāra
acirāt kṛṣṇa tomāya karibe uddhāra

> "Be patient and return home. Don't be crazy. One can transcend material existence and reach the ultimate spiritual abode (Goloka) gradually, in due course of time. Don't falsely display renunciation like a monkey who mimics what it sees. Be attentive and fulfill your present material responsibilities while renouncing attachment to them. Keep sound faith in

the Lord within your heart while externally maintaining appropriate behavior toward those with whom you interact. Then, very soon, Lord Kṛṣṇa will deliver you from your present miserable situation." (*Caitanya-caritāmṛta*, Madhya-līlā 16.237–39)

Śrīla Bhaktiratna Ṭhākura added: "According to this instruction of Mahāprabhu, it's not proper to show impatience on the path of worshiping the Supreme Lord. Mahāprabhu said this to Raghunātha dāsa Gosvāmī even though he was not impatient. These instructions were really meant for us.

"I understand your predicament. Your classes will commence again a few days from now. Pacify your mind and go back to Kolkata on January 1. I hope you will pass your examination and secure your chemistry degree, as planned, and that you will bring good reputation to our village. By and large, you will achieve immense benefit if you can squeeze in some time in your busy schedule to meet with Bimalā Prasāda. He is an associate of the Supreme Lord.

"Let me tell you more about him. When as a baby Bimalā Prasāda was fed grains for the first time, it was at Jagannātha Deva's Ratha-yātrā festival. The whole city of Purī was filled with devotees. To reveal to all of us the fact that Śrī Bimalā Prasāda was a great personality, Lord Jagannātha, on His way to the Guṇḍicā temple, stopped for three full days outside Śrīla Bhaktivinoda Ṭhākura's home at Nārāyaṇa Chātā. They could not get the cart to move. When Bimalā Prasāda's mother, Śrīmatī Bhagavatī Devī, brought six-month-old Bimalā Prasāda before the Lord's chariot, Lord Jagannātha's garland immediately fell from His neck. As soon as the *pūjārī* put the garland on baby Bimalā Prasāda, the cart began to move. How could one be so fortunate as to receive such unique mercy from Lord Puruṣottama at Puruṣottama Dhāma if one were not an extremely exalted personality?

"Śrīla Bhaktivinoda Ṭhākura has bestowed an abundance of blessings upon Bimalā Prasāda. He is also the object of my great affection. You will see one day that Bimalā will become a famous spiritual preacher around the world. Many intelligent persons will take shelter of his feet and serve Mahāprabhu's mission. My wish is that you too will serve Mahāprabhu under the guidance of Bimalā Prasāda. If you have doubts or questions, you may write to Bimalā Prasāda. I will also try my best to help you understand knowledge of the Absolute Truth. I have a feeling that Bimalā Prasāda will attract you at an appropriate time and engage you in the service of Mahāprabhu and Śrī Śrī Rādhā-Govinda. Be mentally prepared for this to happen even as you continue your schooling."

After hearing these instructions, Pramode Bhushan's desire to dedicate his life at the lotus feet of Śrī Bimalā Prasāda grew exponentially. He returned home as usual that night, and although in the morning he had no wish to leave Ganganandapur, he knew he had to return to school in Kolkata.

First Job as a Port Commissioner in Kolkata

Eventually, the date for Pramode Bhushan's final examination in the chemistry honors program arrived and he sat for the examination. However, by this time, he had developed such a strong attraction and affection for Bimalā Prasāda that he had not been paying much attention to his studies, and so his examination results were not as high as his family expected. It was as if Bimalā Prasāda was hinting to Pramode Bhushan's family members that they should prepare themselves to accept and approve of Pramode Bhushan's entrance into renounced life. "Although he took birth in your house," Bimalā Prasāda seemed to be saying, "he came into this world to serve Śrīman Mahāprabhu. Pramode Bhushan is very dear to me, and I will soon take him forever into Mahāprabhu's service."

The desire of a saintly personality never goes in vain. Right after the examination, Pramode Bhushan began to look for a job in Kolkata to make his parents and other family members happy, He found a job in the Port Commissioner's Office. After working about six months at the office, he rented a home in Bowbazar and brought his mother and sister from Ganganandapur to stay with him.

He tended to his office work and performed his duties meticulously, but the instructions and predictions of Śrīla Bhaktiratna Ṭhākura surfaced in his mind. He could not forget the sweet words and wonderful personality of the great Vaiṣṇava he had met in Śrīdhāma Māyāpura, Śrī Bimalā Prasāda.

Hearing Discourses at Ultadanga Junction Road

One day, Pramode Bhushan heard that an extraordinary personality was giving daily discourses on *Śrīmad-Bhāgavatam* at Ultadanga Junction Road. After work that afternoon, he decided to go to meet that personality. To his amazement, he saw it was none other than Śrī Bimalā Prasāda, from Māyāpura, although now he was wearing saffron rather than white and everyone was addressing him as "Śrīla Prabhupāda."

Śrīla Prabhupāda, in his *sannyāsa* garb, looked like a fresh new sun risen indoors. When he saw Pramode Bhushan, he immediately asked, "How did you find out I was here? I have been thinking about you in particular. Finally, we meet again!"

Pramode Bhushan replied humbly, "You look very beautiful in these saffron robes."

Śrīla Prabhupāda replied, "Yes, on Gaura Purṇimā day in 1918 I accepted *sannyāsa* as per the order of Śrī Caitanya Mahāprabhu and the previous *ācāryas*. My name has also changed. My name in this particular order of life is Bhaktisiddhānta Sarasvatī. I speak on *Śrīmad-Bhāgavatam* every evening. If you can, come and listen. There is no longer any need to go all the way to Māyāpura for us to meet. Śrīmān Kuñjabihārī Vidyābhūṣaṇa made all arrangements and brought me to Kolkata to reveal the teachings of Mahāprabhu to the learned and thoughtful people of the world. Therefore, if you find time, please come here."

Pramode Bhushan was jubilant. "I will certainly come every day to hear your *Śrīmad-Bhāgavatam* recitation," he said. "I will make my life successful by taking advantage of whatever little opportunity I may find to serve you! I have heard much praise of you from Śrīla Bhaktiratna Ṭhākura Mahāśaya, who is from the same village as me."

Śrīla Bhaktisiddhānta Sarasvatī Ṭhākura Prabhupāda asked, "You have had his association? When you meet him next, please offer him my respectful obeisance. He is Śrīla Bhaktivinoda Ṭhākura's godbrother."

Pramode Bhushan said, "Yes, I have associated with him, and he loves me very much. I have also heard some topics about Śrīla Bhaktivinoda Ṭhākura from him."

After a long conversation with Śrīla Prabhupāda, Pramode Bhushan returned home late that evening to his rented Kolkata room. He was exhilarated; it was as if he were floating on an ocean of bliss.

The next day, as soon as he finished his office duties, Pramode Bhushan went to the *Maṭha* well before the start of Śrīla Bhaktisiddhānta Sarasvatī Ṭhākura Prabhupāda's afternoon lecture. Pramode Bhushan wished to ask Śrīla Prabhupāda about some aspects of worshiping Lord Hari that were unclear to him. But to his astonishment, whenever Pramode Bhushan thought to ask a particular question, Śrīla Prabhupāda would speak on that exact subject before he had a chance to ask.

[Continued in the forthcoming biography, *A Century of Devotion: The Life of B.P. Purī Gosvāmī Mahārāja authored by Śrīla B.B. Bodhāyan Mahārāja.*]

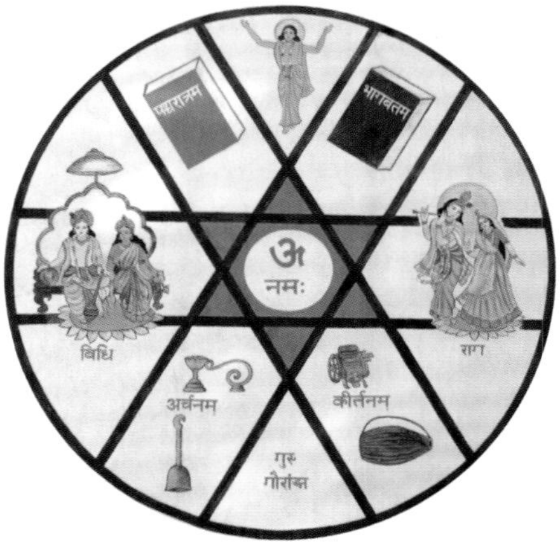

Bibliography

Bhaktiśāstrī, Śrī Hari-kṛpā Dās Brahmacharī, *Prabhupāda Bhaktisiddhānta Sarasvatī*, Bombay: Gauḍīya Maṭha, 1980.

Māhārāj, Śrīla Bhakti Ānand Sāgar, *Śrīla Guru Mahārāj: His Divine Pastimes & Precepts in Brief*, Navadvīpa: Śrī Caitanya Sāraswat Maṭha, 1994.

Mahārāj, Śrīla Bhakti Kusum Śramaṇ, *Prabhupāda Śrīla Sarasvatī Ṭhākura*, Māyāpura: Śrī Caitanya Maṭha, 1940.

Mahārāj, Śrīla Bhakti Pramode Purī, lectures and discussions on audio-cassette, Māyāpura: Śrī Gopīnāth Gauḍīya Maṭha Archive.

Mahārāj, Śrīla Bhakti Pramod Purī, *Śrī Śrīmad Bhaktisiddhānta Sarasvatī Ṭhākura*, Māyāpura, Śrī Gopīnāth Gauḍīya Maṭha, 1992.

Mahārāj, Śrīla Bhakti Rakṣak Śrīdhar, lectures and discussions on audio-cassette, Navadvīpa: Śrī Caitanya Sāraswat Maṭha Archive.

Mahārāj, Śrīla Bhakti Vallabh Tīrtha, *Śrī Gaura-pārṣad Gauḍīya Vaiṣṇavācārya-gaṇer Saṁkṣipta Caritāmṛta*, vol. 2, Calcutta: Śrī Caitanya Gauḍīya Maṭha, 1994.

Mahārāj, Śrīla Bhakti Vallabh Tīrtha, *Śrī Śrīmad Bhakti Dayita Mādhav Gosvāmī Mahārāj Viṣṇupāder Pūta Caritāmṛta*, Calcutta: Śrī Caitanya Gauḍīya Maṭha.

Mahārāj, Śrīla Bhakti Vilās Tīrtha, *Śrī Caitanya-darśane Prabhupāda Śrīla Bhaktisiddhānta Sarasvatī Ṭhākura*, vols. 1–2, Māyāpura: Śrī Caitanya Maṭha, 1974.

Majumdār, R.C., *History of Modern Bengal: Part Two*, Calcutta: G. Bharadwāj & Co., 1981.

McKay, John P., Bennet D. Hill and John Buckler, *A History of Western Society*, vol. 2, Boston: Houghton Mifflin Co., 1991.

Prabhupāda, Śrīla Bhaktisiddhānta Sarasvatī Ṭhākura, *Śrī Śrīla Prabhupāder Upadeśāmṛta*, ed. by Śrīla Bhakti Mayūkh Bhāgavat Mahāraj, Māyāpura: Śrī Caitanya Maṭha, 1990.

Prabhupāda, Śrīla Bhaktisiddhānta Sarasvatī Ṭhākura, *Śrīla Prabhupāder Harikathāmṛta*, ed. by Śrīla Bhakti Vilās Tīrtha Mahārāj, vol. 1, Māyāpura: Śrī Caitanya Maṭha, 1955.

Sarasvatī Jayaśrī, ed. by Śrīpāda Sundarānanda Vidyāvinoda, Calcutta: Śrī Gauḍīya Maṭha, 1934.

Sen, Sailendra Nāth, *History of Modern India: 1765–1950*, New Delhi: Wiley Eastern Ltd., 1979.

Sen, Śrī Sukumār, *Bāṅgālā Sāhityer Itihās* (History of Bengali literature), vol. 4, Calcutta: Ānanda Publishers Ltd., 1940.

Gauḍīya,
Vol. 4, Issue 28, 6 March 1926,
Vol.12, 17 March 1934,
Vol. 15, Issue 33-34, 27 March 1937

Caitanya Vāṇī
9.11 (Dec. 1969), pp. 256-262
10.11, (Dec. 1970), pp. 249-251
13.1, (Jan. 1974), pp. 17-25
13.11, (Dec.1974), pp. 236-45
15.6 (July 1976), pp. 104-107
18.11 (Feb. 1978), pp. 204-210
22.1 (Jan. 1983), pp. 8-14

MANDALA

An Imprint of MandalaEarth
PO Box 3088
San Rafael, CA 94912
www.MandalaEarth.com

Find us on Facebook: www.facebook.com/MandalaEarth
Follow us on Twitter: @MandalaEarth

ISBN: 979-8-88762-105-0

Published by Mandala Publishing for **Bhaktisiddhanta Vani Publishing.**
Readers interested in the subject matter should visit the Gopinath Gaudiya Math website at www.gopinathgaudiyamath.com or write to:
Ishodyan, Sri Mayapur
District Nadia, West Bengal
India, 741313

Sri Gopinath Gaudiya Math (Old Dauji temple)
Gopeswar Road, Vrindavan, Mathura (U.P)
India, 281121

Manufactured in India by Insight Editions
10 9 8 7 6 5 4 3 2 1

ROOTS of PEACE REPLANTED PAPER

Insight Editions, in association with Roots of Peace, will plant two trees for each tree used in the manufacturing of this book. Roots of Peace is an internationally renowned humanitarian organization dedicated to eradicating land mines worldwide and converting war-torn lands into productive farms and wildlife habitats. Roots of Peace will plant two million fruit and nut trees in Afghanistan and provide farmers there with the skills and support necessary for sustainable land use.

THE VRINDAVAN CENTER

Vrindavan, India

The Vrindavan Center is a place where visitors from around the world are presented with a comprehensive overview of the history, devotional culture, and philosophy related to the holy city and saints of Vrindavan. The Center offers visitors an introduction to Vrindavan's temples, deities, founders, and devotional literature by featuring an interactive museum of visual and audio exhibits, cultural festivals, and seminars. The Center also brings awareness to the present ecological challenges and environmental initiatives throughout the area.

Through partnerships with scholars, artists, institutions, and NGOs, the Vrindavan Center facilitates authentic educational and cultural experiences that grant an introduction as well as academic access to the extensive traditions of the greater Braja area. The Center is an extension of the Oxford Centre for Hindu Studies, The Bhaktivedanta Research Center and home of the Yamuna Network, and serves as a space for the cultivation of art, research, events, and environmental awareness.
www.vrindavancenter.org

Restoration Update

Mandala Publishing is also the publisher of academic titles for
The Oxford Centre for Hindu Studies and The Bhaktivedanta Research Center

OXFORD CENTRE FOR HINDU STUDIES

Oxford, England

The Oxford Centre for Hindu Studies (OCHS) was founded in 1997 as the world's first academy of its kind for the study of Hindu culture. Since its inception, the Centre has attracted world-class scholars and students, launched pioneering educational projects, and opened up the field of Hindu Studies for an international audience. The OCHS is dedicated to preserving India and Nepal's cultural heritage and promoting a better understanding of it through a comprehensive program of education, publishing, and research.

And now, for the first time in history, a practicing Gaudiya Vaishnava scholar, Dr. Rembert Lutjeharms, occupies a teaching and research position at the University of Oxford. Dr. Lutjeharms is also supervising the PhD of a practicing Gaudiya Vaishnava student at Oxford. As the OCHS launches a campaign for a perpetual endowment to secure the Gaudiya Vaishnava lectureship, and a graduate scholarship as well, this means that Oxford will always have a lectureship in Gaudiya Studies, cementing the tradition for the first time in one of the world's most prestigious academic institutions. *www.ochs.org.uk*

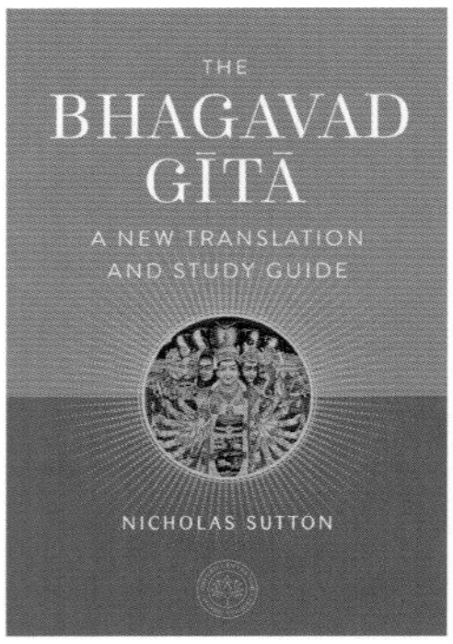

The Bhagavad Gita: ***A New Translation and Study Guide***
Nicholas Sutton
Hardcover, 6" x 9"
$24.99 US

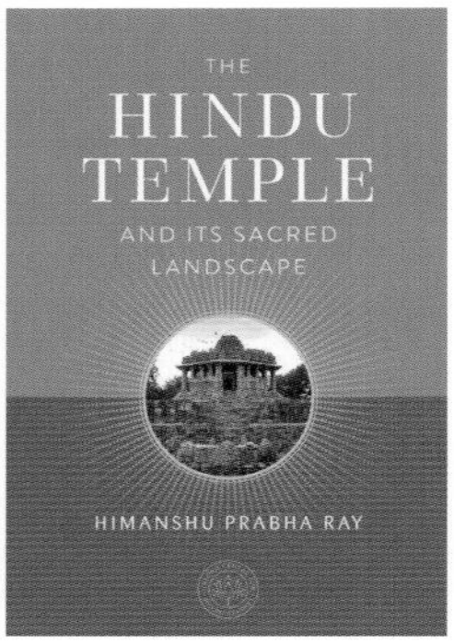

The Hindu Temple and Its Sacred Landscape
Himanshu Prabha Ray
Hardcover, 6" x 9"
$39.99 US

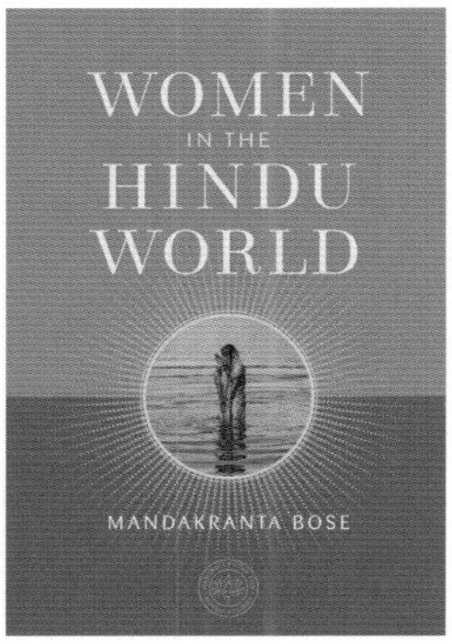

Women in the Hindu World
Mandakranta Bose
Hardcover, 6" x 9"
$39.99 US

Coming Soon

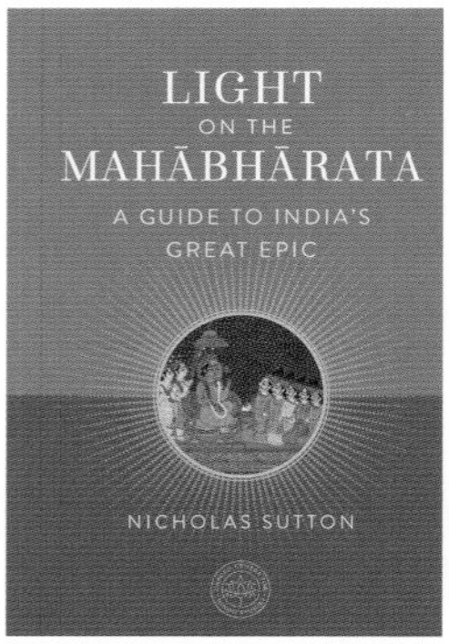

Light on the Mahabharata
Nicholas Sutton

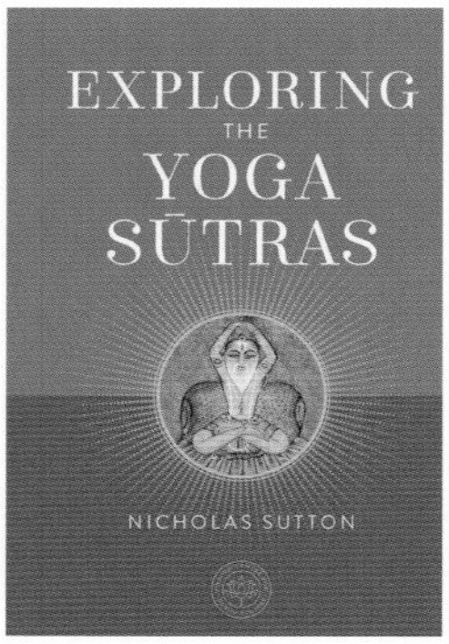

Exploring the Yoga Sutras
Nicholas Sutton

Colonial Hinduism
Amiya P. Sen

Bhaktivedanta Research Center

Kolkata, India

The Bhaktivedanta Research Center (BRC), established in 2009, is a premium research institute headquartered in Kolkata with branches across various cities in India such as Mumbai, Pune, Jagannath Puri and Vrindavan. Its aim is to be a leading research center and an academic institute dedicated to preserve, research and disseminate the rich history, philosophy and cultural heritage of India in general and Bengal in particular, as well as to create awareness and foster cooperation on these studies internationally. The BRC houses a library of rare books, journals, manuscripts, letters and memoirs, encompassing the history, philosophy and culture of medieval and early modern Bengal. This library has already proven to be a treasure chest for scholars searching for unique documents. In addition, the BRC, in collaboration with Mandala Publishing, is publishing the work of many scholars who are compiling and translating significant and rare Vaishnava publications into English and other languages.
www.brcglobal.org

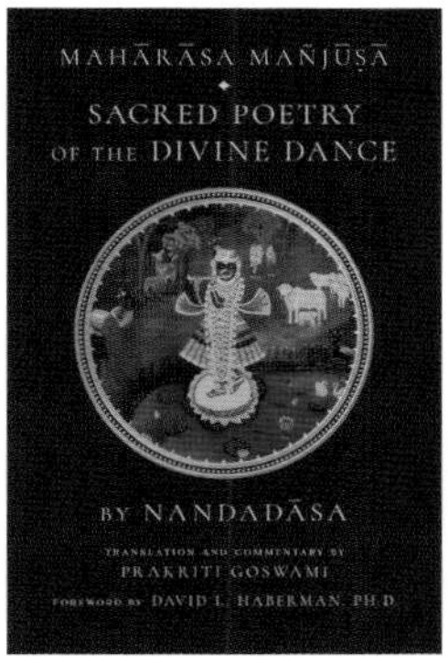

Maharasa Manjusa:
Sacred Poetry of the Divine Dance
Prakriti Goswami
Hardcover, 6" x 9"
$59.99 US

Coming Soon

Madan Mohan:
An Enchanting Saga
Sushant Bharti
Hardcover, 6" x 9"
$45.00 US

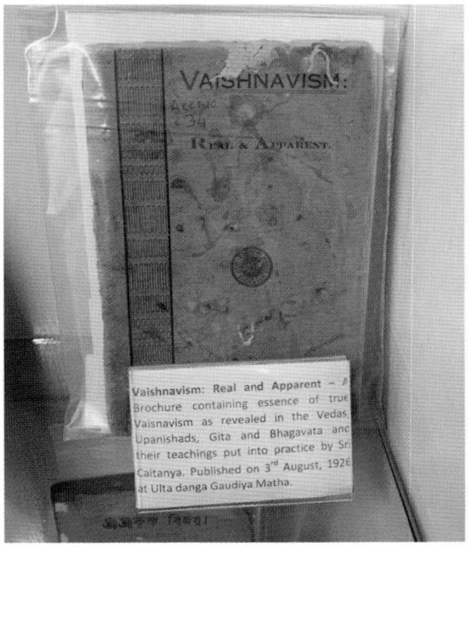

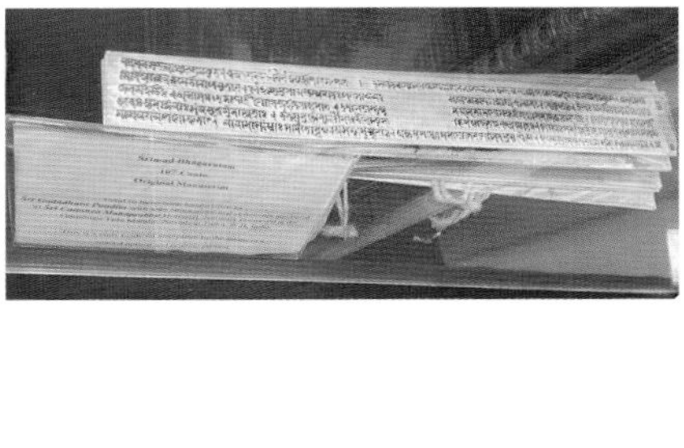

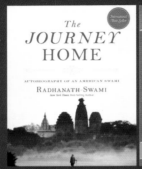

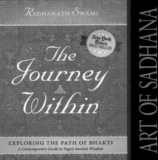

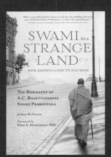

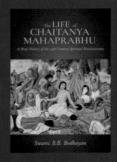

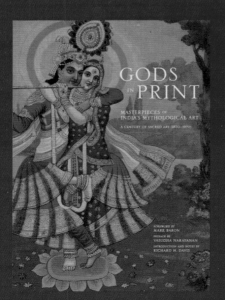

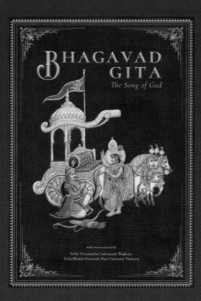

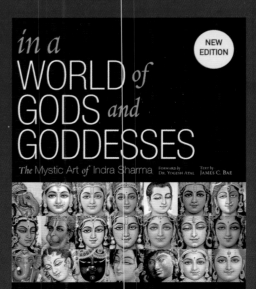

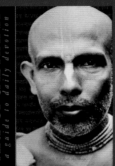

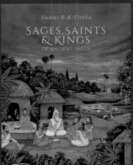

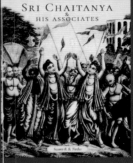

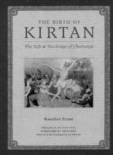

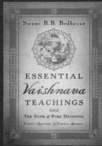

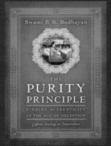

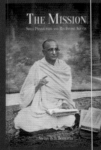